CHRISTIE BLATCHFORD

HELPLESS

CALEDONIA'S NIGHTMARE OF FEAR AND ANARCHY, AND HOW
THE LAW FAILED ALL OF US

Doubleday Canada

LIBRARY AND ARCHIVES CANADA CATALOGUING IN PUBLICATION
Blatchford, Christie
Helpless : Caledonia's nightmare of fear and anarchy, and how the law failed all of us / Christie Blatchford.
Includes index.
Issued also in electronic format.
ISBN 978-0-385-67039-5
1. Caledonia Land Claim Dispute, Ont., 2006–. 2. Iroquois Indians—Ontario—Caledonia—Claims. 3. Six Nations Indian Reserve No. 40 (Ont.).
I. Title.
FC3099.C34B63 2010   971.3'3705   C2010-905555-1

Book design: Andrew Roberts
Printed and bound in the USA

Published in Canada by Doubleday Canada,
a division of Random House of Canada Limited

Visit Random House of Canada Limited's website:
www.randomhouse.ca

10 9 8 7 6 5 4 3 2 1

This is in memory of Corporal Marcel Lemay of the Sûrété du Québec, a 31-year-old father and husband who was shot and killed in a standoff with Mohawk Warriors at Oka, Quebec, on July 11, 1990. No one has ever been arrested in Corporal Lemay's death.

Contents

———

Author's Note   vii
Map   xii

PART 1: JUNE 9, 2006   1

PART 2: BEFORE   21

PART 3: DURING   51

PART 4: AFTER   171

Appendix A   247
Appendix B   248
Acknowledgements   249
Index   251

Author's Note

—

THE NIGHT BEFORE I sat down to write this sucker, I was at the National Newspaper Awards dinner in Toronto and ran into a dear colleague I hadn't seen in years. Photographer Len Fortune and I had worked together at *The Toronto Sun*. I asked what he was doing, and with little preamble he announced he was producing a book for teens about Aboriginal assimilation, that he was part native and that his family had relatively recently decided to acknowledge their heritage. Towards the end of a passionate soliloquy about all this, he raised the subject of the Caledonia occupation.

The previous fall, I'd covered the civil lawsuit of a couple from the town, and Len had read some of that in *The Globe and Mail*. I let him talk a while more before I mentioned I was working on a book on the same subject.

What I told him that night is what I say to the reader now.

This book is not about Aboriginal land claims. It is not about the disputed one in this particular case—disputed because the Canadian government doesn't recognize that there even is a valid claim—which takes in Douglas Creek Estates in that lovely small town, or, more generally, about any of the more than six hundred other claims pending across this country. Academics, government officials and native Canadians have devoted entire careers to the study of those issues, and they haven't begun to figure it out. Besides, I am old enough already that I don't have a career's worth of life left to devote, even if I wanted to do so.

The book is also not about the wholesale removal of seven generations of Indigenous youngsters from their reserves and families—this was by dint of federal government policy—or the abuse dished out to many of them at the residential schools into which they were arbitrarily placed, or the devastating effects that haunt so many today.

Neither is it about the dubious merits of the reserve system, or the dysfunction and infantilization it arguably engenders, all of which may better serve those who wish to see native people fail than those who want desperately for them to succeed.

I do not in any way make light of these issues, and they are, in one way or another, in the background of everything that occurred in Caledonia. But *Helpless* is about what happened to the rule of law—the dry legal term for the noble arrangement a civilized society makes with its citizens, rendering us all equal before and bound by the same laws—in that town and environs.

It officially began on February 28, 2006, when a handful of protesters from the nearby Six Nations reserve walked onto Douglas Creek Estates, which was then a residential subdivision under construction, and blocked workers from entering it.

Over the ensuing four years—and then some, as the occupation continues to this day—the rule of law was utterly decimated. The citizens of Caledonia were, for more than a month—during which period the site was barricaded by occupiers, major roads were closed and lawlessness ran rampant—held hostage. Those who lived adjacent to DCE, and there are about 450 such households, were outright terrorized. Those who lived on Six Nations, just a stone's throw away, were less affected, but still subjected to intimidating forces within and without their community.

Despite frenetic activity—meetings, negotiations at main tables and side tables, talks, reviews, and reports involving various actors from both federal and provincial governments—the town was, for all practical purposes, abandoned by the state.

It was an echo of the truth that Indians have seen for too many years at negotiating tables—that it is when the state seems to be at its very busiest that it may be achieving the very least, and that this may even be part of the plan.

So, what the book is really about is the failure of government to govern and to protect all its citizens equally.

In many instances, documented in the pages to follow, the officers of the Ontario Provincial Police, the force under contract to Haldimand County, stood by while occupiers broke the law, often violently, right under their noses. Arrests, when they were made, were not made contemporaneously, as is the normal course, but weeks or months later.

As it turns out, the front-line officers of the OPP were sold down the river too, by their senior ranks, in particular by two commissioners of the force, Gwen Boniface and Julian Fantino, who either subjugated themselves to government will, held their tongues or respectively dreamed up the disastrous operational plan for Caledonia and then stubbornly held onto it for dear life.

I don't claim to be able to prove which way it happened. But there is considerable evidence that, both at Queen's Park, the seat of the Ontario government, and at OPP headquarters in Orillia, there was the stink of fear in the air, and that what everyone was afraid of were the native occupiers. This, after all, was not the first time in OPP history that such a thing had happened.

Eleven years before Caledonia, a native man named Dudley George was shot and killed by the OPP at what was then Ipperwash Provincial Park, on the shores of Lake Huron. The provincial Conservative government of the day, led by Premier Mike Harris, was for months—if not years—battered by questions from the opposition Liberals, led since late 1996 by Dalton McGuinty. McGuinty promised a full-blown inquiry into Ipperwash if elected, and made good on his word when, after an unsuccessful try in 1999, he led his party to victory in 2003.

By the spring of 2006, with McGuinty in his fourth year as premier, that expensive inquiry was finally winding to a close in Forest, Ontario, just 200 kilometres west of Caledonia.

The shadow thrown by Ipperwash reached the halls of power within the OPP and government and informed every action the state and police took—or, as accurately, every action the state and police didn't take.

This is the story of how all these factors came to a boil in Caledonia.

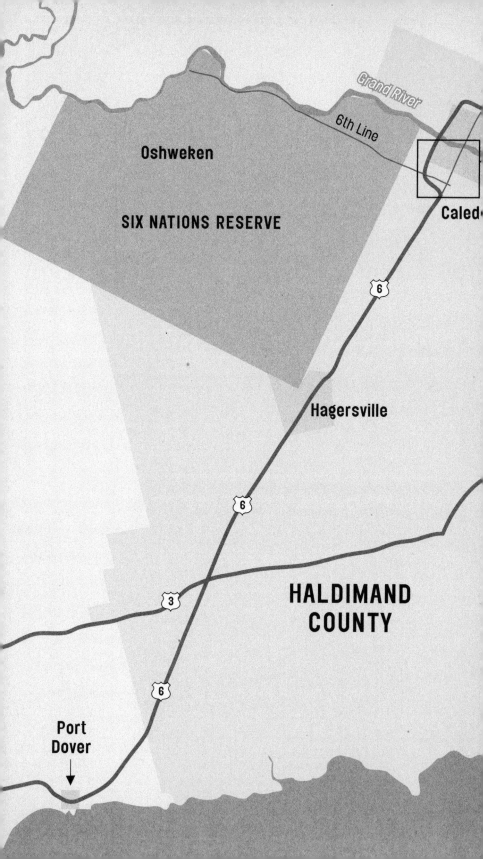

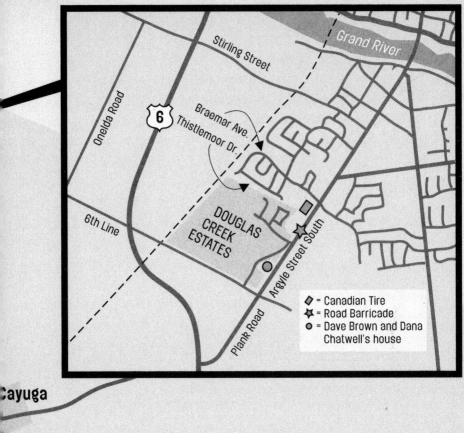

Stirling Street

Grand River

Oneida Road

6

Braemar Ave.
Thistlemoor Dr.

6th Line

DOUGLAS
CREEK
ESTATES

Argyle Street South

Plank Road

◇ = Canadian Tire
✪ = Road Barricade
● = Dave Brown and Dana
    Chatwell's house

Cayuga

Grand River

Dunnville

Lake Erie

N

Friday, June 9, 2006

———

If you're telling us we have to take the law into our own hands—that's happened at various times in history—let us know. Send us the memo. But I think the preferable thing to do is uphold the law and apply it equally to everybody.

—PAT WOOLLEY, CALEDONIA RESIDENT

By June 9, the worst of the occupation seemed to be over.

The mayor had just called an end to the state of emergency imposed after the riotous Victoria Day long weekend, when native occupiers destroyed a Hydro One transformer, plunging much of the county into darkness. The Argyle Street barricade, which for thirty-three days blocked traffic on Caledonia's main drag, had been down for almost two weeks, the financial assistance office set up by the provincial government for businesses affected by the blockade was open, and a fragile calm appeared to have been restored. The situation wasn't normal by any stretch, even by Caledonia's deteriorating standards, but there was reason to hope.

In fact, on June 8, Michael Pullen, the Haldimand County tourism manager, sent out a giddy email announcing that the province had approved the final chunk of money for a $210,000 media campaign for the beleaguered town and burbling cheerfully about "some outstanding fishing photos" that had been taken for the print ads. "Caledonia: Close By, But A World Away" was the slogan of a publicity offensive designed to highlight the area's bucolic charms and improve the town's image. It was the classic government response to trouble: in the absence of actually fixing the problem, mount a public relations operation.

At the start of the season that Environment Canada was later to declare southern Ontario's "Goldilocks summer" because of its just-right amounts of sun and rain, this day dawned cool and overcast. Before 1 P.M., three of the most alarming episodes of the entire occupation, each more violent than the last, occurred within two hours. All took place off the occupied site and well beyond any legitimacy arguably afforded the occupiers by the disputed land claim. These incidents happened instead on a public road, in a busy parking lot and in a pleasant subdivision, in front of citizens left disbelieving, enraged or weeping. In all three events, OPP officers were not only present, but also tantalizingly close to the action, well positioned to intervene.

Yet, with one exception, the police did nothing.

They failed to assist six of the eight victims, including one of their own, a fellow OPP constable. They made no arrests. They chased no perpetrator. They prevented no crime, and in one instance, either outright enabled (by handing over the keys) or allowed the theft of a car.

It all began when Kathe and Guenter Golke, then 68 and 66 respectively, decided to go for what Mr. Golke calls a fun drive. Both retired, they live in Simcoe, a country town spread low and thin, as though there isn't enough of it to fill the space, about forty klicks southwest of Caledonia in the neighbouring county of Norfolk. The couple was heading towards Hamilton when, at the last minute, instead of hopping onto the Highway 6 bypass that skirts the town, they turned right onto Argyle Street, the main street through Caledonia.

"It occurred to me, after hearing so much about that Indian problem there, I wanted to see what it's all about, what this property is all about," Mr. Golke says.

He slowed their cream-coloured Ford Taurus as they pulled even with Douglas Creek Estates, and had a good, long gander at the site across the street. Suddenly, a motorcycle came flying up towards them. "Why are they driving so fast?" he thought to himself, as he pulled over to the shoulder and stopped to let the bike pass. But it drew up to his window, so he rolled it partway down. A furious woman in motorcycle leathers said, "Is there a problem?" and then let fly a torrent of verbal abuse, accusing them of coming to "look at the bad Indians."

"This I don't need," Mr. Golke snapped, and floored it. "The minute I stepped on the gas, all hell broke loose," he says. "From the ditches, a whole pile of First Nations came out, trying to stop us." But the car was already moving—in fact, some of the natives were so close he was afraid he'd hit somebody—and he high-tailed it into Caledonia.

At the Canadian Tire parking lot just up the road, he spotted an OPP cruiser, drove right to it and was trying to explain to the officer inside what was going on when two pickup trucks and some cars materialized beside them. From these vehicles, more than a dozen people, some in camouflage-patterned gear, came running, surrounded the car and began jumping on the hood, whooping. Quickly, the crowd around them grew to about twenty.

"They were trying to bang on the windows, open her [Kathe's] door, but it was all locked, fortunately," Mr. Golke says. Then one of the men made a move for the steering wheel through his half-open window. As he was trying to roll it up, he saw that the officer had grabbed the man's arm and was holding him back.

The officer somehow got them out of the Taurus and into his cruiser. By about noon, they were taken to the police substation a few blocks away. Minutes after arriving there, the police called for an ambulance for Mr. Golke. A diabetic who'd already had two heart attacks, his heart was now pounding and he was grey. He spent about twelve hours in hospital, diagnosed with heart fibrillation, an abnormal rhythm that, untreated, can lead to heart failure or stroke. The couple remain grateful to the officer who rescued them—as Mrs. Golke says, "I win the lottery, I send him off to a nice vacation"—and completely untheatrical about the entire incident. They were just happy to get their car back—damaged to the tune of three thousand dollars, but their insurance covered it—a couple of days later.

The Golkes had no idea that their attackers had merrily driven away in their beloved Taurus, having either been actually handed the keys by a member of the OPP's Aboriginal Relations Team (known as the ART), as some officers believe, or having hot-wired and stolen it in front of a gaggle of cops. Certainly, although seven occupiers were later charged with a variety of offences in relation to the two events that day in the parking lot, no one was ever charged with theft of a motor vehicle.

Self-sufficient German immigrants (Mr. Golke arrived in Canada in 1961 with twenty-four dollars to his name and, when the customs official remarked upon his lack of funds, he smartly replied, "I came here not to bring it; I came to make it"), the couple claim no lasting ill effects but for the way Mrs. Golke starts at the sound of a motorcycle. Still, Mr. Golke says, "You picture this happening in Third World countries, but you don't think Canada can be like that." Canada is still "No. 1 for Germans," he says, and their friends back in the old country "couldn't believe it happened in Canada."

———

The Golkes didn't know the half of it.

About the time they were being surrounded by what can only be described as a mob, Ken MacKay and Nick Garbutt were at CHCH-TV in Hamilton, about fifteen minutes from Caledonia, when someone on the news desk heard over the police scanner that something was happening there.

Something was always going on in Caledonia—CH crews had been there almost daily and knew the atmosphere was highly charged—so when MacKay drew the short straw, he decided, "I'm only going if someone else comes with me." Mostly, he wanted the comfort of knowing someone had his back—holding the camera means the operator can't see much on his right side. Earlier that week, a couple of cameramen had been confronted by hostile occupiers, "and we just felt it wasn't safe to go up there by ourselves anymore," MacKay says.

Nick Garbutt was the next guy up in the rotation, so in two separate trucks, they headed for the Canadian Tire lot. They pulled into the north end and could see something was going on at the south, but not what exactly it was. As the Golkes never saw the CH crew, so Garbutt never clamped eyes on the Golkes' car, let alone on the couple themselves. But MacKay, the shooter, says he could tell the crowd was around a car and that police were in there with them, talking to them.

"My story was to show here's natives around the vehicle, here's the police standing, over here . . . and nothing's being done."

MacKay grabbed his camera, Garbutt following, and as they got closer, an OPP officer—whom Garbutt assumed was in charge and refers to as the sergeant—raised his hands for them to stop.

"Ken and I realized we're sort of a distance away from the scene," Garbutt says, "so I said I'd go back and get the tripod." They set up by a white tradesman's van, and MacKay started shooting. What they could see was the crowd milling about and a group of uniformed OPP officers standing, spread out in a makeshift line.

The natives spotted them. "Three or four of them start approaching us," Garbutt says. The natives walked right past the officer who had waved to the news crew to stop. "They walk quickly past the sergeant," he says. "The sergeant's eyeballing me. I sense trouble and I put my hands up to the sergeant to go, meaning 'What's going on here?' My thoughts are, 'A little help here?' Because I sense trouble."

"Here they come," he told MacKay.

"I see them," MacKay replied, taking the camera off the tripod and sort of backing up.

"They were telling us, 'Stop taping, put the camera away!'" Garbutt says. "So Ken says yeah."

Garbutt stood his ground, but the natives were running now, and the first guy shouldered past him, spinning him around, and began wrestling with MacKay, trying to get the camera.

"Give me the fucking tape, give me the camera," the man told MacKay. "I said, 'I'm not doing that, not doing that.' So I'm stalling, hoping that these guys—the cops—are going to come and help us."

By this time, there were six natives around MacKay, who was trying to protect the camera and using the tripod as a guard. When someone managed to grab his arm, it was Garbutt's cue to step in and help. He hooked onto the lead assailant by the elbow, trying to spin him away from MacKay.

"They grab Nick," MacKay says, "and they put their arm across his throat and throw him up against the van and put him in a head-lock, and they punch him." MacKay saw "there's cops right there, three of them . . . and I turn around and I yelled, 'Do something! Do something!' And they just looked at me."

Garbutt was briefly released, or so he thinks now, and saw that MacKay was still in a struggle over the camera, while other officers stood right there.

"How can that happen?" Garbutt asks. "It should have ended there. So I go into the melee and I start trying to help Ken out. Again. Then I'm surrounded by three or four natives, who jostle me and start . . . I'm getting jostled and surrounded, and that's when the actual assault on me takes place."

Garbutt was getting hit from behind on the top of his head; he remembers taking between four and six blows. "And I remember thinking, 'Oh, this won't last long.' All the OPP officers are on scene, this was the first actual physical violence that has happened. This won't last long, because obviously the officers will step in now because they've seen this. They were so close to me." All of a sudden, Garbutt "felt two hands on my shoulders and someone's telling me, 'It's okay, it's over, just start walking backwards,' and I look up, expecting to see an OPP officer in uniform. And it wasn't an officer in uniform. It was somebody in plain clothes, and I thought, 'Ah, it's an officer in plain clothes who's come to rescue me.'"

MacKay was thinking much the same thing. "My whole tactic was to keep stalling," he says, "because eventually more cops are going to show up and get these guys off of us, because Nick's actually being hit, and I'm having a forty-thousand-dollar camera taken out of my hands."

Only a few minutes later, as Garbutt profusely thanked the "offi-cer" and asked for his name, did he discover that his rescuer was not a provincial policeman, but a Caledonia civilian named Ken Sullivan. He led Garbutt and MacKay back to their news trucks.

"I was still itching to get back in [the fight]," Garbutt says. But now he felt the blood dripping down his face, and allowed himself to be persuaded.

MacKay, an ex-CBC employee who was enrolled in teachers' college at the time and working for CH only for the summer, is now an elementary school teacher not far from his home in Port Dover, on Lake Erie. But the then 46-year-old journalist-turned-teacher had had a third career: he is also a former soldier, a member of the 1st Battalion of Princess Patricia's Canadian Light Infantry.

"I was in the regular forces way back when, '78 to '81," he says. "There was nothing happening back then. But it teaches pride for the uniform, and that's what I said to these guys [the police]: 'How can you guys wear that uniform?' My buddy's over there bleeding. And they wouldn't look. Nick was over to their right, he was on a car, civilians were cleaning him up with towels, and they're standing there, and they're covering up their [badge] numbers, so I can't get names or numbers, and I asked, 'Who's the sergeant in charge?'

"And they said, 'We don't know.'

"I said, 'Give me a break. There has to be a sergeant in charge, with this number of people, there has to be a sergeant in charge; I want to know his name.' Nobody would answer me."

Finally, MacKay says, an officer wearing gloves took a look at Garbutt, called for an ambulance, and "the cops just disappeared—vapourized."

One officer, furious and embarrassed, climbed into the ambulance to whisper to Garbutt, "You should sue the OPP!" He went to hospital in Hagersville, where he got a tetanus shot and four stitches to the biggest of the cuts on the head. And MacKay, with only a few bruises, quickly got the camera back, minus the videotape inside (the natives refused to give police any of the pictures, as they also refused to be interviewed later).

Garbutt and MacKay decided to file formal complaints. They did this on June 27 with the Ontario Civilian Commission on Police Services, which sent the complaints right back to the OPP for investigation, as per the governing legislation. OCCPS may advertise itself to be, and may be perceived to be, an independent agency that investigates citizen complaints against police, but as its spokesman Cathy Boxer succinctly puts it, in practice the agency acts "as a post office" and just forwards the beef to the police force that is the subject of the complaint.

The OPP asked the Ottawa Police Service to conduct the actual probe, two sergeants were assigned, and after extensive interviews with thirty OPP officers and about the same number of citizens who had witnessed all or part of the events in the Canadian Tire lot, they reported back to Garbutt and MacKay one month shy of a year after their attack. I have both reports, and while no one could argue that the investigation wasn't complete, it was also weirdly nitpicking, with an odd passive-aggressive tone, almost as though the investigators set out to minimize what had happened. Where the cameramen complained that they had begged the police for help to no avail, for instance, the report offers detailed breakdowns of where various groups of officers were, and goes to extraordinary lengths to explain why their views may have been blocked or limited, or why they failed to act. In an especially galling illustration, the reports note that officers from one "vehicle were immediately confronted by Six Nations people and were stopped from going any further by these Six Nations people," and make no further comment, as though it were the norm that police are routinely stopped from doing their job by civilians who say, in effect, please cease and desist.

As MacKay, paraphrasing, says: "'The natives were in our way?' Go around them! Arrest them for obstructing justice!"

And while two intelligence officers who arrived at the parking lot early on—one of whom went into the Canadian Tire store while the other stayed in his car—took a total of 157 pictures, neither managed to get any of the first part of the initial struggle-cum-assault, when Garbutt was thrown up against a white van and MacKay was fighting to hang onto his camera. The first officer, the reports say, was changing memory cards and it took him two minutes, by which time "the incident beside the white van had already occurred." To this, MacKay snorts, "I teach photography; it does not take two minutes to change a memory card."

The second intelligence officer "wasn't interested in the cameraman," the reports say, because he was trying to photograph as many of the Six Nations people as he could. As MacKay scrawled furiously in the margin of his copy of the reports, "Both police intel photogs stopped taking pictures at the same time . . . How convenient."

In the end, the Ottawa officers acknowledged that the assault and robbery took place and that the police made no attempt to arrest a single, solitary soul. But they also said the perception that the OPP hadn't intervened was refuted by pictures showing officers involved at various points in the melee (which is not the same thing as going to the aid of the cameramen).

The conclusion? There was "insufficient evidence" to support the allegations.

Only Garbutt appealed the decision to OCCPS, which again sent it straight back to the OPP, which decided there had been a splendid investigation and no further action need be taken. Garbutt appealed to OCCPS again, and in April of 2008 the agency wrote him to say a review panel had examined the file and was satisfied. Twenty-two months later, it was over.

Garbutt, who was then 53, went back to work in the business he'd been in for almost three decades; CHCH gave him the choice of staying away from Caledonia if he wanted, but he returned frequently.

For a time, the station hired a private security firm to accompany crews, but the firm was based in London, Ontario, and the arrangement was sometimes awkward and time-consuming, so the cameramen sometimes still ended up going on their own. Garbutt became very aware of his surroundings, but never again felt threatened.

"In the grand scheme of things," he says, "what happened to me is reflective of probably the big picture, but I don't put much stock in what happened to me. That was my fifteen minutes of fame, that I didn't want, and it was probably one of the more visible hooks that was a tipping point—a journalist got mugged up. So what happened to me, my suffering, is minimal compared to what all the people of Caledonia were being put through, the businesses, the homeowners who live near the property lines who suffer the intimidation at night . . ."

Ken MacKay never went back. "That was it," he says. "I asked not to go." He figured with all the publicity there had been, he was too easy and recognizable a target. To this day, he still drives around the town in order to get home to Port Dover. He finished off that summer with CH, went back to teachers' college, and began working in a school in the fall of 2007.

Buried in the reports, however, were fleeting glimpses of the new Caledonia reality. Officers were clearly confused by their marching orders, with some, including at least one sergeant, believing that the OPP were not to "use any use-of-force options on the Six Nations people" and that, in general, "they were to stand down when dealing with the Six Nations." These officers couldn't, or wouldn't, point to anyone who had said those specific words, but it was clear that the occupiers were already well recognized as being in the do-not-disturb category, untouchable. And at least one officer said that when he saw the camera being stolen, "he questioned one of the sergeants why the person was not being arrested, but there was no answer."

Police officers have the individual discretion to make arrests, to act; they don't need a superior's permission, and neither do they usually ask for it. The hard truth of the OPP's new way of doing business was perhaps better measured that day by Inspector Brian Haggith. Haggith is a Caledonia resident and veteran OPP officer who, from the very start of the occupation, was delegated by his force to act as the OPP liaison with townspeople, precisely because he is so well liked and trusted. Faithfully, he had for more than three months toed the company line: officers were to keep the peace; negotiations were underway and looked promising; residents should be patient.

By June, he was in his third week of working out of the OPP's Western Region Headquarters in London—his superiors were concerned the steady diet of sixteen-hour days and endless meetings with frustrated residents was wearing him down and thought he could use a change of scenery. But he still lived in Caledonia, and June 9 was a day off for him. In shorts and a shirt, he headed to the Canadian Tire store purely by chance. He arrived at the tail end of the confrontations, but saw enough to sicken him—the blood on Garbutt's face, for one thing. As he testified on December 9, 2008, during examination for discovery at the civil lawsuit of Caledonia couple Dave Brown and Dana Chatwell, he overheard numerous citizens complaining that the OPP had stood by and done nothing as the Golkes were swarmed and the cameramen attacked.

Haggith was, he testified, particularly shaken by the sight of a woman on a cell phone, obviously talking to a 911 dispatcher and oblivious to the fact that the man in shorts beside her was also a cop. "The police won't do anything," Haggith heard her say. "Who is going to help us?"

Haggith testified that the dispatcher asked for the woman's name, and she replied, "I will not give you my name because I don't want my name to get out because you will not protect me." "Basically," Haggith explained, the woman was saying "I don't want the natives to find out that I called you because you won't protect me." As she spoke, he said, she was weeping. And as she shut the cell phone and gave it to another woman, she started crying again, got into a car and drove away.

Haggith headed to the Unity Road command post and found Superintendent Ron Gentle, the incident commander that day. "I asked, 'Are we going to be arresting these people?'" Haggith testified. "I also told him that this violence, that this has gone on too far: citizens are concerned for their safety, and that was what was relayed to me on the site. There were ladies crying, saying the police will not protect us, the police, you know, allowed the CH man to be beaten up or assaulted. So I expressed those comments to the superintendent . . . . I told him it's time to make arrests."

What Haggith also said, according to OPP sources, was this: "We can't cower anymore." He testified that, more generally, "we were dealing with this incident [the occupation] differently because it was a land claim situation, and we were trying through peaceful negotiations to get a peaceful resolution, and we tried and we tried and we tried." And compared to the way the OPP normally did business, Haggith said, he "would have to agree" with the widespread view in town that the police weren't doing their job. He agreed that there were earlier incidents "where the law was broken and officers were in sight to observe it, yes."

But the distinguishing factor common to the June 9 events, what made them unusually alarming, was that they all occurred off the DCE site, off the site of the protests surrounding the land claim.

"Yes, that was an act of aggression," he testified, "and it was lawlessness . . . that had nothing to do with the land claim. It was strictly lawlessness and they should have been arrested, and that was my opinion."

While at the command post, Haggith also learned from other officers of the third incident, the one before which the others paled. What he found out was that one of his friends, Detective Constable Norm Ormerod, an intelligence officer, had been seriously hurt. Ormerod never returned to work. He spent some time in hospital, some time on disability, and then put in his papers, as cops call it, and retired.

———

Dave Hartless had just got out of the shower and was on his way to work—he's a detective constable with the Hamilton Police—when he walked out into the middle of chaos at the end of his street, Braemar Avenue.

In this part of the newish development of single-family homes, Braemar hits Thistlemoor Drive and ends abruptly in a little cul-de-sac. Thistlemoor backs directly onto the western edge of the Douglas Creek site; Braemar backs onto the railway tracks and hydro right-of-way, areas that, while not part of DCE, nonetheless had also been taken over by the occupiers.

By this stage, Braemar was one of eight or nine hot spots in town that the OPP had designated as checkpoints, and to which it had assigned cruisers 24-7 and given military-style code names. Braemar was Hotel checkpoint; the cul-de-sac where Braemar hits Thistlemoor was Golf; Quebec was the corner of Thistlemoor and Kinross Street, and so on.

What Hartless saw was this: a native man got out from behind the wheel of a vehicle and stood right in front of the two officers in the cruiser permanently stationed at Golf. The man spread his arms wide and shouted, "Arrest me! Arrest me!"

"They [the two officers] do nothing," Hartless says. "'Come on! Arrest me!' They do nothing. So he turns back and he says, 'See? Your fucking cops can't touch us! You're all next!' He gets in the truck and fucks off and drives it across Graeme's [a neighbour's] lawn, down onto the DCE and across the tracks."

What Hartless was seeing—as were other residents of Thistlemoor who had gathered, drawn by the noise—was the end of perhaps the most egregious example of brazen lawlessness of the entire occupation.

In Caledonia that day, according to documents filed in U.S. District Court in Buffalo, New York, were Mike Powell and Thomas O'Brien, two agents with the U.S. Border Patrol, an agency of Customs and Border Protection (CBP)—the largest arm of the Department of Homeland Security and the one responsible for keeping terrorists and other bad guys out of the States—and Steven Dickey, a special agent with the Bureau of Alcohol, Tobacco, Firearms and Explosives (still known by its old abbreviation of ATF), another U.S. law enforcement organization, which tracks criminals involved in the trafficking of firearms, explosives and illegal tobacco.

With Detective Constable Ormerod, the three were in a blue Chevy Tahoe parked in the little Thistlemoor cul-de-sac, conducting surveillance and sharing intelligence on DCE because, as Hartless notes wryly, some of "their badasses have come up to join the fight against injustice with Six Nations." At about 2:15 P.M., the lawmen, unarmed and in plain clothes, were about to call it quits for the day when two vehicles suddenly appeared and blocked off one exit. A pickup truck arrived within seconds, shutting off the only other route out: Graeme Fisher's unfenced back lawn. About fifteen men emerged and surrounded the Tahoe, and two of them, later identified as Trevor Dean Miller and Albert Kirk Douglas, both then 31, both from Six Nations and both dressed in green camouflage, began banging on the hood, arguing aloud about whether the men inside were cops and whether to run them off—or worse.

The four officers saw the large knife Miller had attached to the front of the military-style web gear he wore, and that he had his hand on it. Miller began shouting at the four to get out, making "lunging movements" with the knife.

According to the affidavit sworn on July 7, 2007, by Philip Knapp, the lead border agent for the Buffalo office, Detective Constable Ormerod "instructed the American law enforcement agents to comply with the attackers' demands to exit the government Tahoe." Powell and Dickey, the driver and front-seat passenger, got out. Dickey was wearing his ATF badge on a chain around his neck. One of the attackers, "wearing a mask," grabbed for the badge, but Dickey pushed him away.

At that point, Miller began advancing towards Dickey "in an intimidating manner and began to pull the knife out of the sheath." (Hartless, ever the trained observer, later spotted this knife in its sheath during the denouement he witnessed.) Dickey, now essentially engaged in hand-to-hand combat, delivered two karate chops to Miller's collarbone and neck, causing his arm to go numb and stopping the attack. Powell, meanwhile, was confronted by Douglas, who looked into the car, spotted the U.S. government radio in the console and began shrieking, "What the fuck is this?" and "They're spies! They're spies!" He pushed Powell aside and got into the driver's seat.

Because the Tahoe was a police vehicle, the rear doors—as a safety feature—had to be opened from the outside. Just as Douglas began to drive off, Powell got the driver's-side rear door open and

O'Brien leaped out. But Ormerod was still frantically trying to exit the Tahoe, which was now accelerating. Dickey working the handle from the outside, Ormerod kicking against the door from the inside in the rear seat, the door finally opened—and Ormerod jumped out, landing violently on the pavement. He was knocked unconscious.

Douglas then put the Tahoe in reverse and tried to run Ormerod over, "narrowly missing" him only because the other three officers and some of the residents who had been watching managed to drag him out of the vehicle's path. As they took cover behind one of those big community mailboxes that are a feature of the modern subdivision, Douglas got out of the car and approached the OPP cruiser—and at that point, made the threats Hartless saw and heard, before taking off in the Tahoe.

The officers in the cruiser called for backup, and within minutes, Hartless says, the area was flooded with cops, which meant that within another minute or so, "we've got a big fucking crew of natives coming up because the OPP are here." By now, this was absolutely standard procedure. To paraphrase the New Testament, Matthew 18:20, wherever two or three OPP gathered within sight of DCE, the occupiers would swarm the area. Among them was Clyde (Bullet) Powless, a high-steel worker and Six Nations member who by now was the head of security on the DCE site.

Hartless says one of the residents approached Powless "and says they stole the fucking truck, so Powless has a few words back and forth with some of his guys and off they go on the quads [all-terrain vehicles], and the next thing you know the truck [the Tahoe], about half an hour later, comes back out."

According to the U.S. documents, it was about two hours later that the Tahoe was returned. Powless parked it next to Graeme Fisher's place and walked away, back to Douglas Creek Estates. "And they're all sort of stood off in the field and they're giving the finger and waving the flags and yelling and squawking off," Hartless says.

It appears that a portable toilet—several of which were on the site—had been emptied into the Tahoe. The truck's contents, including various top-security lists of informants and undercover operatives, body armour, handcuffs and binoculars, were gone. Eventually, some of the stolen items were retrieved, if only, as the U.S. court documents note, "after negotiations" with the occupiers. The body armour was rendered useless; the trauma plate had been stabbed several times. The Tahoe was deemed unsafe and was removed from service.

Eight people were eventually arrested—weeks, months, and in one case more than a year later—and charged with a variety of offences in the three searing events of that long day. Only Miller and Douglas did any significant jail time. Of the eight, one was from Victoria, British Columbia, two from Akwesasne, near the convergence of the borders of Ontario, Quebec and New York State, and five from Six Nations. Miller was arrested in August that year. Douglas was only arrested in September of 2007, reportedly on a routine traffic stop. Both spent about six months in pre-trial custody.

Because of that, though Miller pleaded guilty to two offences, including the theft of the Tahoe, he was sentenced to time served and a year's probation. Similarly, though Douglas at one point faced five charges, including attempted murder, it appears from documents at Cayuga court that he was convicted only in the theft of the Tahoe.

Though the Canadian documents are neither clear about the final disposition of Douglas's charges nor complete, they do show that at least one count was withdrawn against Douglas at the request of the prosecutor.

The Hamilton Spectator reported in April of 2008—on the occasion of Miller's arrest in the United States as he entered Minnesota— that Douglas had earlier been sentenced to time served in the theft of the Tahoe. He still faces several felony charges in New York and is considered a fugitive. Most charges against the others involved that day were also withdrawn by prosecutors. In February of 2010, one man pleaded guilty in the theft of the CHCH camera and was sentenced to the time he'd already served—fifty-six days—and fined fifty dollars.

———

As Hartless watched the Tahoe being towed away that day, he was incensed.

"The police call for the flatbed and it's towed off and off they go," he says. "They do nothing else. Are you kidding me? The two officers, at the end of the street, they actually congratulate them for having restraint. That was outright cowardice. They stood there and watched [four] people get carjacked right in front of them; they say, 'We didn't have time to react.' You don't have time to react in that short a space, you're in the wrong fucking job."

The day was by no means over. At 3 P.M., officers at the Unity Road command post were briefed and told that, in anticipation of a reaction from townspeople to all that had happened, the public order units of the Hamilton and Toronto police had been notified. The briefing sergeant also said he'd received word from command staff: "Enough is enough. Anyone committing a criminal act is to be arrested."

This was what Inspector Haggith had been told too, after his impassioned plea for his cops to be able to act like cops.

In a second briefing three hours later, officers were formally told what most of them already knew, and what some had seen evidence of with their own eyes: the brass was finally "satisfied there are long guns and handguns on Douglas Creek." An OPP superintendent in attendance further admitted that things were "now out of control." Yet members of the Emergency Response Team (ERT) were ordered again to wear what might be called "Caledonia hardtack" that night, meaning they could sling, but not wear, the protective helmets that are standard fare for riot squads being sent into volatile situations, and have close by, but not actually carry, their protective shields. Ever since the occupation had begun, more than three months earlier, not once were ERT members allowed to wear their gear as they routinely trained to do.

By 9 P.M., as many as a thousand angry townspeople were gathering not at the usual spot, the Argyle Street barricades, but in the

Thistlemoor subdivision, behind Notre Dame School—the area where the four officers had been surrounded and attacked. Pat Woolley, a land surveyor who was to have done considerable work on DCE, wandered over, and was there when the ERT came marching down. Like many, he'd watched and heard reports of the awful day on the news. "They were all carrying their helmets," Woolley says, but, bringing up the rear, he could see four officers carrying sub-machineguns. He heard what the sergeant said: "Okay, suit up! We're going in and getting them out of there!"

Woolley's heart soared in his chest. He thought, "This is it, they've had enough and they're going in!" But in an instant, he realized the police weren't heading for DCE, where a large crowd of occupiers were gathered, but for the townspeople.

"And they did a clearing manoeuvre," Woolley says, "and cleared these people out."

At long last, the police made a contemporaneous arrest. They arrested a Caledonia resident, one of the throng in the road, and loaded him into a paddy wagon. The townspeople stayed on the road, blocking the vehicle.

"I had kind of gone from being a spectator and I had kind of got involved as well," Woolley says. "You judge these situations, and I judged they [the residents] were standing there, nobody was touching the police or anything, but they'd arrested some guy and [people] said, 'We're going to stop them.' And so they [the paddy wagon] inched forward."

Woolley was moving in and out of the crowd when he had "my road to Damascus moment, not that I hadn't had it before, but I came out and sort of stepped out of the crowd."

People were shouting at the officers, "Do your job! Do your job!"

Woolley approached the police line. "Guys, do you hear this?" he said. "Do you hear what's going on? You're just a disgrace, everybody's just ashamed and appalled at your behaviour."

"I was just really animated," he says. "My grandfather fought against the Germans in Germany for this, for law and order. If these guys came back, they wouldn't have put down their arms, they would have just marched on."

He began furiously pointing at an officer as he spoke, the moment captured in a photograph that is now famous locally. Woolley told the man he'd been talking to his mother, and she too was ashamed of the OPP, and wanted her son to quit and go to work for a real force, like Toronto's. He said, "You guys should be upholding the law."

"They just stood there stone-faced. I was trying to provoke a reaction. It's not in my nature to say 'you piece of shit.' And the other thing I said, I said, 'How can you allow one of your own to be attacked like that? Who *are* you?'"

Woolley calls the incident "a reverse riot, probably the only one in the world," because instead of police trying to calm an unruly mob by urging them to shape up and obey the law, here was the citizenry, at its wits' end, "yelling at the police to behave, to uphold the law, to act responsibly."

Shortly after, the crowd decided they simply were not going to let the paddy wagon proceed.

"So we all sat down in the road," Woolley says. "Yeah, we all sat down right in the middle. There were probably about two to three hundred of us who sat down."

There, in the middle of the night, this perfectly respectable professional surveyor, graduate of Trinity College at the University of Toronto, well-married father of three, joined his equally respectable neighbours in a sit-in. He was wearing a Hamilton Tiger-Cat shirt. It read, WELCOME TO THE JUNGLE.

Before

Haldimand County . . . is a small pastoral county of some 44,000 people. It is a rural county, a peaceful place, and its population has changed little in the last century . . . It is a land of fields and forests that lies in the most southerly part of Canada . . . It is a beautiful land and has a clement climate. Much more kind than most of the rest of Canada.

—THE LATE ONTARIO SUPERIOR COURT JUDGE DAVID MARSHALL, IN AN AUGUST 8, 2006, JUDGMENT

WHEN I FIRST MET DAVE BROWN, the Caledonia man whose lawsuit against Ontario and the OPP in the fall of 2009 first lifted the lid on the DCE can of worms, I noticed that he uses the phrase *you know what?* the way teenagers use *like*, as a weird sort of filler. In a typical minute's worth of ordinary speech, he might say it three or four times, more if he's excited.

I thought maybe it was just him. I figured he might have developed a verbal tic after all those years living right next door to Douglas Creek Estates, much of it under threat. Perhaps it was some manifestation of his diagnosis of post-traumatic stress disorder. But after interviewing several dozen town residents in taped sessions that lasted as long as six hours, I can safely report that practically everyone I talked to says it a lot. It's the *town* tic.

Not fifteen minutes from Hamilton, just an hour and change from Toronto, and, until the DCE occupation, one of the fastest-growing communities in Ontario, Haldimand County remains, if not wholly rural, then certainly of the country.

As one of its most famous citizens, the late Judge David Marshall, once wrote lyrically of the area, "There are no cities, only rural villages and a series of small towns that are placed along the shores of the green valley of the Grand River." In neighbouring Norfolk County just to the south, the soil is sandy and farmers can grow anything, but are known for tobacco (and that's the subject of another story); in Haldimand, it's clay, so they raise cattle. And land—property—is important in these parts in a visceral way it isn't in cities.

Telling is that, of all the commercial developments cancelled in the summer of 2006, the real heartbreaker was a huge TSC store that was supposed to be coming to Dunnville.

I'd never heard of TSC; it stands for Tractor Supply Company, the largest retail farm and ranch chain in the United States. People were very pumped about the TSC store, says Toby Barrett, Haldimand-Norfolk's Conservative Member of Provincial Parliament. "These TSCs," he says, "they're like Canadian Tire . . . if you've got horses or cattle."

So there you have it.

Despite becoming something of a bedroom community for the ever-encroaching urban sprawl emanating west from Toronto—that growth was predicted to skyrocket under Ontario's Places to Grow/ Greenbelt strategy announced in 2006—Caledonia has a quiet air. People here may earn a little less than the provincial average, but they move less often too. Once the place gets under your skin, it tends to be for good.

Sandwiched between two of the Great Lakes, Ontario to the northeast and Erie to the south, with the mighty Grand flowing right through Caledonia on the way to its mouth at Port Maitland, it's a lovely part of southwestern Ontario.

Barrett is a pretty typical citizen: There's still a farm in the family, and even now, at 65, he looks like he knows his way frighteningly well around a barn and a horse; he's descended from United Empire Loyalists, and, like many of those living in the counties, his ancestors fought side by side with natives in the American Revolution before fleeing to Canada.

He is Theobald Butler Barrett, a descendent of the famed leader of Butler's Rangers, Captain (later Colonel) John Butler. First mustered at Fort Niagara, even the Rangers' uniforms, such as they were, reflected their dual native/British makeup—the best historical guess is that they wore fringed hunting shirts, buckskin leggings, moccasins and forage caps as, with Joseph Brant, the great Mohawk leader, they carried out fearsome guerrilla-style raids on horseback.

Guy Carleton, then the governor general of British North America and the governor of Quebec (his successor was Frederick Haldimand, after whom the county is named), even issued a "beating order" in September of 1777 to Butler. He commanded Butler, "by beat of drum or otherwise, forthwith to raise on the frontiers of the Province, so many able bodied men of His Majesty's loyal subjects as will form one company of Rangers, to serve with the Indians as occasion shall require."

The point is only that the natives and non-natives in this area have had contact and been neighbours, and sometimes platoon mates, for more than two hundred years.

"We came over here from the Mohawk Valley [in New York] at exactly the same time and fought side by side," Barrett says. "And there's been so much intermarriage."

This is true even of Haldimand Mayor Marie Trainer, who was marched off by the municipal council for sensitivity training in Los Angeles during the second spring of the occupation, punishment for having said something deemed inappropriate. Her nephew married a woman from the Mississaugas of the New Credit, a small reserve just south of Caledonia, and two cousins had children with Six Nations men.

It's a common story for local families. And those who haven't intermarried went to school together, played on the same hockey and baseball teams, or, as Barrett says with fond remembrance, hung around Six Nations as teenagers if only because it was easier to drink beer there.

This is not to suggest all was perfect.

"There's a romantic notion, as some suggest, we all used to get along before this happened," says Doug Fleming, a Caledonian born and bred and a hard-nosed realist. "There were always differences there, but they would only bolt to the surface from time to time."

Nor was Six Nations spared the systemic racism all natives have suffered at various points in Canadian history. Despite the glory of that shared fighting past, for instance, Indians, being considered wards of the state, officially weren't allowed to enlist for Canada in 1914, when the First World War began. The policy didn't endure beyond the next year—the war effort needed soldiers, and bands across the country were knocking on the government door. But as a result, the Haudenosaunee Confederacy Council, the traditional government on Six Nations, declared war on Germany as an ally of Great Britain, though the band ended up sending more volunteers, as Canadians, to the front than any other.

What has tempered things in Haldimand County is what usually moderates prejudice: the saving grace of small personal connections wrought by daily dealings.

———

The first hint that trouble was heading for Caledonia came during the summer of 2005, when archaeologists working for Henco Industries, the company developing Douglas Creek Estates, reported being harassed, their vehicles vandalized, by natives. Archaeological surveys are a standard part of the development process in Ontario, the idea being to find and preserve as much of the province's heritage as possible. DCE was subject to at least two such surveys—one paid for by Henco, to the tune of $200,000, and a second—and perhaps a third— paid for by the province after the occupation was well underway. It is among the most carefully studied land in the province.

Though arrowheads, pottery fragments and traces of a possible building were discovered, the finds were insignificant, and despite claims to the contrary, there was absolutely no evidence of an Indian burial ground. In the early days of the occupation, there were rumours that human bones had been found, hidden in 300,000 cubic metres of dirt alleged to have been secretly shipped off the site by Don and John Henning, the brothers who own the company. Actually, they were chronically short of dirt—they were doing a road upgrade, after all—and were in negotiations to get more when the occupation began.

The archaeologists were working on a forty-acre triangle of land on the western edge of the site, which backed up against the rail tracks; the Hennings had mortgaged it to finance development of the first 100-acre parcel. They'd also sold off a nine-acre commercial strip, just south of the main entrance. They were stretched so thin that they could afford to put up only their office, in one house on the site, and start a lone semi-detached. It was the other builders who had the place buzzing, with between ten and twelve houses in various stages of construction.

Henco Industries is a formidable-sounding name, but the company was small and intimately connected to the county—developers, certainly, but with none of the baggage sometimes carried by their big-city counterparts. DCE was, by a long stretch, the largest project the Hennings had ever tackled—there were to be about 450 houses in the first phase—and they had every penny they could get their mitts on invested in it.

The site was also the repository of some of their dreams, and would have moved Henco into a new league, enabling them to make their mark in town as surely as their late father, Jack, had made his. They named the streets in the subdivision by opening up either a map of Scotland or a bottle of whisky. But there were two exceptions. One street was named after Albert Marshall (no relation to the judge), who had loved the Hennings' father and had sold the brothers some of the DCE land. "We had always told him we were going to name a street after him when we developed his land," Don says, "but he got sick not long after Dad died." They got the street sign made up to give to him to show him they had remembered; he died before the occupation started. The brothers also had a Forbes Street on DCE, named after Don Forbes, whose family was the last still living along Highway 6 to have been granted land by the Crown.

Such gestures matter to the Hennings. For men disinclined to sentimentality, they are thoughtful and funny. As Don says, "There will never be a McGuinty Street in any of my subdivisions." The brothers love to work, and work hard, and had envisioned spending the next half-dozen years doing that on DCE; they estimate that if they'd been able to build out the subdivision, they would have made more than $30 million in profit over the course of about seven years.

At the point the archaeologists were being bothered, the brothers got a call from a woman from the Six Nations council, and they ended up going to the reserve to meet with her and another official.

"And they basically said, 'Out here, we've been told it's a ninety-nine-year lease and that that has run out,'" John says.

The Plank Road Tract, named after the old name for Highway 6 and which encompasses DCE, is disputed. Ottawa insists it was properly surrendered in 1841 and then properly sold in 1844, and this the Six Nations elected council acknowledges, though it claims there's never been fair compensation. But the Haudenosaunee (it means "people building a longhouse") Confederacy Council, or traditional chiefs, forty-seven of whose predecessors were the fellows who signed the deed that sure seems to authorize that long-ago sale, claim the original chiefs were tricked, that they'd meant only to lease the land, and that the Plank Road Tract was thus effectively stolen.

A lawsuit for Plank Road, and more than two dozen other Six Nations claims, was launched in 1995, but was put in abeyance in 2005 when the Six Nations returned to the negotiating table in the faint hope that the pace there would be, if only marginally, less glacial than in the courts.

In any case, the council officials the Hennings met that day "went on to say they understand that we have done absolutely nothing wrong, followed all the protocols, done everything we were supposed to," Don says.

As per the "duty to consult and accommodate" Aboriginal people imposed by the Supreme Court of Canada, Haldimand County had given the Six Nations notice of the subdivision plan. On July 28, 2003, Roberta Jamieson, then the Six Nations chief, replied by letter, noting the land "is the subject of outstanding claims" and that "resolution, in the way of accounting, is being sought in litigation against the federal and Ontario governments."

In other words, this battle was about money, not land, and it was with Ottawa and Queen's Park.

Chief Jamieson requested copies of all archaeological, stormwater and sewage reports, and even asked that the Stirling Street bridge be upgraded and a new traffic light considered. Certainly, there was no suggestion anywhere in the letter that Henco should not proceed.

And that appeared to be that until October 25, 2005, when a handful of protesters, no more than ten and most of them women, showed up at the site first thing in the morning and blocked the road. The sole OPP response was to put up some orange cones on Argyle Street and direct traffic safely around the protest.

"We were in the middle of road construction," Don says. "The cops came and did nothing. They [the protesters] stayed for two days. I think it was a test run."

Still, it didn't amount to much at the time.

John Henning keeps a diary, though I hesitate to call it that because it's the furthest thing from modern journaling, where angst and feelings are routinely laid bare. Meant as a pragmatic record of daily tasks and business, and important dates such as birthdays and the start of various hunting seasons, his notes for that day are purely work-related—"Stairs for Lot 14," that sort of thing.

The next month, there was what may have been another tentative probe of the strength of the collective will. On November 16, police were again called to Argyle Street and the Sixth Line for a "native information" session.

Again, police put cones on the road.

Again, nothing seemed to come of it.

———

Ray Robitaille, whose company, R.J. Robitaille Homes, had built homes throughout the county with the Hennings' dad, had two single-family houses on DCE that were nearly finished and had just dug a basement for a semi. February 28, 2006, was his day at the site—his three sons are also in the family business—and as he arrived about 7:30 A.M., he found the entrance blocked by a group led by two Six Nations women, Janie Jamieson and Dawn Smith. According to current Six Nations chief Bill Montour, the two had approached both the elected council and the Confederacy before taking action, "but they couldn't get a definitive answer" from either group about what, if anything, they were going to do about the coming development.

"I think this [the indecision] is what precipitated it," Montour says.

He wasn't the chief at the time—he was working in Vancouver for the National Centre for First Nations Governance—but got regular updates and has brought himself up to speed since his election in November of 2007. As a councillor from his earlier stint as chief, between 1986 and 1991, used to tell him, "There's going to come a day when the young people are going to say, 'Get out of the road, you old political fuddy-duddies, because you sat around here for the past century, talking. Nothing's happened.'" Later, as the occupation took shape, that changed: the elected council supported the protesters financially and the Confederacy backed them morally.

Montour is also skeptical that a notice from the county about a development about to break ground constitutes either consulting or accommodating. "That's the fallacy of that," he says. "I've seen this all across the country and I worked seven years for Indian Affairs [Indian and Northern Affairs Canada, or INAC], and I've seen it every time, the notion that negotiations are going on in a lot of cases, but still development's going on.

"Our fight is with Ontario and Canada, not Caledonia," he says. "In fact, we're neighbours. We've always been neighbours. And that's what really bugs me . . . allowing these major governments to say, 'Oh, we delegated that [the duty to consult].'"

But again, the quarrel appeared to be solely about compensation, not land.

For most of the three years of the planning process, the Six Nations had not expressed a peep of concern about the development, and the only government that is able to negotiate land claims—Ottawa— didn't even recognize there was a valid claim. Into that mine field came Jamieson and Smith.

"They were blocking any contractors from going in," Robitaille says. "We couldn't get our trucks in, trucks that were in were still in there, behind them [the protesters]."

At least one of the contractors demanded that the OPP show him something "in writing" that would explain why the protesters were being allowed to conduct a blockade unmolested, and, one by one, every builder tried to talk his people through the line. But the best they could manage was an arrangement that allowed them onto the site briefly in small groups to turn off the hydro, shut off the water and lock up their houses.

"We didn't know," Robitaille says. "We didn't know if this was going to last two days or two weeks. So that's what we did."

By 4:30 P.M., OPP Superintendent Ron (Spike) George appeared on the site for the first time. George was the head of Aboriginal Issues, Operations, the most powerful native cop in Ontario and per- haps in the country. He reported directly to the deputy commissioner of field and traffic services and to Commissioner Gwen Boniface. As he had explained to the Ipperwash Inquiry exactly a year earlier to the day, unlike Aboriginal liaison officers, whose work was largely admin- istrative, George was on the operational side, which, as he described it, meant "patrol, investigation of crimes, those kinds of things." In Caledonia, it meant he was directing the ART, the Aboriginal Relations Team, the special OPP unit formed in 2004 as part of the force's response to Ipperwash and which, at Caledonia, had the lead on all dealings with the occupiers. All ART officers were either natives or had received significant "native awareness" training.

George testified for two days—February 28 and March 1, 2005—at the Ipperwash inquiry. Given the astonishing number of hats he has worn in his life, sometimes at the same time, what is remarkable about his appearance is the complete absence of questions about potential conflicts of interest he might have had, even if only those of the heart.

Fifty-five years old when the Caledonia occupation began on that last cold day of February, George is a lawyer with a master's in law and a sometime law professor. He was also a student of the "sociology of Aboriginal protest" at the University of Western Ontario in London, a year of study reflected in a diploma with honours standing (he already had a degree in sociology from Western). And he three times has been a member of the elected council of the Chippewas of Kettle and Stony Point—this was Dudley George's reserve too, near Sarnia on Lake Huron—and was still a sitting member when he testified.

On the night Dudley died, Ron George also represented, as a lawyer then in private practice on the Kettle Point reserve, some of the individuals involved or injured in the occupation at Ipperwash.

Most significantly, he was also Dudley George's first cousin. Ron's father, Robert, and Dudley's father, Reg, were brothers. Dudley and Ron grew up together, just five years between them, as part of the sprawling clan of the extended George family section of the Kettle Point reserve.

Ron George also had the ear of Commissioner Boniface. For a couple of years at Western, starting in 1996 when Boniface was a chief superintendent, the two had co-taught a course in Aboriginal law together. Like George, Boniface was a lawyer, and like him, she made her bones less through on-the-job experience (according to her resumé, she spent eleven years as a constable, but some of that was as an analyst) and more on the strength of her commitment to Aboriginal policing. It was under her leadership that the OPP became the first force in Canada to have a stand-alone Aboriginal police division, an achievement that meant the force beat the RCMP to the punch.

And, his high rank notwithstanding, it would not be accurate to say George had a stellar career in the OPP. What he had was a magical one.

Though two of his eleven siblings, brothers Vince and Luke, put in long years of unbroken OPP service, Ron George was in and out of the force so often he was the revolving-door officer. One of the OPP's first thirty-five Aboriginal "special constables" in 1976, he took at least three leaves from the force, once to get his sociology degree, once to go to law school and once for two years to get his master's in law at the University of Ottawa. He was clearly earmarked for great things, considered a golden child, from the get-go. In his first incarnation with the force, for instance, as a rookie with only a couple of years under his belt among fifteen- and twenty-year veterans, he was pegged to take the prestigious criminal investigation course. When he went to law school at Western, he testified, there wasn't really a formal "leave" program in place, but there was "some manoeuvring within the OPP to grant me those opportunities," so away he went, always with the clear understanding he would be returning "to something" good.

Duly rehired after graduation, he told Ipperwash Commissioner Sidney Linden, he was no sooner appointed as a provincial constable than "within a minute I was, the Commissioner [then Thomas O'Grady] used his prerogative, and I was promoted to the rank of inspector." But he stayed on the job only a year, leaving again in 1992 to set up a law practice on his home reserve. He returned to the force in 1997 on a six-month contract, and was formally rehired the following January. But a year later, with Boniface now a chief superintendent, he was gone again—this time to the University of Ottawa for his master's. From 2002, he also served as the first Aboriginal aide-de-camp to Ontario's first Aboriginal lieutenant-governor, James Bartleman.

All of this information—some of the dates, by his own admission, less than crystal clear—is found in the transcript of George's lengthy Ipperwash testimony. What is apparent from his evidence there is that he is a thoughtful, well-spoken man who, throughout his adult years, was drawn to learn more about his Aboriginal roots and to find a role for himself in the awakening that was taking place on his reserve and others across the country. While he testified he was not "prone to occupy" as a form of civil disobedience, he described himself at the inquiry as "a soft activist."

What is equally striking is his shallow on-the-ground experience and the absence of any expression of affection for policing or even the law, except as it was seen through native eyes. As he told the inquiry once, there is "an overriding principle of justice in the Aboriginal community that suggests that social control comes by virtue of one's adherence to the idea that you must do good things and do good things in a good way."

On March 1, George was asked by lawyer Anthony Ross about the Mohawk Warriors. The organization was first formed in 1972 as a voice for native sovereignty, but had since evolved into a group associated with illegal tobacco and gun smuggling and become better known for muscle than idealism. In fact, at the civil suit of Dave Brown in 2009, virtually every OPP officer who went through the discovery process (where witnesses are questioned under oath) testified the Warriors were akin to a full-blown criminal organization.

Certainly, almost any police officer in Canada, particularly those who work on or near reserves where the Warriors are a force, would still subscribe to that description.

But not Ron George.

Ross had asked George if he could help dispel the unfortunate widespread public perception in Canada that "warrior" necessarily equates to "violent or militant." The lawyer was clearly lobbing in a big, fat beach ball. But George began by mentioning how he'd once visited at length with a couple of men involved in the Mohawk Warrior Society at the Akwesasne reserve near Cornwall.

Ross immediately tried to clarify he wasn't speaking about the big-W Warriors, but rather more generally. But George insisted on saying that what he'd learned from those Warriors is that they are "men within a community who are responsible for the protection of lands and people." Later, he said, he asked an elder from northern Ontario, and the elder confirmed the definition, he said, but added that women could also be warriors. "So that would be my understanding of them," he told Ross. It was a little bit more complex than that, he acknowledged, but "that's the general basis upon which I have formed a belief."

It was, at the least, a preposterously disingenuous description of the Mohawk Warriors.

On the night Dudley George was killed, Ron George—then working as a lawyer, on one of his approved absences from the OPP—drove Dudley's brother Reg to the crime scene, where they learned for the first time it was Dudley who had died. Ron George approached OPP Inspector John Carson.

"Did you at least put a gun in his hand to make it look good?" he asked furiously.

"Yeah, I said that," he told the commissioner at the inquiry. "I was angry and I was being sarcastic."

Just one year later, the first cousin of the man killed by the OPP at Ipperwash, the man who saw Mohawk Warriors as protectors, arrived at Caledonia as the guy now calling the shots in the most significant native occupation on OPP turf since 1995.

His first order of business was a meeting with Dawn Smith, one of the protest leaders, and then, back at the OPP's little Caledonia sub-office, with Inspector Haggith and a couple of ART members.

The die was cast.

————

By the very next day, the OPP had adopted the protesters' language and officers were formally referring to the occupation in notebooks as a "land reclamation," the ART was delivering mini-lectures to other officers on the various groups at play on Six Nations (the elected council, the Confederacy, clan mothers, etc.), and everyone was made acutely aware of the "sensitivity of the situation." Almost overnight, officers stopping cars without licence plates or with invalid tags, or making other arrests, found themselves being asked, when they first called in the information over the radio, a single shocking question: "Are the occupants white or non-white?" If the answer was "non-white," meaning native, the reply from the command post would be, "Get their names, disengage, and if there are any charges to be laid, you can lay them later."

This rule of non-engagement also affected officers from the Six

Nations Police, the first stand-alone Aboriginal police force in Canada and a proud, tough and professional unit. Before the occupation, the two forces had an agreeable working arrangement: if the local OPP was short, Six Nations would lend a hand, and vice versa. But now, Six Nations officers who came into town to back up the OPP also learned when to walk away.

An infamous incident happened early one night behind the Kentucky Fried Chicken on Argyle Street, where there was a bit of a dustup involving both Six Nations and Caledonia kids. A Six Nations Police officer arrived to find a Six Nations youth "all but spitting in the face of this OPP officer," who was, in the first officer's view, "standing there and doing nothing, not arresting him for creating a disturbance, not arresting him for assault, not arresting him for threatening, nothing." The Six Nations officer later told a colleague about it, saying, "He's not on DCE, he's not on the reserve, he's a fucking asshole, arrest him!" But, like his OPP colleague and against every instinct in his body, the Six Nations officer also left without making an arrest.

On the police grapevine, word was spreading: if natives were involved, the OPP was to back off, and if officers didn't like it, they were well advised to keep their concerns to themselves.

By the end of March, Mary Ann Burns, the OPP Association president for the No. 3 branch, which takes in Caledonia, was formally told for the first time that her members were concerned: they had no clear instructions, they had been flat-out told not to drive past the site unless it was necessary, and at least one officer had been banned outright, not just from DCE but from the town. This dated back to the first day of the occupation, when the officer in question had been stationed by the main gate where the protesters had set up the barricade. One of the occupiers approached him and demanded that he remove a contractor who was just sitting in his car.

The officer said politely that he couldn't order the man to leave, as he was on a public roadway.

"We'll see about that," the woman snapped and got on a cell phone. Two hours later, the officer was called back to the OPP's sub-office in town and told he was not to go near the site, not even to drive past it, unless there was an emergency of some sort. Why, he was told, his very appearance—he is a huge man, with a shaved head, who is known to his colleagues as a gentle giant—was upsetting to the occupiers, an affront.

"And that," says another veteran officer, "was where the natives on the DCE started to wag the dog, just to see how far they could push it. And you know what, they pushed it and got zero pushback."

On March 31, in an incident that became widely known inside the OPP, the same officer who'd been banned from the site heard a call on the air about an impaired driver. Not two minutes later came a reply from two ART officers who had just stopped the car on the Sixth Line. By the time he arrived, only one of the ART officers was still there. They had been ordered to leave because, as reclamation officers, they couldn't be seen in confrontations with natives; they were supposed to be building trust. Apologizing as he went, the second ART officer left.

But now, occupiers were showing up in force, at least a dozen of them converging on the lone OPP officer, who had already determined that the driver had no licence, no permit and no insurance—oh, and that the car had no plates. He called for backup, a plea that, in the normal course of events in the policing world, usually brings an enormous, instantaneous, gut-level response: every cop who can get there does.

No one arrived.

In what was probably the single most important early indicator of how the OPP was disintegrating from within, its officers were no longer answering a call for help from one of their own. The constable had been left to fend for himself.

Furious, heartsick, he did what he could—cautioned the driver—and left before things got ugly. Back at the station, he filed a formal complaint. Within a matter of weeks, he was verbally disciplined for having created a possible "flashpoint."

It was a sign of things to come: whenever OPP officers dared speak up about the way things were going, they were slapped down, disciplined or punished. As one officer puts it, the occupation was just a month old, and already members felt "fear of repercussions from command" if they complained.

Local president Burns was also told that officers were concerned at how intelligence—a specific tip from the RCMP had come in through unofficial channels about weapons having been spotted on the site—was being discounted by the brass as coming from a "non-proven" informant.

About the same time, Burns was briefed on a disturbing development that had happened at one of the town's two Tim Hortons, the one nearest DCE. An officer posted to the site was on a break and was in the parking lot when he spotted a driver, not wearing a seatbelt, pulling in. As the fellow was heading into the coffee shop, the officer approached him and asked to see his licence.

"What for?" the man asked.

"You didn't have your seatbelt on when you pulled in," the officer replied.

The man immediately went ballistic, yelling, "You don't police here anymore, you aren't doing your job! Friends of mine are out of work for a month because you aren't doing anything and you want to give me a ticket?" Pointing a furious finger, the man snarled "Fuck you!" and walked away. In the lot, the crowd that had gathered broke into applause.

This was a new vibe, foreign to this naturally conservative corner of Canada. Toby Barrett was hearing it too. "So many Caledonia people, business people, would tell me, 'Yup, the cop would be sitting there, so I would slowly drive through the stop sign and not stop, to see if he'd pull me over.'" He mentions a fellow he knows well, a big-time cattleman. The OPP would often sit on the man's gravel road when they were on a break. Well, said Barrett, the cattleman watched for days as young natives on DCE tore about on ATVs, not a helmet to be seen. One day, the fellow decided he wasn't going to bother loading his ATV onto a pickup to drive over to a far-flung field to check on his cattle; he was just going to drive over in the ATV, with no helmet, and go past the OPP cruisers.

"And that's what he did," Barrett says, "and they pulled him over, and he said, 'I'm just making a point: you arrest me, go ahead and arrest me. But this is what you're letting go on.'

"Now this guy," Barrett says, "really represents Haldimand County: a steelworker, a cattleman, two hundred pounds more than I am. Great big guy. People listen when he talks. And the fellow was saying, 'This is not right.'"

Mary Ann Burns duly passed on the members' concerns—this startling new disrespect for police among them—to Karl Walsh, the newly elected OPPA president, for whom Caledonia was his first major test.

"We got involved from the get-go," Walsh says, pounding the table at the memory, "albeit we got involved because of the groundswell of concerns that were coming from the members on the ground. We were getting daily—hourly—reports from members on the ground that they were concerned about the operational plan, or the lack of an operational plan, the approaches that were being taken, the safety that was being put into jeopardy."

But the most jarring was banning of the shaved-head officer, particularly the way he'd been left to fend for himself when he called for assistance.

"What was it?" Walsh says, trying to remember the phrase. "'He looked too intimidating?' What *is* that? I don't understand that concept; it's bizarre."

———

By Friday, March 3, the Hennings' lawyer, Michael Bruder, was in Ontario Superior Court in the lovely old courthouse in Cayuga. There, Judge Barry Matheson granted Henco a temporary injunction ordering Smith, Janie Jamieson and other protesters off Douglas Creek Estates and forbidding them from blocking the entrances.

The Henning brothers didn't appear, but, Don says, "We thought it [the injunction] would give the police something to go on." They were talking to the OPP, of course, chiefly Inspector Haggith (whose house the Hennings had built) and Inspector Mel Getty, who was brought in from nearby Brant County as the site commander.

"They were the ones that were dealing with us," Don says, "and understand, I have the full belief that those guys were being led by above, and I don't even think they were being told . . . I think they were being lied to, quite frankly."

On Saturday, the Hennings had a meeting with some Haldimand councillors, Mayor Trainer, the Six Nations' elected council chief David General, and others. Basically, they were told "the natives want another level of government and another approval process through them, and they want to be paid a development charge on every lot, and then they want a toll," Don says.

"They wanted taxes," John says, "on a yearly basis."

"And his [General's] words were 'revenue stream,'" Don says.

Mayor Trainer remembers that too, and how it was just the beginning of a trend whereby natives would show up at almost any building site in the county and, under the umbrella of the new Haudenosaunee Development Institute, demand a percentage of virtually every fee the county charged. "Development fees, culverts, everything that the county would have, they wanted a portion of that," the mayor says.

She replied by asking if Six Nations would then contribute to the cost of county services—snow plowing, street lights and the like. "And they said, 'No, that's your problem.' They wanted perpetual care; they wanted the land looked after forever and ever."

In John's diary were entries that began to reflect the brothers' grim new reality, notes about "injunction, liability, who are we dealing with? . . . Schools that are close by [DCE], peace is absolute . . . . Builders meeting."

By then, Don says, "we were starting to worry about our guys (the builders]." All were locals, and the biggest of them might put up fifteen houses a year.

"We felt that the product [the Henco brand] was going to be poisoned now," John adds. "We assumed that this would end, and we were going to change the name of the subdivision. We were not going to put our company name out there at all, because it was in the media by this time."

As Don puts it, "We fronted all the media stuff, hoping they [the builders] could keep their names in the background."

That Sunday, when the local sheriff tried to "serve" the protesters with Judge Matheson's order, they wouldn't accept delivery. Dawn Smith even burned the document, an event seen on local television. The motion to continue the injunction hearing had been slated for Thursday, but with the protesters brazenly failing to comply, Bruder brought a motion asking the court to find them in contempt of court. The matter was heard by Judge David Marshall, he of the poetic description of Haldimand County, a lifelong resident and the area's own Renaissance man. As well as being an Ontario Superior Court judge, Marshall was a qualified M.D., former provincial coroner, pilot, author and an honorary chief of the Six Nations, the honour bestowed on him for his work on the reserve where, for years before the advent of universal health care, he had worked for free at a Six Nations clinic one day a week.

Marshall did three things on March 9: he made Matheson's injunction permanent, adjourned Henco's contempt motion to March 16 and set the same conditions for service of the new injunction as Matheson had. What was galling for the Hennings is that Haldimand County distinguished itself by opposing the injunction—the county argued it shouldn't have been named in the motion because it hadn't yet formally assumed the roads on DCE, a dubious position since the land registry showed they already were in the county's name. This stance, Mayor Trainer hints, was the result of legal advice to the county's then CAO, Bill Pearce, a man Don Henning describes as having "nuts the size of a chickadee."

"The county has abandoned us," John wrote that day.

Though none of the protesters appeared, by then a group calling itself the "Trustees of the Mohawk Nation Grand River" had served the parties with what's called "a notice of constitutional question." This bizarre four-page document summed up the perplexing absurdities of dealing with groups that claim not to recognize the authority of the Canadian state, but simultaneously quote, or misquote, Canadian law in order to challenge it.

On the first page, the document gave notice that "the Haldimand is the Supreme law of the land" and merrily declared that "Canada does not exist as a country." On the second, it cited the Charter of Rights and Freedoms—the foundation document of the "nonexistent" country—as the overriding reason why the Criminal Code, the Indian Act, etc., were unconstitutional and why the contempt motion should be tossed. (On March 13, in Texas, a group with the same name, the Trustees of Mohawk Nation Grand River, filed over the Internet a purported lien against Henco for $110 million. Bruder had to use a lawyer there to make sure the lien had no force in law.)

When court resumed on March 16 to hear the contempt motion, the room was jammed with protesters and supporters, and though they several times refused to acknowledge the court's authority, a number, including Dawn Smith, were allowed to stand and speak nonetheless, and "spoke eloquently," as Marshall noted kindly in a later decision.

"They outlined their reasons for the blockade," he wrote. "They were frustrated with the slowness with which their land claims were moving . . . Their sincerity in their frustrations is not in question."

Yet, "on the evidence," as Marshall put it, he found the protesters in criminal contempt. Even so, he extended them every possible courtesy, giving them thirty days in jail but ordering the sentence be instantly suspended once they'd been arrested and fingerprinted. If they complied with the injunction for six months, Marshall said, that would be the end of it.

"He allowed them so much latitude," Don says. "I think he tried to explain to them nicely how everything worked and why they should do this."

Marshall also imposed a deadline for the occupiers to be arrested—
2 P.M. on March 22—and the local media duly reported it. By the time
D-Day, as the Hennings call it, rolled around, townspeople were in
position to watch what everyone expected would be fireworks. On the
site, the occupiers' group, reinforcements having coming in, linked
arms and were braced for action too.

"Remember the crowd?" John asks. "Everybody came to watch.
There were people on the rooftops. Waiting and parked on the [side
of the road] because the time had run out."

"Yeah, and of course everybody was waiting for the police to come
and roust them," Don says.

"They were watching because they assumed the police or the military were coming to remove them," John says.

It was then that Don Henning got a call from Inspector Getty.
"And he says, 'Where are you?' And I said, 'I'm at home, why?' And
he says, 'Oh, well, the Indians are upset because they think they see
your truck there, watching to see if anything's going to happen.'"

If this was astonishing—the OPP's site commander was personally calling to make sure the Hennings weren't anywhere near the
property they owned because the sight of them would give offence
to those illegally occupying it—the brothers didn't have time to
worry about it.

"At this point now," John says, "our people are preparing us for
financial disaster."

Between the usual securities to the county and the mortgage they
had on the forty-acre parcel where the archaeologists had been working, which their credit union had piggybacked to another credit union,
they were terrified their bankers were starting to get nervous.

"They *were* getting nervous," John says.

Henco's financing was done through the Hald-Nor Credit Union,
a local four-branch company headed by Ralph Luimes, who "kept
the other guys calm and said, 'Let these guys work, they'll get you
looked after,'" Don says. "And in hindsight, they did a great job. With
a traditional bank, we would have been done."

The brothers braced themselves for the possibility of liquidation. "We had to sit and say to our wives that we may have to sell our homes," John says. "And we had taken great care to pay for our homes . . . We didn't have a way to pay a mortgage at the time. Nobody would have given us a mortgage."

In John's notes from that period, the following: "We were fighting for our financial lives." And they were still infuriated that the county opposed their injunction in court, "which can only be perceived as aiding the native occupiers," as John wrote. They had tried, in an in-camera meeting with Haldimand Council, to impress upon the politicians "how serious and grave this situation has become," Don remembers. They told them, "It's not about a handful of homeowners. Realtors are having people who do not want to live in Caledonia; they can't risk not owning their homes. Local lawyers are getting calls from clients wondering if they should sell their homes now . . . What impact will the occupation have on other developments? What investor would risk coming to Caledonia or Haldimand when surrounding lands already have their value diminished? Who's going to buy them? Will all development lands now be challenged by the natives?"

"I tell you," Don says now, "we were already right, and this was only two weeks in."

It was at one of these March court appearances—probably over the two days when the contempt motion was heard—that something extraordinary happened. By this point, documents and affidavits filed with the court showed that the Hennings had more than $6 million invested in DCE.

"This was when some of the Indian smoke shop guys came to us and you know, you got $6 million invested—this was right in the courtroom, at a recess—and said, 'We'll buy it from you. We got investors that'll come and buy the property from you.'"

Then an advisor with the Six Nations council, an old schoolmate of Don's, approached the Hennings. "He said, 'Stay away from those guys, they're smoke shop guys.'"

"At this point," John says, "we're just trying to be polite, talk to everyone, not making waves."

Nothing ever came of the purported offer, though it was reported in the press about five weeks later, with traditional chief Allen McNaughton saying such a buyout was a possibility. But it feeds into the persistent rumour that the real raison d'être of the occupation may have been the desire of some of those involved in tobacco— legal or otherwise—to build a casino on DCE. While there is a perfectly law-abiding, taxpaying native-owned cigarette manufacturer on Six Nations—Grand River Enterprises—illegal factories also proliferate on the reserve.

Two years ago, the RCMP guessed at least seven of the country's then-estimated thirty illegal and unlicensed plants were on Six Nations, with as many as three hundred roadside shacks on the reserve selling bags of two hundred no-name rollies, as they're called, for a fraction of the retail price. The industry has taken over as a major Six Nations employer, with, Montour estimates, about 4,500 people out of a total work force of 17,000 in the business in one way or another.

"So every family's got somebody in the trade, so to speak," he says.

That makes it tricky, if not outright risky, to have an honest discussion about the problems associated with contraband smokes, notably their links to organized crime. At the drop of a hat, Montour can rhyme off criminal groups he believes are among the financial backers of illegal plants on Six Nations, and give him credit, he does just that: "Right now we have the Mafia, Hells Angels, the Philippines, the Asians, the Koreans, the blacks, the Russians—they're all here. And it's scary.

"We've only got thirty-one officers," Montour says. "And they're severely outgunned. So that is the scary part.

"But what really makes me mad is that they're [the industry] destroying our youth through drugs, and they're giving these kids fifteen dollars an hour to sit there and sell cigarettes. So we [council] said, 'You gotta be 18 to work in the damn things.'

"But kids say, 'Well, why do I need to go to school?' I keep telling them cigarettes aren't going to last very long because society in general has shunned it [smoking]. So I would suggest the key part is, [the industry] has got one foot in the grave and the other on a banana peel.

"They're going to be gone."

Montour fought this battle once before, in 1988, in what is known on Six Nations as the Cigarette Wars; his house was even shot up during a drive-by. He rushed outside with his own gun.

"I was going to blast them," he says in the no-BS manner you hear a lot from people in this part of the world, "but they were down the road."

––––

The Hennings, beleaguered on all sides, were immersed in an interminable round of meetings that seemed to go nowhere.

Intensely private, they came to the galling realization, as the high beam of media attention focused on them for the first time in their lives, that, like it or not, until this thing was settled, they would have to learn to deal with the press if they were to have even a prayer of having their voices heard.

In early April, they hired a Hamilton-based public relations consultant, Tricia Hellingman, and, with her guidance, were soon booking sessions with local newspaper editorial boards and doing occasional interviews. The story of the occupation was getting significant attention in the area, and certainly in Hamilton, but it had yet to crack the radar at either *The Globe and Mail* or *The Toronto Star*.

The builders were growing frantic at the evident reluctance of the OPP to act. At one stage, they were threatening to march, with their tradesmen, right onto the site.

"We were actually going to have the First Annual Douglas Creek Road Hockey Tournament," John says with a sly grin. Everyone would show up, hockey sticks in hand, and just go through the barricade. "We were going to push our way on and go back to work. That was what it was about."

But the OPP pleaded with them not to do it. "The police were 'No no no, don't do it. Give us time. We're working it out. We're talking to the chiefs.' On and on and on," John says.

On Wednesday, April 12, the Hennings were summoned to a meeting at the Best Western hotel in nearby Brantford. "At the top-secret location," John remembers sarcastically, because reporter Al Sweeney of CHCH-TV and a crew beat them there.

Before they went in, the OPP begged them to say nothing.

"We sat in this room," Don says. "It was probably, without exaggeration, a hundred natives and maybe a total of ten white guys, of which we were two." Their lawyer, Mike Bruder, was there for part of it; Mayor Trainer was there, and a councillor or two.

"So then we got, and it just got ridiculous. They [the natives] all stood up and they yelled and screamed at us: we were responsible for all the drugs and misfortunes of the reserve; we were raping the land—"

John interrupts: "Their children couldn't eat because of us. It was our fault their teenagers were on crack cocaine. And we sat there and took it."

"We didn't say anything," Don says.

The Hennings had played hockey on the same team as some of those now publicly berating them. They knew and liked these folks. Some were friends.

"You've got to understand," John says, "we'd had native carpenters at this point for like fourteen years. We didn't treat . . . like, when you're in construction, it's got nothing to do with the colour of your skin. It's just whether you do what you say you're gonna do. And we've got Germans and Irish and English and Jamaicans and God knows what [working for them], it doesn't matter. The Indians were there and we never had any problem with those guys, you know? They've been working for us for years and we're stealing from them and starving their children? It was disgusting. I was really offended."

They sat there, mute, absorbing the verbal abuse. "We sat there and let them curse us and tell us," John says, with Don finishing his sentence: "'It [the land] was all ours, and there's going to be violence, it's your fault. It's on your shoulders if somebody gets hurt.'"

But no one *had* been hurt, and, publicly at least, the occupation still had a peaceful profile. Behind the scenes, though, silent alarms kept sounding. In early April, Walsh of the OPP Association sent a director, Kim Williams, down from headquarters in Barrie to take the pulse of the town and talk to their members, who had a new worry: an unidentified native male had been spotted taking pictures of officers' personal cars at the Cayuga detachment. This was important because it suggested that the occupiers were sophisticated enough to be conducting surveillance.

The OPP also had reports that one of the protest leaders had been dispatched to reserves in Quebec to round up support. And sure enough, by the end of March, Michael Laughing, the leader of a group of supporters from the Akwesasne reserve, was both on the site, helping to shout down the poor beleaguered sheriff as he tried for the third time in less than a month to read Judge Marshall's injunction to the occupiers, and in the pages of *The Hamilton Spectator*, proclaiming his willingness to die for the cause.

The OPP was put on heightened alert for signs of natives running reconnaissance missions. The townspeople, who had noticed increasing numbers of people on the site and increasing numbers of out-of-province licence plates on their cars, were already uneasy.

Toby Barrett had been on DCE almost daily since March 2. That day, just before Question Period in the provincial legislature, he'd quietly asked David Ramsay, who was then the provincial minister of Aboriginal affairs and northern resources, who was in charge of settling this thing. Unusually, Ramsay showed him his briefing books, which were open, and let him read them. "Everything said it was the federal government," Barrett remembers. "I said, 'Okay, that's good enough for me.'"

The next morning, he drove down to the site. "I was just doing what I thought . . . I was thinking, but I was more on instinct, 'I'm the MPP, I've got to be there.'"

At the time, Six Nations was also part of his riding—the following year, it became part of the Liberal-held riding next door, Brant—
so he approached the occupiers and introduced himself.

An addictions counsellor by training, he'd also worked on the
reserve, mostly in anti-drinking and driving programs, for a number
of years in the 1980s, and had lots of friends there. As far back as
university, he'd studied the factions on Six Nations and thought he
might have a feel for it. An ex-reservist, Barrett was even an honorary member of the Six Nations Veterans Association, and would go
on parades and attend powwows with the group, where, he says
cheerfully, "I was the only white guy dancing. I wouldn't say dancing. I was kind of shuffling."

At DCE, despite his self-introduction, he says, "I'm not really
sure some of them knew who I was, but they wouldn't talk to me."
He hung around anyway, watching four or five young men chop
wood. Eventually, Janie Jamieson came up to him. "She seemed to
feel kind of bad," he says. "She said, 'Look, we can't talk to you. We'll
talk only to the federal government.'"

But at some early point, Jamieson and Dawn Smith let down their
guard a little. "And I would say right off the bat, they made it very
clear to me—and I don't think this was really bullshit speaking
notes—they made it very clear to me why were they there. Because
of the unbridled growth of Caledonia. They made that very clear."

That was an issue of some concern to Barrett too. The government's Greenbelt/Places to Grow plan, which protected some agri-
cultural and parkland in southern Ontario and pegged other areas,
such as Hamilton, as points where development would "leapfrog"
the greenbelt and growth would take place. Under the plan,
Caledonia was set to become one of the leapfrog destinations.

"The people on Six Nations," he says, "they read all those government reports. That's what they do; they're government minds, many
of them. They knew about the Greenbelt. They knew about the leapfrogging, same as we knew. And they pretty well knew—and I think
I knew it at the time—that probably from Caledonia ten miles down

this Number 6 highway to Hagersville would have been subdivisions on both sides, because of the Hamilton growth area. So they knew that, and I agreed with their analysis of what was going to happen. Brantford: leapfrogging. Still is a leapfrogging area now, because of the greenbelt and the natural unbridled population growth that I see coming out of the Greater Toronto Area.

"And Six Nations, the people at the front, they talked about this a lot. They knew they [the reserve] were going to be hemmed in on the east, and on the north. They knew. They were so close. And that was one [of the reasons], and certainly I would say for Janie Jamieson and Dawn Smith, that's why they did that."

He was sympathetic. "In a way, I respected what they were doing, and I agree with them. I said, 'Yeah, the world's in trouble. There's too many millions of people in this world, and you're seeing it right here, and I kind of know where you're coming from.'" He kept returning to the site every other day or so. "I would say, 'I'm your MPP. What do you want me to do?'" He made himself useful, or at least unthreatening, and blended into the background. Ultimately, "They said, 'Well, we're here, but everyone's ignoring us, and nobody will talk to us. The federal government won't talk to us.'" So Barrett offered to send out a newsletter by email, and did, and it made one of the local papers. "I went back there sixteen, eighteen, times," he says. "I got to know people, I was helping out."

He even agreed, at the request of the clan mothers, the respected female elders, to drive copies of their treasured documents to the governor general in Ottawa, and within a week or so, Barrett and an assistant did just that, delivering a package to Michaëlle Jean's aide-de-camp. The package included a letter in which the clan mothers warned the governor general, in writing, that if the OPP came onto DCE, they would consider it an act of war. At the request of the clan mothers, Barrett read that particular paragraph of the letter aloud to the aide.

In the early going, when to the outsider things seemed so quiet, Barrett also did something he almost never does. He had one of his assistants type out a letter for him, "saying how serious this is, how the shit's going to hit the fan . . . I never do this," Barrett says. "I never work with the Toronto media. I'm just a local guy out here. But I had it dropped on every desk in the Toronto media [in the press gallery] and I was astonished—they wouldn't do anything . . . Nobody would listen to me. They thought it was just a little demonstration down here."

By this point, Barrett had developed considerable regard for Janie Jamieson. "I thought I got to know her very well," he says, "and I thought she did an excellent job, for handling such a volatile situation there."

But one day, when he showed up, Jamieson was sporting a Mohawk Warrior ball cap. "I just looked at her and, non-verbally, just my feeling, I thought, 'Things have changed.'"

During

———

There's this borderline where people still know what is right
and wrong. A lot of those people didn't have that anymore.
They were ruthless.

—MARIA RAUSCHER, FORMER RESIDENT OF
THE SIXTH LINE IN CALEDONIA

On April 13, weeks after the "best before" date on Judge David Marshall's injunction had expired, the OPP's Emergency Response Team was deployed to the Yorkdale Holiday Inn on Dufferin Street in northwest Toronto in anticipation of a foray onto DCE. The ERT is the OPP's public order unit—in layman's parlance, its riot squad. There are about 240 members drawn from across the province; on this occasion, only those from the OPP's three districts in southern Ontario were called upon, meaning about 120 officers met at the hotel. Within two hours of arriving, they were "stood down": nothing was going to happen immediately. The next day, they were put on standby, given a briefing, stood down again and sent back to the regions from whence they'd come.

The following Tuesday, April 18, they were back at the Holiday Inn and, after a day of waiting about, gathered in the hotel conference room at about 7:30 P.M. for a full briefing from Inspector Robin Jones. She gave them their "mission statement." It was a classic of modern police corporate-speak. The Haldimand Reclamation Operations Plan, dated April 12, read as follows: "By executing the arrest warrants issued by Justice Marshall, peacefully bring an end to the occupation in a professional manner that addresses the safety of all concerned." Officers were to tell the protesters, "You are in contempt of court. You must accompany these officers immediately off the property. Failure to do so will result in you being arrested for contempt."

Superintendent Ron Gentle also addressed the group, as did a couple of staff sergeants. Then they waited, jammed into a room too small for so many big cops, to hear from Superintendent Ron George. After almost an hour, he arrived in plain clothes, walked up to the front of the room and whispered something to Inspector Jones. She then turned around and told the crowd, "Ah, Superintendent George has decided he's not going to speak to you at this time."

If it was plain to many in the room that George was disappointed that the ERT was poised to go in, his failure to address them was still surprising. The eve of possible peril is the traditional moment when superiors deliver last-minute pleas to watch one another's backs. As the fictional Sergeant Phil Esterhaus used to say at the start of every shift on the old *Hill Street Blues* police drama, "Let's be careful out there." The omission was stark.

Forty-five minutes later, the unit was again stood down because of "ongoing negotiations." These were preliminary talks, at best. The federal government's fact-finder, University of Western Ontario professor Michael Coyle, had just produced his twenty-five-page report in early April. His summary of the parties' positions showed just how bewilderingly complex any real negotiations were likely to be: Ottawa claimed it had no authority to intervene because the feds considered DCE to be privately owned land; Ontario argued Canada should have the lead; the Six Nations elected council, which officially pronounced itself neutral on the occupation (though later it financed the occupiers to the tune of at least $60,000), declared it was the appropriate party to engage in talks; the Haudenosaunee Confederacy council supported the occupation but demanded official recognition as the traditional government. The conflict, Coyle concluded, appeared "difficult to address, not hopeless," the description, in the circumstances, constituting sunny optimism.

Wednesday the 19th dawned warm and clear, and the ERT team leaders met to discuss the intelligence they had on DCE—there were observers on rooftops and sentries posted at the vacant houses, more Mohawk Warriors had responded to the call for support, and there was a report of someone spotted with a barrel of weapons. If that sounded alarming, the ERT members were nonetheless told not to wear their helmets or carry their shields—standard protective gear for a public order unit. Rather, they were to go "soft tack," meaning they'd be indistinguishable from regular uniformed officers, in baseball caps and blue shirts, with only their blue tactical pants and perhaps an ERT patch as clues to their public order expertise.

Certainly, they were not to take their C-8s—compact assault rifles just like those used by the Canadian Forces—which were deemed provocative. The rifles were to be made "loader safe," meaning a magazine is inserted, but the weapon isn't charged. The C-8s, the officers were told, were to be left behind, purportedly "accessible," in gun bags in a fleet of fifteen-passenger window vans rented from Hertz. With eight officers per team, that meant that eight C-8s, along with six thirty-round magazines for each gun—a total of 1,440 rounds—were to be left in each of the vehicles.

The officers met in small groups well into the night, and by two in the morning on April 20, without ever having hit the sack, they had a final briefing in the hotel parking lot. By 4:45 A.M., they were in Caledonia, and after a quick stop at the Unity Road command post, were in position at the staging area at the Stirling Street bridge, ready to move onto the site.

There were the 120 ERT guys, a couple of canine units, intelligence officers and a group of regular officers (augmented with as many females as could be rounded up, the rationale being that in native culture, women are respected and therefore wouldn't be assaulted). A team of a dozen members of the OPP's Tactics and Rescue Unit (TRU), had been there, on the ground, for three days. In total, the OPP was almost two hundred strong.

The seasoned among them, however, were filled with dread. The operational plan was seriously deficient. There was no acknowledgement of the fact that the western edge of DCE is less than two kilometres from Six Nations and its twenty-two thousand residents, or of the hard truth that, by waiting as long as they had, the site was no longer sparsely populated, as it had been in the first weeks, nor solely populated by the likes of Janie Jamieson. In fact, Superintendent George, as court documents reveal, was aware that "extreme activists" were on the site, and that the Confederacy "was unable to manage them." In the discovery for the Brown/Chatwell lawsuit, Superintendent John Cain, the OPP's major incident commander in overall charge of DCE from March, testified that this information came from George in early April. Cain also said that, in his view, "extreme activists" meant Mohawk Warriors, whom he described as being akin to Hells Angels in that the Warriors deploy themselves in a quasi-military manner and, as he succinctly put it, they "use guns, have guns."

Never was there any attempt to answer the question that was the elephant in the room: assuming the OPP secured Douglas Creek Estates, what was the backup plan if the occupiers returned en masse? In other words, three of the four great tactical principles by which virtually every tactical squad in the world lives—isolation, containment and evacuation—were virtually ignored in the grand plan. As for the fourth principle, negotiating a peaceful resolution, it was put into use in novel fashion when the OPP was left with only one possible resolution *to* negotiate: their own retreat.

————

If very few people in town had specific warning of when the raid was coming, on DCE and Six Nations they were certainly braced for it.

"Confederacy, federal and provincial talks break down, protesters refuse to leave, OPP raid expected" was the front-page headline on the *Turtle Island News*, a native-owned weekly published on Six Nations, on the morning of April 19. The story went on for two full pages inside, and among the photographs was a shot of OPP Deputy Commissioner Maurice Pilon and Superintendent George talking to one of the Haudenosaunee chiefs, Steve Maracle. In the piece, various of the chiefs were quoted as telling the protesters the police were coming, that the OPP already had told them "they're down to their final hours."

On the Caledonia side, detachment commander Brian Haggith, drafted into an unofficial police–community liaison role because of his local popularity, had in his discreet way put the bug in only a few select ears. He called Mayor Trainer and, as she remembers, said, "Do you want to know when we're going in and that sort of thing?"

Even then, Trainer had a decent grasp of her own frailties. "And I said, 'No, don't tell me. Then I can't leak it and can't accidentally tell somebody. You tell me when it's all over.'"

At 4:30 A.M. on April 20, Haggith phoned the Hennings and gave them a heads-up. The brothers had hoped to get onto the site themselves before this point, to clear out their office, but didn't get the opportunity. That the office was thus far untouched gave them a small measure of comfort. As John says, "The alarm was on and the red light on. We could actually see it from the main road." Then people began to call, as word spread around town, and soon they were watching the raid live on CHCH—Don at his house, John at his, the two talking non-stop on the phone and wondering, Don says, "if we should bust into a bottle of something."

"It was euphoria," John says. "It had been so long, it was so frustrating, and then we're starting to watch, it's starting to go downhill."

About the same time, just as he'd promised, Haggith phoned Marie Trainer to say it was over. She remembers the call well. Haggith was telling her, "'We're just cleaning up, it's okay, everything went well.' And as he was talking, he went, 'Gotta go! All hell's breaking loose!' And it did."

The arrest warrants had been quickly executed, the sixteen (by day's end, the number would total twenty-one) people taken into custody already were back at the station in Cayuga for processing. But other occupiers had called Janie Jamieson and Dawn Smith at home, and the two young women made quick work of their prearranged phone trees: within fifteen minutes, dozens and dozens of people were pouring onto the site from Six Nations on the other side of the rail tracks on DCE's western border.

The fifty or so ERT officers stationed there immediately called for reinforcements. From other parts of the site, ERT teams responded, driving along the Sixth Line and parking their rented vans on the side of the road, their loads of gun bags visible through the windows to anyone curious enough to look.

Some of the officers were constantly checking back over their shoulders, as if to will the vans to remain unnoticed and unmolested. No one was left behind to watch over them or their lethal cargo. The officers barely got going before they were greeted by at least a hundred natives, coming onto the site on foot, on ATVs, in pickup trucks—and that was merely the first Six Nations response.

Many supporters, some wearing bandanas over their faces, were armed—with baseball bats, axe handles, shovels, steel table legs and at least one chainsaw. They wove in and out of the small knots of police, who were now standing back to back to cover one another, petrified at the thought of having to use lethal force. Ken (Tex) Deane, the well-liked OPP officer who was convicted in the shooting of Dudley George at Ipperwash eleven years earlier and who had died in a car crash just three days before the occupation of DCE began, was probably never more in the thoughts of his former colleagues than he was in these moments. No one wanted to be the next Tex Deane.

A couple of fights broke out; heavily armed TRU team members were caught on camera, looking sheepish as they emerged from their hidey-holes; the fellow with the chainsaw tried to start it up; one officer was hit with a bag of rocks and went down; a few officers used their Tasers, pepper spray or batons; a few protesters cried, "Take their gun belts!" or "They're ours now!"; a couple of people were arrested, then quickly de-arrested.

"Not that I was scared," an ERT officer says, "but I was scared. We were so vastly outnumbered immediately . . . we know we're in the shit."

By 6 A.M., the police were allowed to turn their vans around in anticipation of withdrawal, this thanks to Superintendent Gentle, there on the front lines with his officers, who negotiated the police retreat with the occupiers. By 7:25, to whoops of delight from the crowd, the OPP began to withdraw. At 7:53, the OPP formally gave up DCE to the natives. They had been on the site for about three hours, and held it firmly for less than an hour.

For one ERT officer, Constable Jeff Bird, the retreat was personal and particularly painful. A Caledonia resident, Bird is also a good friend of Dave Brown and Dana Chatwell, the couple whose house on Argyle Street was uniquely located relative to Douglas Creek Estates, bordered by it on two sides and, for all practical purposes, surrounded by it.

"We're trying to get everybody off the site," Bird remembers, "and now the natives, they're empowered, they're just nuts now. I'm looking across, I can see Brownie and Dana on their deck, I can see literally a hundred natives running across DCE and coming towards us, and we are so fucked here."

The police were being pushed back, and then, Bird says, "We jump in the vans and we fuck off . . . and then there's the big *whooooo*— 'We win! We win!' We saw the fires had been started, the gravel had been dumped, and of course my phone starts ringing off the hook."

It was Dave Brown, and he was screaming, "Where are you guys going? What the fuck's happening here? You can't leave me here!"

————

When things started to go pear-shaped, John Henning jumped into his truck and drove down to Russell Douglas's field directly across the street from DCE, not far from the pond where in winter they skated as boys. The old farmer is the Douglas in Douglas Creek Estates; the Hennings share a huge affection for him, bought the land from him, and in his honour arbitrarily anointed the drainage ditch that ran through the site a proper creek, "Douglas Ditch Estates" lacking the proper gravitas.

John walked into the field.

"There were now other people there," he says, "and I took my binoculars, and I went with a friend and I sat there, and now the tire fires were burning. And I actually watched them rob my office with my binoculars, watched them carting stuff out into vans, things like that. And this is all being televised." The OPP now had officers in other houses close to the site, videotaping it all. This practice of videotaping criminal acts instead of investigating and policing them, ostensibly for later use in prosecutions, would soon become common.

The Hennings are both talented competitive marksmen, and at that moment, John says, looking through his binoculars, "I'm just wishing there were crosshairs in it, I was so . . . I was so frustrated.

"I walked out of there onto this field, nearly in tears, and these people are there now, and it's hard to explain. There's a dead-end road where I walked in, and these people are there and they're going, 'Arrgh, our wedding's going to be cancelled on the weekend.' I went over and apologized to them, and they didn't know who I was, and I felt so bad, because we'd pressured them [the police] to do this and now the whole thing, it was our fault."

In the brothers' office was the usual stuff—family pictures, a copier, their grandfather's table with its big, hand-turned legs, a Robert Bateman print their mother gave Don for his fortieth birthday. But it was also a real construction site office, filled with the valuable tools of their trade, everything from shovels to generators to hammer drills and measuring tapes and sanders. And just about every scrap of personal information they had—including banking information, chequebooks, social insurance numbers, phone numbers of old customers (including several of the OPP whose homes they'd previously built), tax returns and gun registration certificates—was also in there, as well as confidential information about their builders and their new homeowners.

Later, they learned someone cashed one of the stolen cheques, for a couple of thousand dollars, in Niagara Falls, then crossed the border, and that a native man who was arrested in northern Ontario was found with a blank Henco cheque in his wallet. Later still, their lawyer, Michael Bruder, started getting calls from "guys trying to sell us our own information back," Don says.

But now, like everyone else in Caledonia, they had bigger worries. Their beautiful town looked like a war zone. The natives had parked a dump truck across part of Argyle Street and deposited its load of gravel across the rest, shutting down the main drag, but also had thrown up makeshift barricades on Highway 6 between Argyle and Green's Road, preventing anyone from going north or south, and at the rail line. Some of them also moved into and occupied the bush on the hydro land and the tracks behind the houses along the western portion of Braemar Avenue, where it intersects with Thistlemoor Drive at the north end of the site. This area was never part of DCE, though it was, from the get-go, treated and patrolled by the occupiers as part of the disputed territory. Had the natives wished to seize even more land that day, they probably could have. Such was the state of shock and paralysis that, as one senior OPP officer who was there says now, "I honestly think if they'd [the occupiers] kept going that morning, if they'd wanted to go as far as the Canadian Tire or right into town, they could have."

Caledonia itself seemed to be burning: There were grass fires, at least three tire fires, and bonfires going on the site. Black smoke billowed throughout the day from a van that occupiers dressed in camouflage had tossed over the Highway 6 overpass and which had landed smack on top of one of the piles of burning tires, as well as from the old wooden bridge that crossed the train tracks, providing a direct route into town from Six Nations by linking Stirling Street and the Seventh Line, which was burned to the ground.

By nightfall, both the OPP and natives quoted in the local press offered the same wide-ranging estimates as to how many occupiers were on DCE now: between five hundred and a thousand. The only thing the Hennings could imagine happening, and they were torn about whether they wanted it to happen, was that the military would be called in. "It was the only thing that *could* happen in our minds," John says. "What else could be done now? The police can't do it; the military's got to come."

John got his kids from school—he remembers the teachers being white with shock—and packed up them and his wife and sent them to a hotel out of town; Don got his two youngsters and they went with his wife to her parents' place in a city a safe distance away.

At about six o'clock, as some of the OPP were having supper at the Unity Road command post, in walked some of the Emergency Response Team from the Royal Canadian Mounted Police.

An OPP officer asked, "What are you doing here?"

"We're here to back you up," one of the Mounties replied.

"Little late, aren't you?"

"Yeah," said the Mountie, "well, we've been here for two days. We got paged last week."

The RCMP had answered the OPP's call for help, rented a hangar at Hamilton's John Munro International Airport—about ten minutes away—and one hundred of their ERT members had been sleeping and eating there for two days. Yet somehow, no one thought to call upon them in time for the morning raid.

For the Hennings, April 20 ended with a group of their friends starting to sleep in shifts that night at their homes, so "someone was always awake in case there were drive-bys and so we could actually sleep a little while." It was a ritual that was replicated by families all over town, and would continue to be for many months—people would send their kids away, emergency-board their pets and keep packed bags at the ready, either by the front doors of their homes or in the trunks of their cars, should they need to leave at a moment's notice.

———

Maria and Dieter Rauscher, one of fourteen families who live on the Sixth Line just east of Six Nations, are early risers, a habit born of a lifetime of hard work and the ingrained discipline of those who come to Canada as immigrants, as they did from Germany, with the dream of giving the next generation a better life. They had lived in their rambling old farmhouse on a small acreage since 1978, having moved there when Dieter transferred into a management position with Lake Erie Steel (now U.S. Steel Canada) at Nanticoke, just a short trip south of Caledonia.

One of the conditions of the new job was that he be within a half-hour of the plant, close enough to be on call. The Rauschers didn't want, and couldn't afford, an actual farm, but they wanted to be in the country. In Hamilton, when Dieter worked for Stelco and Maria at a home for mentally and physically disabled youngsters, they'd had a typical city house with a handkerchief-sized yard. But there, Maria had her first "gardening experiences," as she grandly describes it, and she was ready to tackle something bigger. They spotted the red-brick house with the big maple tree out front and, Maria says, "I just fell in love with it, eh? Isn't that stupid? Plus it had four bedrooms; we had three kids, and it was old.

"All of a sudden I have this property. We had six and a half acres [though they later sold off a parcel of that, before the occupation began]. We were like landowners," she says, making fun of herself in a Bavarian accent that remains thick, "because we come from Europe—who has that? So we walked our own land, we looked at every shrub, we found an old foundation from the first settlers, Irish people. So we were absolutely in love with our property." And every time they had a little extra, they bought and planted a tree.

On the morning of April 20, they were still in bed when they heard police cruisers speeding by on the Sixth Line, heading east toward the train tracks.

"As we look out the window," Dieter says, "there was a Suburban or something like that, a big one, stopped, and cops get out. They were standing there with hands behind their backs. Six or eight of them. And there were about three or four Indians who came out the back here."

The trees weren't in full flower yet, so the Rauschers could see clearly. Dieter watched as one of the officers pulled out a piece of paper and began reading something—presumably the OPP's warning to protesters—aloud.

"All of a sudden, there was a big kerfuffle," he says. "Out of the bush came another twenty people . . . there were already people coming from Six Nations down the road. And they all walked by our entrance to our driveway, they all had sticks, baseball bats."

The OPP, seeing the crowd, just "high-tailed it" and took off.

"That," Dieter says, "was the last police we saw."

He doesn't mean for the next few days, either, or even weeks: the OPP, by its own admission, did not police the Sixth Line for the next forty-seven months. As then-OPP deputy commissioner Chris Lewis wrote Mayor Trainer in March of 2010, there had been "a verbal agreement" among the OPP, the Haudenosaunee and the Six Nations Police that, as "an interim measure," Six Nations "would police the DCE property, as well as the 6th and 7th Lines." That "interim" measure lasted one month shy of four years.

The Rauschers went outside again a bit later, when there was what Maria calls "a commotion"—residents of the Sixth Line use *kerfuffle* and *commotion* to describe the most harrowing events—just up the road from them at a little bridge.

"Before we knew it," she says, "we see guys throw that [Chevrolet] Lumina over the bridge."

"We saw it," Dieter says.

"The thing is, people were heaving something," Maria says, "but you don't for one minute think they're going to throw it onto a highway, do you? Oh my God, oh my God."

The Rauschers didn't know the occupiers had already closed the bypass and that there were no cars below. "We were thinking," Maria says, "what if that goes on a cop? So the next thing you see is flames, smoke."

"That's when they set it on fire," Dieter says.

"Because the whole road was burning," Maria says.

She had someone else to worry about now. A few houses up lived a native woman with young children. "There was all this smoke and this toxic stuff," Maria says. She phoned the woman and suggested she grab the kids and get out of the house. "Her answer to me was, because she must have known, 'We [natives] have to do what we have to do.'"

What the Rauschers call "the victory parade" was next: a constant flow of cars and trucks up and down the Sixth Line, horns honking to celebrate the defeat of the OPP. In the open bed of one pickup, they both saw a young man coolly sitting with a rifle across his knees. Still a little later, Maria was in the kitchen, and when she looked out the window this time, the smoke she saw was close. She ran outside and saw her neighbour Bob Masecar's front lawn was on fire.

"All I could think of was, 'Oh my God,'" Maria says. "We didn't know Bob very well [then]. His house, which he built mostly by himself, is going to go up in flames . . . it was very dry."

The Rauschers had had a fire once. Their barn burned down in January of 1981, and it left them with the deep-in-the-bone fear of fire that is so common in the country. Dieter, who was in the house, dialled 911; Maria was outside, weeping, as dozens and dozens of cars passed by. Only barely can she talk about it now.

"They all slow down," she says, "and this is why I hate them [the occupiers], I hate them with a passion: they laughed.

"They were laughing because they thought this was my house [about to burn]."

As Dieter came flying out with a couple of watering cans, they could hear the siren.

"The fire trucks," he says, remembering the relief that washed over him, and the crushing realization that followed.

"We can hear the fire trucks: okay. Hear the noise, hear the noise, wait and wait, and nobody shows up. They had closed it [the Sixth Line at Argyle Street] off already, with that tower and a truck, and they wouldn't let the fire department in," he says.

At last, a pickup stopped, and two young native men got out and, with Dieter's watering cans, some water bottles and a lot of stomping, put the fire out. The Rauschers decided to go into town, but with Argyle Street closed, the only way was the long way around, through the reserve. There were already sentries on the bridge, checking every car that came through; there was also a checkpoint on Oneida Road.

"They were way better organized than the police," Maria says.

In town, they headed straight for the fire department to ask why they hadn't come. "This guy was livid," Dieter says. "He was the assistant fire chief; he said, 'They wouldn't let us through.'"

The chief called the OPP, and two detectives showed up to interview the Rauschers; Dieter reminded them of the tank cars that passed by every day carrying liquefied petroleum gas.

"By this time," Maria says, "we know already it's out of control. We know already. We looked at each other and we said, 'Oh, we lost. We have lost.'"

Next, they went to the OPP substation in Caledonia, which is in a small plaza on Argyle, beside the beer store. They asked for an escort home.

The young officer breezily said, "Just drive home. I'll call you in half an hour."

As with the police videotaping, this also became a standard practice: the OPP, unable or unwilling to act, would either offer to call residents to check up on them or would give out their cell phone numbers so the residents could call them.

Back through Six Nations the Rauschers drove, but of course, once home, they realized they couldn't stay the night and that they had better get Pete, their Labrador retriever, into a kennel. They dropped Pete off, found themselves a motel room in Hamilton, and the next night moved to a now-defunct inn in town.

Months before, they'd booked a trip back to Germany. Both their mothers were elderly (Dieter was then 64 himself, Maria 60), and they were due for a visit. Before they left, the OPP asked if they could move into the Rauschers' house while they were gone, to use it as a stakeout. "I said, 'You make just one little mistake [and get caught] and I can't live there anymore,'" Dieter says. "Or my house is burned down."

"When we came back," he says, "I thought it would all be over."

———

Debbie Thompson, who lives up the road from the Rauschers, wasn't so lucky as to get away for a couple of weeks.

At first, like a few of the other Sixth Line residents, Debbie and her husband Carl didn't want their real names used; their son Ryan is an OPP officer, who started to work in Caledonia in 2007, and they didn't want to complicate things for him.

The Thompsons are the fifth generation to live in what is Carl's family home. They used to live in town, and Debbie was wary of moving into the country, but quickly got used to it and liked it. She has been in Caledonia and environs for almost forty years. "I used this road almost every day, saw the people, knew the people, visited here or rented land," she says. "There were all kinds of connections."

She describes April 20 as the day "a war broke out."

"The first thing I saw were hundreds of vehicles on this road, lots of burning torches, guns, people everywhere, screaming, yelling, 'Kill this, kill that.'"

"Guns in whose hands?" I ask. "The police?"

She laughs, derisively. "Oh, there was no police. No police. What happened is my dog started barking early in the morning. We didn't know what was wrong, because the road didn't seem any different. My husband went to go to work . . . he could see all the flashing lights and stuff, because the police had put all their cruisers across the railway tracks."

Carl thought there'd been an accident, so he turned around and went up through the reserve, tried to use the bypass but couldn't, and only realized there'd been a raid when he finally got to work and called Debbie. By then, everything had changed noticeably. The Sixth Line was jammed with parked cars and protesters; she saw at least three of them carrying long guns. She phoned Carl and asked him to come home, but he didn't think he'd make it, so she set out in one car, while her daughter, who had an exam that morning, drove another.

"We were met by protesters with baseball bats," Debbie says. They begged their way through. She arranged to meet Carl at the OPP substation by the beer store. She had to wait in line to speak to an officer, told him where she lived, and asked how she was going to get home.

"You're a native woman?" he asked. "Just walk in."

"I'm not a native woman," Debbie says, "and even if I was, it's not something you'd expect an officer to say to anybody. That's like painting everybody on Six Nations with a brush—you know what, you're all bad, or you're all protesting or whatever—and that wouldn't be the case."

The remark was her first clue that the OPP, already drawing upon officers from out of town to boost their numbers, was under the mistaken impression that on the Sixth Line, as with all the other Haldimand County lines, the railway tracks marked the start of the reserve, and anyone who lived where Debbie did must therefore be native. The police even had a map, used to orient the hundreds of officers who had come to Caledonia from all over Ontario, showing the reserve beginning at the tracks. Off and on that summer, officers would point to the map and tell Debbie, "Look, this is where you tell me where you live—it's Six Nations!"

"Well, it's wrong," she would explain. "I live there and I pay taxes to the town of Haldimand and I'm not a native."

The Thompsons went to their son's, and stayed there that night—and a few others.

"When we did finally come home," Debbie says, "we thought, 'We can't just leave our house forever.' And I really thought—this happened on a Thursday—and I thought, 'Okay, it's bad, whatever. [By the] time Monday morning comes they'll have all this cleared up, right? Just gonna be a bad weekend, whatever.'

"But it didn't. It didn't clear up."

———

Dave Hartless of the Hamilton Police was home on Braemar Avenue the day of the raid, and he saw it unravel as the OPP were driven off the site. As a police officer, he believes the operation was properly executed and that the on-the-ground commander did the right thing by having his people retreat.

"I think where they misstepped," he says, "is that they didn't take into account the possibility of such an uprising against it. They essentially had officers in reserve, but they didn't deploy them."

From that moment, he says, "My nice, quiet neighbourhood, where I'd moved my kids, became a war zone."

Hartless is one of those highly compartmentalized people. At work, he's a cop; at home, he's a dad and husband. He had no desire to mix the two halves of his life, and for the longest time, even as his world changed unrecognizably, he kept quiet. He stayed inside for most of the day on April 20, figuring it was more prudent to be behind brick walls. At about 4 P.M., he looked out the window, saw it was quiet and went down to pick up his mail at the end of the court. Occupiers were there, "yelling their various obscenities. I had one of them say, 'I know that guy; he's a cop!' Then they start talking about 'We're gonna kill you, we're gonna burn your house down.' Yap, yap, yap. I blow 'em off, I go back inside."

He headed to the Unity Road command centre to report the threats. The OPP inspector wanted to know how the natives knew Hartless was a cop. "Well, I don't know," he says. "They're all masked . . . is it possible I arrested one of them?" Perhaps, but how could he know since he couldn't identify them?

That night, at work in Hamilton, he asked his supervisor if he could have permission to take home his gun; he was refused. Thus began a two-month-long internal battle with his own force.

All the while, the natives who had moved into the area behind Braemar were making their presence felt. The first week, Hartless and his neighbours got rocks and garbage thrown over their back fences. "It was an annoyance," he says, "but it wasn't anything of significance. And most people can't throw from the tracks to my house.

I wasn't worried about the windows getting busted." Plus, he had his dog, a Chesapeake retriever. "Three traits I wanted in a dog," he says. "I wanted a good hunting dog; I wanted a family dog; I wanted one that would die protecting me or my kids, and a Chesapeake was the only one that fit with all three."

So, despite the garbage and the constant lights from the ATVs and the noise, he was managing.

"Then I had the wing mirror on my truck shot out with a pellet gun," he says. "That was an expensive nuisance, but again, not something that was particularly gonna get my back up."

That Hartless so quickly adjusted his vision of what was tolerable is typical of how Caledonians adapted to their changing reality. It was happening all over town. In fact, at the beginning of what became known at the Brown/Chatwell trial as the "barricade period" in Caledonia, Hartless and his neighbours were grateful for the OPP car that was always posted at the end of the street. Linda Hartless would bake for the police and take goodies to them, and the couple's middle daughter, excited at the spring crop of baby frogs, would collect them and then sell them to the officers for a penny a pop. What galvanized Hartless was the day his wife called him "and said she'd lost a wheel and crashed on Highway 6," with all three kids in the car. He tore out of work and raced to the scene. "I get to where she is," he says. "I look at the wheel. Now, I'm just fuming."

The truck had been in for service the month before, so, he says, "I could understand if there'd been one lug nut that hadn't been tightened down properly and had come off." But that wasn't the case: all five nuts on the wheel were off; it appeared that someone had tampered with it.

Hartless was bouncing off the walls.

"So now I'm battling with myself over my rage and desire for vengeance and to create a learning curve for them [the occupiers] that they just fucked with the wrong guy, over my oath and duty as a police officer to collect evidence and ensure that the right person is charged."

The real problem, he says, "is that I've got nowhere to focus my rage because I know what group did it, but I don't know *who* did it." He slipped into a bit of a depression. "I pretty much shut everybody else out of the house off, getting less and less apt to go outside," he says. The kids weren't allowed out, he says, "until I'd scanned the tree lines. I wouldn't let them out front unless I'd scan the area first, and I'd stay out with them. If they were out, I was out. If Linda was out, I'd come back in. If Linda wasn't here and the kids were out and I had to come in to use the washroom, I'd bring all the kids inside."

It wasn't because he was paranoid, either. One day, he says, "I'm doing my standard checks of the back yards, I find someone all camouflaged up, sitting in a home-constructed tree stand with a rifle across his leg." This was in the tree line at the back of the house, about four hundred yards away. He reported it immediately.

"I went down and talked to the OPP," he says.

"The ones who were always at the end of the street?" I ask.

"Yes," he says. "They said they'd call it in."

"Did anything happen?"

"No," he says.

———

At least at Thistlemoor, there were cops—an oppressive number, it felt like some days, but their stolid presence offered a reassurance of sorts. In the time before June 9, there was still a die-hard belief that, if push came to shove, the OPP would act to protect citizens.

After April 20, on the Sixth Line on the other side of DCE, policing was nonexistent, just one of many civic services residents didn't receive.

"We didn't get garbage pickup," Debbie Thompson says. "We didn't get mail."

And there were the blockades: the first just outside her driveway, at the little bridge; another along the road to town; the big main barricades across Argyle Street; and then, of course, the OPP line, which was maybe a hundred metres up the road, at the south end of the Canadian Tire.

"And we had curfews," Debbie says. These were imposed by the occupiers. They changed constantly and were designed solely for the occupiers' convenience or amusement.

"I was only allowed out till eleven," she says. "My daughter was allowed out till 9:30 P.M. Twenty-one years old, she was, and she worked night shift at the time, so there were a lot of shifts she couldn't take. So she didn't continue with that job. There were just protesters always here, chanting or singing, whatever they do. Fires. I don't hate fires, but you knew they were there because you could always smell it. And you know, when you tried to go out, they'd be mad if you went out too often. That wasn't really necessary, they didn't think."

At the time, Debbie had a grandmother who lived in the retirement home in town, and was in the habit, long before the blockades, of taking her lunch or something special she'd made. "I went to see her three times a day usually," she says. "She was, like, 99, and I would go . . . we were so close, a minute and a half away. And she didn't hear that good, so talking on the phone wasn't the same anymore.

"Like I said, I'd make something—the dinners get sort of [institutional]—and if I had something I knew she liked, salmon in particular, I'd take stuff to her, or go and get a coffee for her, whatever. Just to be with her sometimes."

Every single time she left the house, she was interrogated. "Where I was going, how long I was going for, the reasoning, why. I mean, I've got kids who live in town, I've got friends that live in town, my grocery store's in town, my doctor, my dentist, my grandmother. To get out, to see the rest of my family, I've got to go through town.

"I mean, this is my town, right? This is where I do things.

"And even the police would hassle me about how many times I went through. Now, I guess to them, they thought I was doing it on purpose, I don't know. I had to go through one, two, three barricades, and then the police," she says. "Three barricades and the police, and sometimes townspeople would have a block up, and they were no better. Because if they didn't know you, well, you're not coming through.

"Well, you know what? I bloody live there. I'm not a protester.

"So you had to put up with them as well."

And she found she sometimes simply *had* to leave the house. She hated being there. Even if all she did after leaving was to sit by the Grand, in the park, she would. "Just to not be here," she says.

Sometimes, the natives would demand body searches. "They'd just announce it," Debbie says. "'It's a body-search night'—and you had a choice whether to come through or go the other way." Her daughter, Lindsay, who was then twenty-one, bore the brunt of these requests; she would turn on her heel, furious, and go stay in town. "She never went through one," Debbie says.

They demanded it of Debbie only once. "I think they were drunk," she says. "I could smell alcohol, beer, whatever, and I basically laughed at them and said, 'Yeah, that'd scare the hell out of you, wouldn't it?' and kept going. Nothing happened."

She might be under the occupiers' thumb, she might hate herself for her uncharacteristic subservience, but she was 52 and she was damn well not going to subject herself to a body search. "I just took them [the occupiers' demands] as a joke. My daughter didn't take it as much of a joke, she turned around and left. She wouldn't tell her dad. I guess she feared what he'd do, and it was a long time before she let him know."

Debbie went to the OPP to report the body searches, saying, "Like, 'What can we do about this?' And he said, 'Well, at 21, really, don't you think she should move out?'

"That is not something you say to anybody's mother," Debbie snaps. "I don't care if that girl was 50; you don't say that."

Then came the "passports"—nothing more than pieces of coloured paper with residents' licence plate numbers written on them, issued by the natives. But they had to be proffered nonetheless, and checked. Visitors, such as her parents, who used to come for Sunday dinner, had to be preapproved. "They wouldn't go through the barricades," she says. "I think they were nervous. Plus, there were days they couldn't get through anyway, to visit.

"I mean, you had to be okayed," Debbie says, "and if you weren't okayed . . . I had people who didn't come because they weren't okayed."

"Sometimes, you'd go out, and we'd get to this thing [the first barricade] and they'd turn you back and say, 'You're not going in, you're not going to town today.' What choice do you have? Call the police? For what?"

She stopped taking pictures of her flowers or her grandchildren. "If they [the natives] saw me," she says, "they'd come and check my camera. And I'd say, 'Do you really think I'm taking pictures of you? Look here, look at what I've got to take pictures of.'

"I did not like them asking to see my camera," she says. "I didn't think they had the right."

It was during this period, too, that a couple of natives approached her when she was outside and demanded she take down the Canadian flag. The Thompsons had two flags flying, Canada's and Scotland's. "They drove in, said, 'That Canadian flag's gotta go or we'll burn it.' So down it come. You know what, I don't want it burned. Down it comes. Yet we had Warrior flags and Six Nations flags all over."

She was afraid, at a low level, all the time. There were always occupiers' cars parked on the road just past the driveway. Sometimes, there was a car sitting *in* the driveway. "I always try to be nice," she says. "You know—did you run out of gas, are you sick, do you need a phone, whatever."

The answer she would get: "This is our land, and I'll sit here as long as I want."

"Normally, it was a car that doesn't have a licence plate on it. And I'd just sit there and wait it out. But what am I gonna do? Like, some people will say to me—they think I'm odd—they say, 'Just phone the police.' And I'm," she says, derision in her voice again, "'What are they going to do?'"

Yet it was the control and humiliation that got to her most. "I mean, I *knew* the police weren't coming, so I knew whatever they [the natives] wanted, or said, or whatever, they were in control of us. And I mean, I'm not somebody who keeps quiet, usually. [But] I did. I was really nice to them. My husband wasn't. And they'd tell me, 'He's horrible.' Yeah, I know. What am I gonna do?

"Basically, it was kissing their ass. You know, to survive and to try to get as much peace as I could."

The Thompsons' two approaches began to take a toll on them as a couple, too. They'd been married for thirty-four years at the time. "We get along good," Debbie says. "He's a good man, blah, blah, blah. But during that time, it was like, you know what? I believed that DCE, after that first weekend, was going to go to the natives. He's very patriotic. I was, too, but not to the extent he was—'Our government this, our government that.'

"Well, our government has just left us here. So we had a lot of issues. We'd argue, we'd fight and then we'd say, 'Okay, nobody can talk about Indians, blockades, whatever.' Then something would go on and we'd start again. I saw the anger in him, and the hurt—this is my house."

She began to dream about escaping, about leaving Carl, about going to another country—she fixated on Germany.

"Why Germany?" she wonders aloud. "I'm not German, never been there, it was just where I wanted to go. I figured no one would look for me there, I guess."

———

The Rauschers got back from Germany in May, though they can't now remember precisely when. "We come back to Caledonia," Dieter says, "and there's still barricades up. He [an occupier] asked us for a passport."

"Did you get out your real one?" I ask, knowing they would have been in travel mode and would not have had a clue about what had happened to Caledonia in the interim.

"Yes!" Dieter says, laughing.

"So we get home," Maria says, "and then the misery was every day, every day."

At first, she says, seeing the new reality, she feared she wasn't going to have a garden that year. Then she decided, "to show them, I'm going to have a garden."

Still, she was careful: she could do most of her work behind the trees and shrubs and not be seen. She would do it in the mornings, when the occupiers were still sleeping; that was also when Dieter would mow the lawns.

"We were hiding most of the time," she says.

"We stayed out of sight," Dieter says. "We were like mice."

If friends came to visit, the occupiers went crazy. "They monitored every car that came into our driveway," she says.

If they drove into town, the natives at the roadside shack would speak into walkie-talkies; by the time the Rauschers got to the main barricade, others were waiting for them.

"It was totally a military operation," Dieter says.

The fires on DCE were always going. The old generators, on their last legs, roared and there were lights on constantly at night. Sometimes, the Rauschers could hear the drumming from the other side of the site, at Thistlemoor.

Maria, who is a heavy woman, plotted her strategy if the occupiers came to the house or set it on fire. She thought she might be able to run towards Bob Masecar's house and hide in the culverts. She kept Pete inside a lot more, especially if they were out in the yard and heard gunshots. Dieter bought blinds for every room in the house, a house where there had been none before. "When things got wild," he says, "we'd let the blinds down and close it off."

"You just didn't want to see," she says. "The doors were closed, the windows were closed, some of the noise was blocked out. Some. The night was the worst.

"I said this openly in meetings, because they were shoving it down our throats—they are not my neighbours anymore. Neighbours don't behave like that. There is, in my mind, absolutely no excuse for it. If only one of them had come to our house and said, 'It's going to be a bit unruly around here for a while, it's not directed at you, it's blah, blah,' I would have felt okay.

"This was not the case," she says. "They hated us. They let us know, 'You are intruders; you are not supposed to be here.' I don't care what anyone says, that's how it was."

Dieter adds: "And when all is said, 'You got to realize you live on Indian land.'"

What he can't forget is one distinct noise, "the sound of large flags that are mounted on a vehicle and make this flapping noise" as the cars went flying past their house.

"I get goosebumps," he says.

One morning, when what Maria calls "this circus" was going on, she awoke to the smell of freshly burning tires. Still in her night-gown, hair uncombed, she marched down to the rail tracks and told the two young natives there, "You know what, I don't care what you do. I don't give a shit what you do. Just remember not to make a tire fire anymore and watch it doesn't go over to my side. The rest, do whatever. I don't care.

"And actually, he took his mask off. And with that, I turned around. I went back to my yard, I picked up my garden hose and, in my bloody nightgown, I watered my plants and I moseyed along. This is *our* property. This is how you see me. This is how you get me, and that's what I'm going to do and nobody is going to stop me.

"And I think that made the rounds a little bit," she says, a little proud. "I must have looked a sight. Oh my God. But I didn't care. For once, I think they knew there is a limit; do not push anymore."

By now, the occupiers were regularly roaring along the rail tracks on ATVs, and one day, Maria walked up towards the tracks, intending to have a look. "As I'm approaching," she says, "there's already a van coming" to greet her. That was one of the things that most unnerved them—the sophistication of the surveillance.

"You would almost think they had a satellite up there," Dieter says, "watching everybody."

"They were continuously watching you," Maria says. "Continuously."

There was a particular knoll with a tree on top, and a tent pitched there. "That was the lookout for the whole area," Dieter says. "You could see the whole area, all the way around."

Just going to town was fraught with tension. The Warriors—or, at least, occupiers wearing Warrior paraphernalia—would some-times play a game of chicken with them. As the Rauschers came out of the driveway, one pickup truck would be in front of their car, one behind. "They were dictating your speed," Dieter says. "You were just carried along. There was always someone in the back [of the truck in front], facing you, so you know, your adrenalin is going like crazy."

They knew there was no help. "If they stop you or if they would take you physically out of the car, or attack you, you know there is no help. You know that then," Maria says.

Dieter gave up his long walks to town with Pete, along the tracks. They drove around for months with two suitcases in the back of the car. "At all times," Maria says, "because we moved out more than once. And you never knew if you would be able to go back to the house, so you had the suitcases in case. I'm not some little person who can go in any old store and just buy underwear."

Once, during this period, there was a widespread rumour—false, as it turned out—that the police were going to rush the site. "The whole of Caledonia was convinced of that," Maria says. The Rauschers went to the OPP substation, where they ran into an offi-cer who told them that, yes, off the record, it was true.

"So then I said I'm not staying at the house," Maria says. "I don't want to go to a motel either this time. You know what? This time, we gonna go to the police station on Unity Road and we are going to be camping there. I had enough. Because, what other place is there?"

They pulled into the parking lot, where a security guard asked why they were there. "We're going to be here all night," Maria told him.

It was their version of the old saying, "If the mountain will not come to Mohammed, Mohammed must go to the mountain." The

OPP wouldn't come to the Sixth Line, so part of the Sixth Line, in the form of two seriously fed up sixty-somethings, went to the OPP.

———

On Friday, April 28, eight days after the raid and Day 60 of the occupation, the ERT had a major briefing at the Unity Road command post. Inspector Getty told the assembled crowd that the operation had been a smashing success, and said, pointing to the door, "If anyone doesn't agree, you can get up and leave the room right now."

An officer who was there says, "As a gymnasium full of ERT guys, we all should have got up and walked on this cocksucker."

Then Getty said something even more astonishing: The new mission, he said, "is protecting natives now from non-natives."

It was about this time that crowds had begun to congregate at the OPP barricade, the occupiers at theirs down the road. The "Friday Night Fights," they came to be called, though they weren't always that night of the week. People from both sides would hurl insults, and sometimes objects, at one another.

The first of these confrontations took place on April 24, after a rally at the fairgrounds drew an estimated two to three thousand frustrated Caledonians. The event also marked the birth of the group—headed by local financial planner Ken Hewitt, Ralph Luimes of the credit union, and Jason Clark, president of Clark Poultry Farms—that soon coalesced into the Caledonia Citizens Alliance. Afterwards, a smaller crowd, perhaps five hundred people wound up like tops, marched down to the OPP line, waving Canadian flags and chanting, "Let us through!"

If, as Chris Pickup, the editor of the *Regional News This Week*, wrote in the April 26 edition of her weekly paper, "it wasn't pretty," neither was it end-of-the-world material.

And that was the thing about the new OPP mission—never disclosed publicly of course, but apparent—to protect natives from non-natives. There was no evidence that Caledonians were breaking the law, behaving in a threatening manner or otherwise turning en masse upon the occupiers. The intimidating conduct, and the lawlessness, was almost exclusively coming from the native side. It was the occupiers, after all, who had torched the bridge, blocked all the roads, burned the tires and who were trespassing, harassing and threatening residents in their homes on a daily basis.

In fact, what was instructive about the Friday Night Fights was how much of the citizens' fury was directed at the police. Certainly, there were clowns hurling racial epithets at the natives occasionally, just as there were natives flinging insults back. But the citizenry's real venom was aimed squarely at the cops. People were angry and frustrated that their town was being held hostage by the natives, to be sure. But what they were incensed about was that the OPP was doing nothing about the law-breaking they'd already seen with their own eyes, out their own kitchen windows and on the streets of their subdivisions.

Within six weeks, Ontario Provincial Police Association boss Karl Walsh would coin the lasting phrase that still best describes the phenomenon. In a lengthy interview in the June 8, 2006, *Hamilton Spectator*, Walsh told columnist Susan Clairmont that officers were being ordered not to wear their tactical gear because the OPP didn't want to give the media or the occupiers the impression "there's an increased level of aggressiveness" in what the OPP brass—and politicians and government spokesmen—were publicly insisting was a "peaceful" operation.

As for the minuscule number of criminal charges laid by the OPP against the occupiers, Walsh said simply, "That is a two-tiered justice system."

And down at their Argyle Street barricade, the OPP was regularly doing something that absolutely everybody noticed. On their line, they were always facing the townspeople, their backs to the occupiers. The message couldn't have been clearer: the threat, if there was one, and the lawlessness were going to come from Caledonians, not natives.

It was insulting and galling to the townsfolk, and fairly so—they hadn't started this quarrel, though they were suffering for it, and now they were being treated like the enemy.

Karl Walsh had heard about it, plenty, from his members.

"How can you stand in a crowd," he says, "as a crowd management officer and discern who's the one who's going to turn on you? Hence the reason you face both sides. But to simply tell a professional group of crowd management people, 'Turn your back on a possible threat . . .'" He was gobsmacked.

It wasn't until August 25 that the OPP, for the first time, reverted to the time-honoured public order practice and finally had one line of officers facing the occupiers, another facing Caledonians.

———

In May of 2006, Dave Brown was still working at the Nicholson and Cates lumber yard, operating the lift truck, still hanging on to the remnants of his old life.

Until the natives moved onto DCE and into his yard, Brownie, as everyone calls him, was a man so happy in his own skin, his disposition so sunny, that his best friend, Jeff Bird, says he was like a big old Lab, impossible not to love. Brownie liked to party. He loved to barbecue and have friends over; he was the Q King. He worked hard, played hard. He was a loyal and reliable friend, a good teammate and a trusted employee. He loved his glamorous wife, Dana Chatwell, her teenage son, Dax, their border collie, Hunter, and his friends.

I don't want to make Brownie seem unsophisticated—he's not. He has lived and worked in Europe and is bright. But he was a stable man, content with his lot, not locked into the more-is-better cycle. He had all he wanted.

In August of 2005, he and Dana bought her family house from her dad. Right on the west side of Argyle Street, with commercial zoning, it was perfect for what she had in mind: a hairdresser who once had owned her own business, the entrepreneurial spirit ran deep in her and she had a hankering to do it again. She and Dave sank everything they had into the new house, renovated the lower level to the tune of $30,000 and a lot of their own sweat, and she hung out her Shear Body Sense sign. With five employees, posh new digs and a potential mother lode of new homes and customers coming right next door, things could not have looked rosier.

The house, as OPP Commissioner Julian Fantino was later to acknowledge in court, was "almost within" the occupied site. People on the Sixth Line had more barricades to pass through and nowhere to run when things turned ugly, and there were many more folks directly affected in the Thistlemoor subdivision at the north end of DCE, but no one lived more intimately with the occupiers than Brownie and his family.

That month, Nicholson and Cates had rented a limo bus, invited some employees to a Blue Jays baseball game in Toronto and laid in some beer and a big buffet for them. Brownie was one of them. It was exactly his sort of night—lots of people, a Jays game at the centre of things, a bit of a road trip and a few pops. He testified about this in the fall of 2009, during his lawsuit against the government, and his delight at the memory even then was evident. The Jays were playing the Los Angeles Angels, and won 5–1. Brownie estimates that, over the course of about seven hours, he had twenty-five chicken wings, garlic bread and anywhere from seven to nine beers.

The bus pulled into the Nicholson and Cates yard about midnight; he'd invited his friend Harold to stay with him, instead of going to his in-laws' place in town so late.

The routine was familiar by now: Dave would stop at the OPP barricade, say he lived in the house on the highway, one of the officers might joke, "I'm sorry to hear that," and off he'd go to the native barricade.

"You know who I am," he told the natives at the barricade. "Going home."

But, one of them replied, tonight there was a curfew, it had come and gone, and he couldn't go through.

"That's not going to happen," Brownie told them. "My wife's at home."

He drove through the tape that was strung across the road and tore home, dragging a pylon behind him.

"They followed me, of course," he testified. "Right away, I was scared. They started yelling at me that the curfew was posted." His friend was disbelieving. "He'd never seen anything like this," Brownie said. Filled with outrage, Harold began yelling at the natives, and got into a shouting match with one of them.

Dana was inside, in their TV room, looking straight into the driveway. She saw Dave come flying in, then saw all the lights as ATVs, trucks and a van arrived in hot pursuit. She ran out the front door.

"They all swarmed in," she testified at trial. "An ATV drove by him, smashed a concrete light stand." She was yelling at Harold, "We've never had a curfew!" He stormed off down the road, heading for the police barricade.

"I yelled at Harold not to go," Brownie testified. "It was dangerous." He told Harold, "Nobody's gonna help you if you get into a confrontation!"

Dana called the OPP, she said, laughing at herself for her folly. "I don't know why I called the police; I knew they wouldn't come. We knew the police wouldn't come; they would *never* come through those barricades."

Brownie was wild with rage, as if days of living behind the barricades—having to show a passport; being made to wait, and when he'd ask why, being told, "As long as it takes; it's been two hundred years"; watching as occupiers seized groceries and beer from his vehicle—and all the humiliations great and small had loosened some control mechanism in his head.

Then, as the ATVs screamed and circled around Brownie, Brian Skye, a purported native security boss, pulled up. "He told me if I didn't get in his truck, these guys would beat the shit out of me," he told the court. "I looked at Dana, she's scared to death; I'm scared to death. I got in the truck."

April 20, 2006: Caledonia was burning with grass fires, bonfires, tire fires. Black smoke billowed throughout the day—from a van that occupiers pushed over the Highway 6 overpass on to a pile of burning tires, and from a blazing wooden bridge that had stood over train tracks.

April 21, 2006: Makeshift barricades on Highway 6 prevented anyone from going north or south.

April 28, 2006: The OPP stand guard at a rally of non-native Caledonians. Detachment Commander Inspector Mel Getty told officers earlier that day that the new mission "is protecting natives now from non-natives."

Victoria Day, 2006: On the traditional "bread and cheese day," protestor Michael Laughing returns offerings left by Caledonia residents at the Argyle Street barricade.

May 22, 2006: A native protestor tears a Canadian flag following a shouting match with residents. The barricade had just been removed as a "gesture of goodwill" after construction was banned on the occupied site. It was soon replaced.

May 23, 2006: *Shortly after this photograph was taken, the Argyle Street barricade finally came down for good.*

June 7, 2006: *Clyde Powless, high-steel worker and frequent spokesman for the occupiers, pictured with Mohawk Chief Allen MacNaughton (right) and Cayuga Sub-Chief Leroy Hill (second right).*

June 10, 2006: It seemed that anyone who criticized the government or the OPP had become the enemy. Caledonia resident Pat Woolley, seen here protesting, saw the attitude this way: "Attack people personally—anyone who says anything, attack them personally. Make them too afraid. We kind of feel that in this town."

May 2, 2007: Marie Trainer, mayor of Haldimand County, at a demonstration in Toronto. Frustrated by the lack of a resolution in the then 15-month-old land dispute, residents of Caledonia had driven in a convoy in an attempt to get their message heard by the provincial legislature.

"stolen land": Occupiers of the Douglas Creek Estates, in an undated photograph.

Dec 1, 2007: Activist Gary McHale, creator of Canadian Advocates for Charter Equality and the website Caledonia Wake Up Call, is led away from a protest that turned violent. Clyde Powless later pled guilty to assaulting him.

Skye drove him to the OPP barricade.

"I just wanted to go home," Brownie said. "I just wanted to go to my home. Of course, I'm irate. I probably called him [the OPP officer] everything but a police officer. 'How can you watch this happen, you useless piece of shit?' I was angry to the point—I don't think I was ever more angry in my life."

He was thrown into a cruiser. At the wheel was Constable Will Lariviere. It was a measure of the one degree of separation that exists in small towns. As Brownie put it, "Before I started dating Dana, he was dating the roommate of the girl I was dating." Lariviere actually got into an argument with another officer about which of them would drive Brown to the OPP station in Cayuga; Lariviere wanted to do it, because of their previous connection, and he won the day.

The OPP put Brownie in a cell. He was not charged with anything. "It was a long night for me in that cell," he testified, "knowing Dana was home" alone. He paced and shook. He got no phone call, not even a drink of water.

"Just for trying to go to my own house," he said, "I got thrown in jail."

Every bit of this—the occupiers chasing Brown down because he dared defy a native-imposed curfew and try to go home; the OPP doing nothing to help him or stop the occupiers; his confinement, under threat, by Skye; his arrest without charge—was confirmed by evidence given in discovery by OPP Superintendent Cain in October of 2008 for the Brown/Chatwell lawsuit.

Early the next morning, a female officer Brownie knew—as he knew most everyone—came to let him out. "She's crying," he testified.

Brownie apologized to Will Lariviere; Lariviere kept apologizing back to him. His father came and picked him up, and took him to his house. "He gave me a hug," Brownie said. "I walked home." His dad couldn't drive him all the way; he wasn't allowed past the barricades.

As he went through the OPP line, Brownie said, "I watched the OPP watching me." He was almost forty, and "It was like I got a time-out or something," he told the judge. "I was so ashamed. I didn't even want to talk to anybody.

"That was only the first two weeks."

———

The Hennings got the first call from Rob Chadwick, the Bay Street lawyer who was the first of the province's special advisors, on the day after the failed raid.

"You gotta understand," Don says, "we're so enraged at this point, so he calls . . . he starts babbling on a little bit and I just said, 'Rob, this is Don,' and I asked him a question and he didn't answer. Then I asked him another question, and he didn't answer. And then I asked him a third question, and he didn't answer, and he started talking again.

"And I said, 'Stop it! I know you're from Toronto and that means you're way smarter than I am, but I have now asked you three questions which you have not answered. Where I come from, yes or no are the appropriate answers for a question.' And I said, 'If you don't know the answer, you can say "I don't know." But don't bullshit me.'

"I said, 'Can you write us a cheque, because you know what, this is bullshit, and you better tell the guys that you're working for that this is going to get really ugly and really public.'"

That day, the Hennings also had to go to the Burlington Holiday Inn to meet Doug Carr, Ontario's assistant deputy minister of Aboriginal affairs.

"And he's a jackass," John says, "and I'd tell him that to his face."

"Pinch-faced little bastard," Don says.

In Don's words, Carr suggested that "we're going to have a nice little sit-down meeting with these nice guys from the Confederacy and discuss what's all going on here, and I just looked at him and said, 'Doug, if I go into a meeting, the first thing I'm going to do is I'm going to grab one and I'm going to drag him across the table and I'm going to kick the shit out of him. Think it's a good idea to put us in a room with those guys?'"

The brothers had pretty much determined by now that they had no choice but to talk to the government people.

Weeks earlier, John had actually rented the second-biggest bulldozer Caterpillar makes and was set to go onto the site. Don talked him out of it. They often took turns like that, whichever brother was calmer talking down the one who happened to be hot. But the realization was sinking in that they might never get to build on DCE and that they would be caught in the middle, forced to wear the hair shirt of blame, yet unable to work, if they didn't force the government to buy them out.

"We told him [Chadwick] we wanted at least our money out of everything," Don says. "We wanted . . . like, buy us out. If you want to negotiate on our property, buy us out. We'd said that to fifty of them at the time, that we were not going to be in the middle. We said openly to their faces, 'We are not going to be the guys you try to blame this on, okay? We know what you're thinking here. We're not dealing with the natives; that's your job.'"

In John's notes, the following: "Trust is earned, not given."

The brothers' public relations rep had managed to book them a sheaf of media interviews, though at the time she arranged them, no one was terribly interested in hearing from the Hennings. But after the fights at the barricades on April 24, Don and John were suddenly in hot demand.

"It actually became very apparent right then and there," Don says, "that the only time that anything ever happened as far as the government was concerned was when either there was violence or court pressure, because at this point the judge [Marshall] is sitting there, seeing what was going on, the rule of law has been thrown out the window, and he wants to know, 'What is going on? Why isn't my injunction being upheld?'"

Indeed, the judge was growing impatient. Four times that summer, clearly frustrated, he called lawyers for the parties—the various levels of government, Henco, the Six Nations—to his court for updates on the situation. Judge Marshall was concerned about the deterioration of the rule of law, plain and simple. And *ex mero motu*—Latin for "of his own free will," whereby, to prevent injustice, a court makes rules or orders the parties might not be entitled to ask for—he dragged the lawyers back before him.

By late April, the Hennings and Chadwick had begun to talk money—though that wasn't the only thing. John had also decided, only half-kidding, to ask for a bull tag for the next moose hunt from the Ministry of Natural Resources.

"You should have seen the look on the lawyer from Toronto's face," Don says.

They abandoned that demand, but it was a delicious shot at the legion of city slickers in good suits who kept being fired at them as if from the cannons outside Queen's Park.

On Sunday, April 30, they were out of town at a shooting competition—they needed to do something that was normal—when they got a phone call from David Peterson, the former Ontario premier who had agreed to come in to try to resolve "short-term issues," chiefly the barricades of roads and railway. To Peterson's credit, he did the work pro bono.

"He said, 'We want to meet with you,'" Don remembers. "'We'll do it some place secluded.'"

Peterson suggested the north-end Tim Hortons, which hugely amused the Hennings, knowing as they did that both Hortons in town were the least private locations imaginable.

"So we go to the Hortons," Don says, "and here he is, in a bright yellow polar fleece, in a Mercedes convertible—and you gotta understand, there's not too many Mercedes convertibles in Caledonia—and everybody's staring, everybody's looking. And there's an entourage, there's ten guys."

"He's got all these lawyers, all his henchmen," John says.

"We pull up, we're in ball caps and we've been shooting all day, and we're dirty," says John.

Wisely, they moved the meeting to Don's wife's office.

Peterson's big lines, they remember, were "We'll make you whole" and "Think big, boys, think big. Think about how we can make this thing go away."

Wild turkey season opened at the end of April, but neither brother could muster much enthusiasm. "I only went a couple of times," Don says. "I'm afraid I didn't really give a shit about turkey anything at this point," though he remembers being out at John's farm, which is several klicks out of town, and still being able to hear the drumming from DCE.

The Hennings were preoccupied, trying to see through the BS to a path to survival. They'd started to fight with their insurance company over the looting of their office (it took about two years, but they did get paid); they were talking to their accountants, shifting things from one company to another as they tried to protect themselves; juggling constant meetings. At the same time, their lawyer, Michael Bruder, was in hard negotiations with Chadwick; John Burke, the provincial deputy minister of municipal affairs; and Neil Smith, the assistant deputy minister of economic development and trade for the province. Then, on May 16, they found out the province had sneaked in an immediate moratorium on all development on DCE; Bruder had found the information on one of the native websites. No one from Queen's Park had bothered to inform them.

The Hennings met the negotiators first thing the next morning.

"It was a short meeting, believe me," John says.

"We walked in and we had copies of this moratorium and we just flipped each guy a thing," Don says. "They started 'da-da-da-da-da' and we said, 'Stop. Get us an offer by Friday for fair market value on our property.'"

"And they said 'No, can't do that, gotta go through Cabinet, da-da-da-da-da,'" says John. "We said, 'Okay, get us a letter of intent that you will pay us fair market value by Friday.' They say, 'No, can't do it.'"

"Okay," said John. "Meeting's done. Have a nice day." They walked out.

The Hennings then launched a bit of a media offensive. Having decided they had to trust someone, they spent about an hour filling in Jamie West of CHML, a Hamilton talk radio station, shortly before he interviewed Ontario Aboriginal affairs minister David Ramsay on the air. Now well armed with information, West gave Ramsay a rough ride. Ninety minutes after the interview, the government called the Hennings.

"Finally," Don says, "things were serious, because they just got fried. And I was an arrogant prick to them when we walked into that meeting the next morning too, because I knew we had just manipulated the situation and they were denying it, they were denying that that was why they had called. And I just said, 'Well, no problem. If we have to keep the media pressure up, then I guess you've got no problem with it, if it's not doing any good.' [They said,] 'Well, I would advise you not to do that.'

"So I finally forced them into admitting that."

On Saturday, May 20, the Hennings were at the Burlington Holiday Inn to meet government negotiators; right behind them, with their lawyer, were their builders.

It was the Victoria Day long weekend, and by Monday, the occupiers appeared ready to bring down the Argyle Street barricade. In fact, the barricade was actually dismantled early that morning, but to a crowd of townspeople who had gathered in anticipation of this very thing, it wasn't good enough. They began to shout, "Open both roads! Open both roads!" and the natives walked away, back onto the site. The townsfolk now manned their own barricade, as they had off and on that weekend, refusing to let occupiers or Six Nations people pass. The OPP, with only about thirty officers on the line, decided to move in some cruisers to keep the two sides apart, and as they were doing this—moving the cruisers very slowly, being careful—a native man in a burgundy car tried to follow them and slip through the townies' barricade. He had Warrior flags on his car, says John, who was there, and an old fellow with a cane stepped in front of the car and was grazed and knocked to the ground.

"He was being obstinate," John says, meaning "provocative," but the crowd of townspeople went wild and began rocking the car, trying to tip it on its side. The OPP rushed to surround the vehicle and protect the people inside, but, John says, "by now, the police are outmanned, everything's ugly."

Occupiers rushed in to help the people in the car, including Clyde Powless, a high-steel worker and a frequent spokesman for the occupiers. "Someone bangs him right in the face," John says, "knocks him down with a punch to the mouth." John left at that point, but shortly before one o'clock, furious occupiers retaliated, dragging a large hydro tower across Argyle Street and then, as the OPP stood by, proceeding to dig up the public road with a backhoe. The townspeople were enraged, and a full-fledged riot broke out— with the OPP stretched thin across Argyle, people from both sides were able to breach their line and outflank them. There were scraps and assaults as natives and Caledonians fought and screamed obscenities at one another.

And then, at about 1:30 P.M., the lights and power went out. A Hydro One transformer station, located on the native side of the barricades on the way out of town, was vandalized and set ablaze, knocking out power to nearly eight thousand people in Haldimand and Norfolk counties and on Six Nations.

On the lines, OPP officers could hear only the crowd of towns-people as they suddenly roared, "What the fuck is that?" When they turned around—because, of course, they had their backs to the occupiers—they could see a black plume rising into the sky. The arsonist had driven a truck through the gate, cut the lock to get into the station, pulled out some big drawers, poured gasoline in the trays and then lit the works.

No one was ever arrested.

(The damage cost Hydro One $750,000 in direct costs—repairing the transformer, replacing the tower and demobilizing crews—and, since the incident, another $350,000 a year, or about $1.4 million so far, for 24-7 security at the station. As well, its Niagara Reinforcement Project, the last part of which was to be completed near DCE, remains unfinished.)

The crowd went berserk.

That night, after Haldimand council met in camera, Mayor Trainer formally declared a state of emergency.

———

By this time, Trainer had had her knuckles sharply rapped by her own council.

In late April, the day after the first near riot had erupted at the barricades, she was interviewed by CBC Newsworld and said, in part, that Caledonia residents "have to work to support their families. If they don't go to work, they don't get paid, and if they don't get paid, then they can't pay their mortgages and they lose their homes . . . They don't have money coming in automatically every month . . . They've got to work to survive and the natives have got to realize that." Trainer says this was a clear reference to the hundred or so tradesmen who would have been on DCE every day and were now out of work, and that the only comparison she meant to make was between those on a salary, like her, and those who weren't, like labourers. But her remarks were instantly taken as a slur painting natives as welfare recipients, and they sparked an immediate storm of protest—on the site, in the press and among county staff, some of whom were from Six Nations.

At an emergency meeting on April 25, council actually tried to remove Trainer from office, stopping short of that only on legal advice. But they did appoint deputy mayor Tom Patterson as council's spokesman on all matters related to DCE, and furthermore, most of the councillors marched down to the natives' barricade and abjectly apologized for her remarks.

Frankly, this was plainly absurd: if Trainer had insulted anyone, it was surely the hard-working people of Six Nations, not the occupiers, whose numbers by now included plenty of outsiders, unionists, students, non-native supporters and those who clearly weren't, well, working. If the councillors felt compelled to apologize, they might have done it before their counterparts on Six Nations.

But by then, Trainer had long been in the soup with her own council and senior staff.

For such a motherly-looking, gentle-seeming and religious woman, she has had a controversial political career marred by disputes. The most recent of these was with the former mayor's administrative assistant, who in 2005 launched a complaint against Trainer, alleging workplace harassment. After an investigation by outside consultants, the allegation was confirmed by council. The woman was first on leave and then eventually fired in 2007, after which she filed a wrongful dismissal suit, which was later settled.

But when the occupation began, much of this business wasn't entirely resolved, with the result that Trainer was essentially functioning as an island unto herself. Senior staff either weren't allowed to talk to her, or didn't, and she spent most of her days alone in her office, isolated and frozen out.

One of the recommendations stemming out of the harassment complaint was that she should take sensitivity training; the brouhaha sparked by her April remarks only added to that. Eventually, in March of 2007, Trainer was shipped off to the Friends of Simon Wiesenthal Centre for Holocaust Studies in Los Angeles for a "Tools of Tolerance" conference. Though it appears to have been generally understood that the mayor was the one who needed correction, four others went with her, perhaps as babysitters: OPP Staff Sergeant Phil Carter; Scott Miller, whose wife, Susie, is the native half-sister of Dana Chatwell; Rocky Smith of the Six Nations police; and Brenda Johnson, spokesperson for the clan mothers.

Trainer actually found the experience interesting, particularly the Holocaust survivors who spoke. She says that, while her companions expressed themselves rather copiously, "I thought if I expressed myself, I would have been in more trouble. So I just kind of kept chewing my tongue, but it was pretty hard to take, [hearing] how horrible all the county people were."

"Who said, 'Mayor Trainer, you better get your ass to this thing?'" I ask.

"Dianne Woods," she says.

Woods was the coordinator of the government-established Citizens Advisory Group, or CAG—unfondly known to its many detractors as the GAG—and employed by the Ontario government in a mysterious capacity. A recent Caledonia resident, she was described in print as working in community relations for the Aboriginal affairs ministry, though her government email was JUS, for justice. Typically, at the time, it was only employees of the attorney general's office and community safety ministries who had such addresses, including OPP, Crown attorneys and the like.

Woods didn't return several phone messages I left, asking for an interview.

In any case, with all this swirling in the background, Trainer was pretty much on her own, both by dint of her then fragile grasp on council and by inclination. At one point that summer, for instance, she wanted to call in the Canadian Forces, but found no support for that notion. The matter was discussed in camera, so she can't comment except to say that "it was discussed." She says Steve Beatty, from Emergency Management Ontario, a branch of the community safety ministry, advised them of the procedure: council had to pass a resolution asking Premier McGuinty to ask Prime Minister Stephen Harper to call in the army. "And this gentleman [Beatty]," Trainer says, "made it quite clear that he would not be advising the premier to do such a thing. He made that quite clear that it was not going to happen."

In any case, Trainer was, as she puts it, "kind of on my own with that opinion. The atmosphere of the council of the day was to make peace and to sit down and talk to people . . . That seemed to be where people were coming from at the time." In fact, she says, "It seemed like anybody who wanted to take a strong stand, myself included, were ostracized. They were bad—get out the garlic and get rid of them."

At 1:53 P.M. on Tuesday, May 23, the Argyle Street barricade finally came down for good.

One picture—of protester Michael Laughing (in traditional native dress) and resident Jim Meyer walking together, with Meyer carrying a so-called branch of peace—was widely published the next day, to much relief and giddy prediction that the worst was over. Virtually none of the coverage (including my own, for I was in Caledonia for the first and only time in 2006 that day and wrote a column for *The Globe and Mail*) identified Laughing as a resident of Akwesasne, the Mohawk reserve near Cornwall that straddles both the Canada–U.S. and Ontario–Quebec boundaries. His story, revealed in U.S. District Court documents, is a fascinating and tragic one.

Like many Mohawks a high-steel ironworker by trade, Laughing was on a job in Hoboken, New Jersey, just across the harbour from the Twin Towers, in the fall of 2001. Though he happened to be home in Akwesasne, taking a few days off, on September 11, as soon as he heard of the terror attacks, he and others on the reserve met immediately to discuss how they might help in the rescue. As his lawyer, Stanley Cohen, later told the court, "Akwesasne reeled from the blow . . . Akwesasne's contribution in the twentieth century to the structural shaping of the American skyscraper in cities across the continent is well known."

Within a few days, Laughing was back in the New York City area with his brother and cousin, and on September 18 he received his volunteer assignment. For about three weeks, he worked as long as sixteen hours a day on what workers called "The Pile," recovering pieces of human bodies and putting them in designated bags. Where many lasted only a short time at the grim task, Laughing stuck it out, ultimately working on what shifted quickly to a recovery operation. He spent his shifts hovering just twenty feet above The Pile in a bucket hoist at the end of a boom crane, using an oxyacetylene torch to cut through the twisted metal. Once, he saw two bodies in the hole below him, one over the other in the shape of an X. As he burned through the beam, molten steel dripped on the bodies, which then caught fire and burned steadily. As Cohen wrote in a moving sixty-one-page plea for leniency that was filed with the court, every day, as Laughing left the Twin Towers site, his ironworkers' tools and blackened, oily face betrayed him, and as "he walked through a gauntlet of hundreds of people holding photographs of their missing loved ones . . . people stopped him to ask in anguish if Michael had seen their husband, their daughter or son.

"All the recovery workers had been instructed to say that there was nothing but dust and ashes, but Laughing knew the grisly truth. Nevertheless, he could not bear to face the victims' families, or to tell them lies, and hurried quickly from the site."

His heroic and heartbreaking efforts at Ground Zero—he worked 160 hours in thirteen overnight shifts—left him with a variety of physical ailments and a formal diagnosis of post-traumatic stress disorder. Later, as he underwent therapy for the first time in his life, he revealed an incident of childhood rape and was also diagnosed as an alcoholic (though he had been sober for the previous eight years) and as dependent on marijuana. He was unable to work at all for several years, unable even to handle his tools, and at one point, close to suicide, he even gave up his treasured union card in despair.

Cohen wrote that by the summer of 2005, Laughing's life "began to carom into penury and privation . . . broke, depressed, suffering from weekly nightmares so powerful he would wake and leap out of bed in tears, he smoked marijuana in large quantities every day." Desperate, he agreed to help "move a load of pot for money." It was just a few months later that he showed up on DCE, where he became, for a time, one of the faces of the occupation, caught in a widely published photograph standing defiantly on top of the dump truck barricade on Argyle Street.

In early 2007, after Laughing had left DCE and Six Nations, U.S. law enforcement agencies raided Akwesasne. The raid marked the end of a two-year-long smuggling investigation, and for his solitary lapse in 2005, Laughing was one of the ten men arrested in the sweep. The story got press attention because, as *The Hamilton Spectator* noted, Laughing had come to symbolize native protest, being photographed first standing on top of that barricade, a fierce and formidable-looking forty-year-old, and then as one of the peace-makers on the day the Argyle Street barricade finally came down.

Though his role in the drug operation was minor (he was a one-time "mule"), and though he acknowledged responsibility by plead-ing guilty and had no significant criminal record, and though Cohen argued convincingly that he should receive a conditional sentence, Laughing was sentenced in September of 2009 to six months in prison and three years' probation.

The several months he spent at the DCE occupation weren't mentioned in Cohen's lengthy "sentencing memorandum," which laid bare so much of Laughing's life. It was only in an attached psy-chiatric evaluation that Dr. Robert Wolff noted that Laughing told him he'd been involved in something in Canada "related to some land claims demonstration that he participated in . . ."

———

In his condo in Richmond Hill, north of Toronto, Gary McHale looked in disbelief at the front page of *The Toronto Sun* on May 24.

A regular *Sun* reader, McHale had been casually following the events in Caledonia through the paper and the Michael Coren show on CTS-TV, a Christian network based in Hamilton. Though he knew only a fraction of what had happened, he'd heard enough to believe that the story ought to have been a perfect fit for his favourite con-servative, scrappy tabloid. Yet, McHale thought he remembered, until the day after the Argyle Street barricade was removed, the *Sun* hadn't once devoted its front page to the story. The failed OPP raid, with its aftermath of fires, masked occupiers with their bright red Warrior flag flying in the background, the torching of the hydro station—great pic-tures all, McHale figured, but none had made the front.

"Flames at the hydro station or the bridge, or the tire fires," McHale says, "that sells newspapers, regardless of what your view is. That sells newspapers."

The *Sun* was hardly alone.

In fact, from February 28 to May 30 of 2006, the story rarely cracked front pages or led newscasts outside of the Hamilton area. *Globe and Mail* researcher Stephanie Chambers, who surveyed press coverage during the two-month period in *The Globe and Mail* and *The Toronto Star* for me, found that only eleven of a total of seventy-seven stories in the two papers made the front page, and these were divided among the failed raid, the riotous backlash (and in those stories, Chambers was struck by how often the townspeople were referred to as an "angry mob," making their "concerns seem almost cartoonish," as she says) and the dismantling of the barricade.

McHale was intrigued, and started paying closer attention.

"It must have been close to June 9," he says, "when they had the swarming of the seniors, the attacks on the CH camera crew and the attempted murder on the OPP officer, along with the attack upon the border patrol. And to me, that was the last straw."

In the process of doing essentially what Chambers did, he went through the front pages of the *Sun* for about four months leading up to June 9.

"I looked at every single cover," he says, "to see what was important, and I found only one cover picture relating to Caledonia."

He had been remembering correctly; the May 24 front page, with a Fred Thornhill shot of the Michael Laughing–Jim Meyer handshake, was the only one.

"And that's when I made a decision that I was going to get involved in Caledonia," McHale says. "And the [idea] was purely, simply, I'm going to create a website and . . . get the true story out to the public, whatever that takes. The true stories are going to be put on the Internet and are going to be recorded from this point forward."

At the time, as he had for years, McHale was developing customized computer software—accounting and tax information, mostly—for a living, though he and his wife, Christine, had also got into graphic and web design, and from there, into wildlife photography for corporations. They had turned themselves into pretty good photographers, too, and in the previous five years had travelled across North America, created a huge library of stock photos and even won a couple of awards.

In March that year, they took out a second mortgage on the condo to finance a new business—educational software for children—and had produced six DVDs when McHale got hooked on the Caledonia story.

He was uniquely qualified, you might say, to tackle an issue that seemed too hot for the conventional institutions of society—government, police and press—to touch. In 2001, just after the 9/11 attacks, he had begun phoning his local Liberal member of Parliament, Bryon Wilfert, who had, as a member of Jean Chrétien's government, voted down an antiterrorism motion put forward by the opposition Canadian Alliance party. McHale knew perfectly well how Wilfert had voted, but wanted him to have to explain it. So he began calling, emailing and faxing Wilfert's office, with the same message: "I want to know how you voted. Just tell me how you voted."

"So he was ignoring me," McHale says, "as all politicians do, even though they try to claim they're accountable. I didn't realize that the only thing that peeved off MPs . . . They don't care if you leave a message on their answering machine; they're not going to listen to it, it will be some assistant. They don't care if you send an email; they'll just delete it. They don't care if you write letters.

"But the thing they really don't like is you sending a fax."

Having figured this out, he began sending faxes, twenty pages at a time, each bearing his name and asking only, "How did you vote?" He would send one twenty-page fax, wait an hour, then send another. "All I wanted was an answer," he says.

But in one email to Wilfert, McHale, who has a learning disability, misspelled one letter of one word in a sentence. Instead of typing, "Maybe it's time for the people in your riding to start protesting at your office," he wrote, "Maybe it's time for the people in your riding to start *protecting* at your office."

The next thing he knew, he got a call from the RCMP. "I'm probably the only person in Canada who had the potential of being on the terrorist watch list because I can't spell," McHale says. He explained himself, and that seemed to be that. "I said, 'Just tell the guy [Wilfert] to phone and tell me how he voted,'" he says. "The RCMP guy told me he spoke directly to the MP, had to bring him out of Parliament, and I said, 'Just have him give me a call.'

"So I get a message at the end of the day that he had voted against it."

Within days, the Liberals put forward similar anti-terrorism legislation of their own, and this time Wilfert, of course, supported it.

"So then I faxed him another question—just one question again," McHale says. He doesn't remember now what it was, but Christine does: "When will Bryon Wilfert respond this time?"

But this time, McHale says, the response was a knock on the door from the York Regional Police.

"They came in and had a little chat with me," he says. "I said, 'Just tell him to answer the question.' Then they did their little spiel, and I said, 'Look, if he doesn't like it, tell him to have me arrested.'"

"Well," he says the police responded, "that's why we're here." They put him in handcuffs, arrested him for mischief and took him to the station. The MP claimed McHale's faxing had shut down the entire office, tying up the phone lines to the point where they weren't able to do any work.

"The written statement by Wilfert," McHale says, "and I still have this stuff, is the signed statement that I faxed him six hundred times in one day."

Christine was working that day and had the car. She arrived home to find Gary not there, and she thought it was odd. By dinnertime, he still wasn't home. "And then I thought, 'You know what, I bet he's been arrested.'"

Next thing, she got a call from a duty counsel.

"We spent two and a half hours," McHale says, "the cop and me. The cop would come in and say, 'Do you want to talk to a lawyer?' and I said, 'I want to talk to my wife.' 'Do you want to talk to a lawyer?' 'Can I not talk to my wife? Can I talk to my wife?' 'Don't you want a lawyer?' 'Why can't I talk to my wife?'

"This would go on, and then he would leave. Wait twenty minutes, he comes back in . . . So this went on for hours. It was absolutely ridiculous that I was being arrested and put in jail overnight. It was just intimidation—what politicians do. And police, by the way. How was I a danger to anybody?"

By about 8 P.M., McHale had agreed to talk to a lawyer, and it was this fellow who called Christine on his behalf.

He spent the night in jail, and the next morning, was in the sally port area of the cop shop, about to be put into the paddy wagon for the trip to the Newmarket courthouse.

"So there's all these hard guys," McHale says, giggling at the memory, "saying, 'Why are you in?'

"'Oh, I'm in for rape,' 'I'm in for murder.' So they get to me: 'Why are you in here?'"

"I'm in here for faxing my MP," he told them.

"There was dead silence.

"One of these guys goes, 'What's an MP?'"

In court, one by one, the prisoners went up to talk to the duty counsel. "He's writing like a madman," McHale says. "Imagine the cases he hears. So anyway, I go and I sit down and he says, 'Why are you here?' 'For faxing my MP.' He drops his pen and looks at me. I said I asked him how he voted or something. I said that's all I did.

"So anyway, he goes away and comes back and says, 'Oh yeah, they say you faxed him six hundred times.' I said, 'It's not even possible to fax someone six hundred times in one day.'

"So anyway, the only evidence the York Regional Police had was the single fax—not six hundred, but a single fax. As they were pushing this along [through the court process], I was making all these disclosure requests. If we were going through all this, I wanted to know all this stuff—how many phone lines he [Wilfert] has, did he receive any other faxes that one day. I want the reports."

He fired the lawyer he'd got, began representing himself and finally told the Crown, "'You got ten days to drop the charge or I'm doing these four things,' and I think my last thing was, 'And five years from today, when this is before the Supreme Court of Canada, we can still be arguing whether or not a person has the right in a democracy to harass their MP.'"

He had a little ammunition. Unknown to the Crown and police, McHale had bought himself a little pen that was actually a tape recorder and had been taping the many meetings where he'd been asking for prosecution disclosure—a legal requirement in the justice system—to no avail. (What he did was perfectly legal because the Crown has no Charter right to privacy in conversations with an accused person, and because McHale, as one of the parties, consented to the recording.) He played hardball with the Crown attorney, telling him, "It's time for these tapes to go public."

"I'm trying to send a message, right? I'm not giving up. This is going to be five years of your life, trying to convict me on a bogus charge on which you have so far given me no disclosure eight months later."

Within the week, McHale got a fax telling him the Crown was dropping the charge, but wanted him to sign a peace bond whereby he'd agree not to contact Wilfert for a year. Christine says (and this is an indication how rooted in principle and stubbornness both of them are), "I said to Gary, 'You can't take that. If you agree not to contact him, that means you have no representative in Parliament for a whole year. You have the right to have that representative.'"

The charge was duly dropped, without the imposition of a peace bond.

It was McHale's first experience with the arbitrary exercise of power. "It showed me that politicians and the police, they work hand in hand to control the public," he says. "There's no such thing as democracy in Canada; we have four years of dictatorship interrupted by a couple of months of democracy [the election period], and the last thing, and it's true throughout human history, the last thing anybody in a position of power wants is for someone to be speaking out against them. And so they will use every means at their disposal to silence people.

"If it was allowed," McHale says, referring to his Caledonia experience, "I would have been black-bagged already. I would have been missing. It's not that these people wouldn't do it; it's just that they know they can't get away with it."

On June 17, 2006, he officially registered a website called CaledoniaWakeUpCall.com. In mid-July, having made contact with a couple of people in Caledonia, he went there for the first time in his life.

"We're just astounded by the number of cop cars that were just driving by," he says. "I mean, there was nothing going on that day, but it was like every fourth car was a cop car—in a community of ten thousand people. You don't even see that in downtown Toronto. And so there are probably more cops in Caledonia at that time than ever has been anywhere in Canada.

"I wasn't at the stage where most of the residents were," McHale says. "By that time, most of the residents were absolutely in fear—I mean of everybody. And it wasn't just fear of the natives, it was fear of the OPP and, to a large extent, fear of the media.

"And that really has to be remembered, because in the early days, the residents never spoke to media. Refused. They believed the media twisted their words, that they would always paint the residents as the ones inciting the violence, and once their names and photos were printed, they'd become targeted or their kids would be targeted at school." McHale points to a time in August when TV reporters were trying to interview locals, "and all they could do [were allowed to do] was videotape their feet."

With his two local guides, armed with a video camera, McHale got his first tour of town. He spotted a fire on the edge of DCE and an OPP officer trying to put it out, and jumped out to take pictures. In what became the norm for Caledonia, the OPP videotaped him videotaping them.

"That was my approach from day one," McHale says. "See, in every community, there's those who commit violence. It doesn't matter where you go in Canada. The issue in Caledonia has nothing to do with whether or not people committed violence or with whether or not people committed criminal acts. That happens in every community across Canada. The only thing that makes Caledonia unique is that the police did nothing."

He decided early on that he would focus on the OPP.

"I knew from moment one the focus was not on the criminals," he says, "but on the failures of the police, and I added, and still say, the failures of the media to report it."

"And the government?" I ask.

"Yeah," McHale says, but he knew, "if you tell Canadians that 'your politician has let you down,' they'll say, 'So what? Welcome to the real world. They let us all down.' You can't market that to anybody. You know, 'Woe is me, my politician's screwing me.' But if you tell people the police are not doing their job, that they're allowing violence to take place, that their policies are based on the race of the person, it doesn't matter if you're in downtown Toronto or Timbuktu, nobody will tolerate the police standing by while crimes are committed. You go to downtown Toronto, you say to black people, 'Are you against race-based policing?' Absolutely . . . You go to the Asian community, you go to any community in Canada, and ask them, 'Do you think this is right?' they all say no."

In his nimble mind, McHale performed a triage of blame. For him, the No. 1 villain in Caledonia was the failure of the national media, in particular the Toronto media, to cover the story.

"The media cannot report this story properly," he says. "I think that the media were so frightened of being called racists, there's no way they were going to show a photo of a masked Warrior having tire fires or beating the crap out of a resident. It was not going to happen. And the reason I get so frustrated with them is that the media, in my view, is the last line of defence for democracy. And it has absolutely failed to do that job.

"It's been up on my website since day one: the sole reason I got involved is not really just that the OPP didn't do their job, because I'll tell you, that happens across this country. We've had inquiries into the RCMP Tasering that guy in Vancouver (Polish immigrant

Robert Dziekanski, whose death at Vancouver International Airport was the subject of a full public inquiry), we've had numerous examples where police abuse their authority, or misuse their authority, and fail to do their job.

"Why am I not involved in those? Because the media exposes those."

No. 2 was "the complete failure of the OPP to enforce the Criminal Code."

No. 3 "was the absolute willingness on the part of native protesters to commit crimes and to do violence against others.

"And if any of those situations had not occurred," McHale says, "I wouldn't have been involved."

For all those who wanted the story of Caledonia to just quietly go away, for all those in government and business who were already saying it had done that, Gary McHale was about to become their worst nightmare.

———

The day after the OPP raid, by formal resolution, the Six Nations elected council gave the traditional Confederacy the lead at the negotiating table, a move the chief of the day, Dave General, was against, and one the current chief, Bill Montour, describes as a critical mistake.

In fact, General's council, just like Trainer's, at one point tried to impeach him. This complicated things enormously, because almost thee decades earlier, the Supreme Court of Canada had affirmed in a landmark case, Davey vs. Isaac, that it is only the elected council that has the legal authority to speak (or negotiate) for Six Nations or any other Indian band.

"That's the only legal entity that Canada can recognize," Montour says. "Or Ontario. So Allen [MacNaughton, the Confederacy chief] goes there and says, 'Well, first of all, are you ready to recognize the Confederacy as the legal government?'"

The decision had predictable results. It made for confusion, not only at the negotiating table but also on the site itself, where, as Montour says, "You get a whole bunch of people stepping forward—'I'm the leader here, I'm going to do this'—and usually it lasts a day and his ass is kicked down the road."

The federal and Ontario negotiators had set up a process, Montour says, "and they do it for a purpose, because when the shit hits the fan, Canadians say, 'Well, why can't you settle that issue at Caledonia!' [And they say,] 'Oh, we have a process, but Six Nations can't get its act together.' So I can just see *The Globe and Mail* and *The Vancouver Sun* and the Halifax *Chronicle*[*-Herald*] and every other columnist across the country—'Those damn Indians are standing in the way of progress again.'"

On the non-native side, things weren't much better. In early May, though David Peterson was still beavering away as the provincial lead and various senior officials were meeting lawyers for the Hennings and their builders, Ontario also appointed Jane Stewart, former Liberal MP for Brant and a former minister of Indian affairs, as a special representative. Ottawa, not to be outdone, named former Conservative MP and cabinet minister Barbara McDougall as its representative, along with veteran negotiator Ron Doering.

The Hennings, meantime, fast learners both, had picked up a few tricks. "We were learning way more than we were supposed to about media relations," Don says. "We got to the point where we came out—there was talk of them buying us out, but there hadn't been any amounts or anything—so they [the press] said to us, 'What's the property worth?' And our words were that it would generate $45 million in revenue . . .

"Well, of course the government guys jump all over us—'Oh, you guys, this isn't going to be a lottery win for you.' And we just shook our heads and said, 'Guys, you guys do this all the time. It's called conditioning the public.' We said, 'Now, when you guys come in and you give us way less money, you're going to look like heroes because nobody actually read what it said—$45 million in revenue [not profit]. We just helped you.'"

"We never heard another thing about it after that," John says. "Honestly, not to be demeaning, but some of the reporters couldn't even spell our names. They didn't understand [the difference between revenue and profit]."

In early June, a couple of their builders were getting cold feet about the prospect of a buyout.

"We actually went to them," John says.

"We sat down and said, 'Guys, you know what, we've been through this same discussion ourselves, every night as we're lying in bed,'" Don adds. "'But the reality is, we firmly believe that we will be thrown to the wayside and that it won't make a difference, so that we'll get swallowed up, and we'll be broke, and we won't have anything and your families will starve.' And that's what we tried to portray, and I believe that to the core."

By June 7, they were growing frustrated. That night, Jason Clark, one of the movers behind the Caledonia Citizens Alliance, came to see them. Clark was upset, and told them one of the Ontario negotiators, knowing he was the Hennings' friend, had hinted that if they didn't soon sign something, the government was going to expropriate. The brothers immediately start checking out expropriation legislation, trying to find out what they could do if need be.

By June 14, the government was starting to talk seriously about money, and the Hennings were trying to figure out whether they could live with the deal, whether they were doing the right thing. Two days later, the parties were back in Judge Marshall's court.

"Once it got . . . any time court was coming, the pace just all of a sudden . . . the guys [the negotiators] could make decisions," Don says. "It was amazing."

There were twelve lawyers in front of the judge that day, and most of them were brimming with optimism over the splendid way things were going. The senior lawyer for the province, Dennis Brown, spoke of the dismantled blockades, the newly formed "main [negotiation] table" and Ontario's recent handing over of 250 acres of land (Mr. Brown didn't name the land, but this was the former

Burtch Correctional Centre, which Peterson had arranged to give Six Nations in exchange for the removal of the barricades) and various financial supports Ontario had put in place for "the communities" in Caledonia, and announced that the government now had "an agreement in principle" to purchase Douglas Creek Estates from Henco.

The lawyer for the federal government pronounced Canada "very encouraged" and predicted "a process is now in place to resolve, not only the current situation in Caledonia, but as well the broader historical claims that have been brought by the Six Nations."

Ken Peel, the lawyer for the railway, RaiLink Canada, was delighted that, a few days earlier, crews had been allowed in to repair the tracks and trains had begun to run again. Darrell Doxtdator, the agent speaking for the Six Nations elected council, assured everyone he'd heard "the familiar 2 A.M. whistle call" the night before and joined his colleagues in saying "this is a situation that calls for peaceful discussion, not violent confrontations."

Michael Bruder, for the Hennings, was noncommittal, as he had to be, but confirmed that there was an agreement in principle.

And the lawyer for the OPP, Chris Diana, was happy because, despite what he called "a number of violent incidents" in recent weeks, investigations were underway, arrest warrants had been issued and the OPP was "actively engaged in keeping the peace and upholding the law."

But Diana *was* aggrieved about one thing. Earlier in the month, the lawyers had gathered at Judge Marshall's invitation to discuss his concerns. As the judge said that day, "It's evident to everyone that there's great concern in the community that the rule of law has been suspended to some extent in our county." The judge had invited the Haldimand Law Association to attend, and Hagersville lawyer Ed McCarthy had spoken on its behalf, but according to Diana, McCarthy's submissions that day "were unnecessarily inflammatory and inappropriate. Words that are said in a courtroom reverberate throughout the entire community and are not confined within these walls, and therefore have consequences and potential consequences outside the courtroom."

What McCarthy had said was that the government's tactics of negotiating with the occupiers was reminiscent of British prime minister Neville Chamberlain's infamous "peace in our time" speech, in which Britain agreed that part of what was then Czechoslovakia should be given to the Germany of Adolf Hitler, hoping it would slake his appetite for "breathing space."

Suffice to say, it did not.

McCarthy had also told the judge that there "needs to be a stand for the rule of law," that the occupation had to end "forthwith, by force if necessary"—a remark that prompted Denise Dwyer, who was representing the OPP that day, to snap that these were "fighting words"—and that the focus of the proceeding "has to be directed towards compelling the OPP to discharge its responsibility."

But on this occasion, Diana was representing the OPP, and *he* said they were concerned about the impact of McCarthy's words "on officer safety and on public safety . . ." Why, he added, using a great Canadian epithet, McCarthy had not been "constructive." Besides, Diana said, things were so swimmingly improved in Caledonia that "there's no longer the same concern with respect to the rule of law, in terms of the situation on the ground." And, as the OPP had opposed the law association's participation in the first instance, Diana said, he was opposing McCarthy being allowed to speak again.

Brown, for the government, added that if McCarthy did get to speak again, he should keep his comments in line "with what we're trying to achieve."

Judge Marshall was not to be browbeaten; he ruled he'd hear from McCarthy again, saying, "This case is a difficult one, and it's not a case of peaches and cream, so to speak; it's a case that does have a nasty underside."

McCarthy duly addressed the court, though only briefly, and stuck to his guns: "We in the Law Association remain concerned about the rule of law," he said. "We can't help but talk to our clients. We hear daily about matters going on in Caledonia and the concern for the rule of law." He pointed out that none of the lawyers, for all their hearty good cheer, "have addressed anything as to when this occupation of this subdivision is going to end."

The lawyers went into chambers then—I call this super-secret court, because there's no record of what transpires—and came back before the judge a little later. They agreed that negotiations would continue and that, while the judge's oversight might be necessary, for the time being, all was jim-dandy.

Judge Marshall, ever polite, wasn't quite so sanguine. "I want to make a few comments," he said. "Lest one should go away thinking that this is entirely happy on all sides, I can assure that it is not. Early on in this unfortunate matter, after the injunctions were issued and criminal warrants issued, a number of decisions were made to resort to negotiation, temporizing and generally not getting on with enforcing the court's order, the law.

"The negotiating, the temporizing, has emboldened the contenders, which has resulted in damage—physical, social, commercial, and damage to the very fabric of both communities involved, as well as damaging the reputation and the reliance on the Superior Court of Justice. This, unfortunately, has fostered disrespect rather than respect for the administration of justice in our county.

"There are compelling reasons for having and for following the rule of law," he said. "The results of not following the law are evident in this case in Caledonia."

Judge Marshall said he didn't doubt the good intentions or bona fides of the negotiators, but they "cast a grave responsibility, in this court's view, on the negotiators to bring this matter to a speedy and satisfactory solution for both communities."

Of the main players in the courtroom that day, only Ed McCarthy and the judge weren't enthusiastically toeing the party line.

———

The many who were saying of Caledonia, in effect, "Nothing to see here, folks, move along" didn't include Toby Barrett, either.

Having dropped almost everything else, the MPP was in the county all the time, and was on the scene when the rolling Six Nations information picket-cum-blockade first arrived at a construction site in the neighbouring town of Hagersville—where, again, he says, "there were people with masks," workers had to move their equipment out of the site and "again, we couldn't believe it, nobody raised a finger" to stop it.

"Was the OPP there?" I ask.

"Yeah," Barrett says. "They helped put up the barricade that shut 'er down."

Off and on that year, there were native protesters showing up throughout the area—at a dozen sites in Brantford; in Dunnville, where they stopped the TSC store and a planned Walmart (which, unlike in other towns, the locals badly wanted, Barrett says); and in Hagersville, where they delayed, but didn't stop, another small subdivision.

For the first few months of the occupation, Barrett was essentially a one-man office.

"I have a rule," he says with a sheepish grin. "We're a political office, so all the gals in my office, if they get pregnant, you've gotta have a baby in between elections. So I had three people off on maternity leave—three!"

He was unsettled by how orchestrated things became as the occupation progressed. "The planning was incredible," he says. "Military strategy and tactics."

He watched as some of the vacant houses on DCE began sporting slits, basically gunports; he saw the occupiers using a backhoe, supposedly for an archaeological dig.

"I'd talk to them about that," Barrett says. "You don't use a backhoe to do an archaeological dig. You're digging a World War I trench. I was *there*, watching them do it. This isn't an archaeological dig; all the papers were saying it's an archaeological dig. Bullshit."

He was also staggered by the sheer amount of spin emanating from Queen's Park. "All the standard bureaucratic 'community development,' 'community outreach,' 'citizen participation'—all of that was a farce," he says. "It really was a farce."

The policing itself reminded him of the time he once spent in 1969 in Saigon (Barrett is astonishingly well travelled, having visited about sixty countries). In one of that city's many little tea shops or bars, he got to know some U.S. soldiers who were on leave for some R and R. He was a young guy then too, had had some militia training and was interested in the Vietnam War. In fact, it was some of these soldiers who wisely suggested that he might want to skip a planned side trip to Cambodia.

Barrett was shocked by the cynicism of the soldiers, who explained what they did every day when on duty: they'd put up a giant wire fence around a park in Saigon, lit it up like a living room, and every night, when they went out "on patrol," what they'd patrol was the perimeter of the park.

"'That was our patrol,'" they told him. "Then the boss would write it up and they'd fax it to Washington. And it counted as a patrol.

"That's what I'm seeing here," Barrett says: the OPP "going through the motions."

The force was shipping people in from across Ontario; they'd be flown in for seven-day tours, earn so much overtime that the assignment became known as "Cashadonia" and rotate back out. In many cases, they had little affinity for or understanding of the area; in the modern lexicon, they weren't invested.

But there sure were tons of them in town.

One result is that Haldimand County, Barrett says, has the lowest rate of speeding of any OPP jurisdiction in the province. The MPP himself "got pulled over all the time down here.

"It's not a personal thing," he says. "I'm pissed off about that, sure, but I'm just saying—they're going through the motions. They come down here—and I was here virtually every day for I don't know how long, I didn't do anything else for months. I would see these guys come down [from out of town]. They would have their protocols and their action plans and all this stuff . . . They'd come down here, and basically, they'd take a look at Douglas Creek Estates or take a look at Six Nations, they'd take a look at the subdivision [Thistlemoor] and say, 'We're going over there. We'll apply all of our procedures to these people living in this subdivision, because it's a lot easier. We can still send reports every day, that we talked to these people.'

"That's my perspective of what has happened," he says. "And I'm pro-police. I'm with a political party that's pro-police, pro-OPP."

Barrett was also in a good position to monitor the comings and goings on DCE. He saw the various flags—the purple Haudenosaunee flag ("I call it the smoke shack flag," he says, "because that's where you see 'em, on smoke shacks"); the Warrior flag; banners and signs from supportive unions, such as the United Steelworkers, and groups such as the Ontario Coalition Against Poverty; and, from the Niagara Palestinian Association, which sent representatives to the site in May, the black, white and green Palestinian flag. Barrett was there when Palestinian student groups held education programs on the site.

On May 22 of the long weekend, he was on Six Nations, hanging out at the veterans' association. (It was some of his buddies there, incidentally, who coined the term "catch-and-release" to describe how the OPP was policing natives. Barrett passed it on to John Tory, who was then leading the provincial Tories in opposition, and he used the phrase frequently in the Legislature.) But that holiday Monday, while he was on the reserve, one of his native friends told him they were going to open up Argyle Street and that if Barrett left right away and came out on the Sixth Line, he could be the first one to drive through after the barricade came down.

Barrett liked the sounds of that, so he jumped in his notorious old red station wagon.

"It's a reserve car," he says. "It's a total piece of shit, 1990—that's old for a car."

His was the first car through, but then the Caledonia residents shut down Argyle with *their* barricade, and he was caught smack in the middle.

"So anyway," he says, "I got up here, [and] here it's the Caledonia guys who shut 'er down. I couldn't believe it. So I just parked it right in the middle of the highway, I just walked away. I was too pissed off.

"I just walked around and sat on the hood," he says. "It's the kind of car, you sit on the hood, you stand on the roof. I stand on the roof a lot at demonstrations. Just sat on the hood. There was nobody there; I was just in the middle of no man's land."

Then behind him, he saw an excavator start tearing up the road, right up to the back of his station wagon. "So I went around to the back," he says. "But I thought, 'Shouldn't the police do something about this? They're tearing up the main street of Caledonia!' I was astonished at that point. I watched them dig up the thing, and the OPP by then, they had the thin blue line in front of my car."

That night, CHCH broadcast aerial shots of the scene on the news, and there was Barrett's beater sitting between the barricade and the police. Photos of the scene also made some of the papers.

"John Tory phoned my wife about midnight," Barrett says. "I wasn't home yet—I had no car. And he said, 'Is that Toby's car in the middle of the highway?'"

Cari Barrett just laughed and told him, "I hope they torch it."

"It was the only car on the highway," Barrett says. "There was this mass of people, native guys, behind the car, and all the Caledonia people in front of the car, and all the fistfights were on the east side, by the fitness centre. I had a front-row seat for everything." For hours, Barrett just sat on the hood of his car, where he "had a panorama of everything that went on. I had clear vision all the way around."

At one point, the occupiers came running up, tossing some of their stuff in the car. Janie Jamieson threw her notes on the front seat; others stood on the hood. Barrett walked away.

"Down our way," he says, grinning, "you never drive a car you can't afford to walk away from."

The car was eventually towed to the Canadian Tire parking lot, where Barrett found it.

"The native guys, they say, 'You're the only guy who ever had a car *returned* by Six Nations,'" he says, snorting with delight.

Four days after the government lawyer had told Judge Marshall that Six Nations had been given the Burtch lands, near Brantford and just a few klicks west of the reserve, Barrett was on his feet in the legislature, asking the premier if the rumours swirling around were true. Five times he rose to ask if, to get the Argyle Street barricade taken down, Peterson had offered the Burtch property.

What most people didn't realize was that the Ontario government had also put virtually all the land the province owns in Haldimand and Norfolk counties on the table for consideration. Among the land, owned by the Ontario Realty Corporation, that was on the block were the Sprucedale Correctional Centre in Simcoe, the former OPP station on Highway 3, an assortment of salt domes throughout the area, a huge assembly of land near Dunnville, and the old Cayuga courthouse.

"This was all put on the table in negotiations," Barrett says. "It's in Hansard.

"I raised a ruckus, and the two negotiators—the only time I've talked to these bureaucrats—one of them came down to my office and said, 'Yeah, this is on the table, you're right, da-da-da-da . . . but it's only for two years!'

"Now it has been taken off the table," he says. "But just the thought to have put all that property on the table, thousands of acres . . . I mean, nobody told the mayor of Norfolk County—he hit the roof. He was pissed off with me that I was talking about it. He didn't want this talked about.

"A lot of people are like that—don't talk about it. But the various salt domes and ministry of transportation yards along [Highway] No. 3 and the former OPP station," Barrett says, "they're perfect locations for smoke shacks, that kind of stuff."

Barrett then went out to the affected areas and knocked on three hundred doors, telling people that they should know the land had been put on the table.

"And people went, 'Oh, that will never happen, they'll never have an Indian reserve here.' But who knows? I am astonished at some things that happened that I thought would not have been allowed to go on as long as they have."

In fact, given the slight attention paid to the Burtch land transfer at the time, there was no mention of something only Barrett has the nuts to talk about. The Burtch property land wasn't just used in the past for a prison. It was also a former relief landing field for World War II pilots in training and a Royal Canadian Air Force school for wireless operators. The intact runways are still visible in modern aerial photographs.

"Why give two runways to organized crime on native-controlled territory?" he asks. "Is that not a recipe to help business?"

"I sure get pushback when I say things like that."

———

While lawyers were talking in court about the agreement in principle to buy out the Hennings, the brothers were not awash in warmth.

"All we have is a two-page thing with a list of conditions on it that we signed," says Don. "They [the government] had not signed it. Then they went into court and they announced we've come to an agreement."

"And we haven't," John adds. "All we'd agreed to was that we'd sell it. There was no money." There was no figure, no indication of a sale price, attached.

Then, on Wednesday, June 21, Premier McGuinty, answering a question from John Tory, told the Legislature that, yes, "There is in fact a binding agreement to purchase the land, but the Leader of the Official Opposition has a hard time accepting good news and signs of real progress."

That was certainly news to the Hennings, who still had only the same unsigned two-page document—essentially, a letter of intent.

The Conservatives somehow got wind that all might not be as the premier had said, and John Tory began calling Don's house, desperate to talk to the Hennings.

"We did not speak to him," John says, "because, you know, we couldn't bite the hand that was going to feed us, in essence."

"Well, we sat there, looking at one another," Don says. "We're sitting at the kitchen table, and we sat there looking at one another."

By now, their phone was jumping off the hook: Bruder was calling, and the negotiators—Burke, Chadwick and Smith—were calling. "They're [the negotiators] going to release numbers that we haven't agreed on yet," Don says. "We sat there looking at one another. 'What do we do here, John? What do we do?'"

The number they'd discussed, though no final agreement had yet been reached, was an initial payment of $12.3 million.

"And so we thought that if at least we got that out of them, we would survive," Don says. "That was our initial intent."

John says, "At this point, you gotta understand, we're just trying to get out with our skin."

"We're wearing down," says Don. "Our wives were worried about our health." Their advisors were saying, "Boys, you need to end this."

Also on June 21, Judge Marshall, growing impatient, ordered the lawyers back to court on June 29 to bring him up to speed—and, he noted, "so that the communities involved may have some idea when the contempt of the orders of this court will come to an end." That date was later adjourned to July 5.

That same day, the Hennings' friends, Jason Clark and Ralph Luimes of the Caledonia Citizens Alliance, had a meeting with Cabinet ministers in Toronto. "They were told that, upon our sale of the land, it would be given to the natives," John says. "This is more pressure on us—"

Don interjects: "Are we doing the right thing?"

"—because the town doesn't want that to happen," John continues. "It would ruin the town. This is again adding to the burden. If we take this money and they give it to the natives, the town is going to lynch us, you know what I mean? We're known here, everybody knows us, we're selling out the town by doing that.

"But we had little choice by this point."

Their only real option was to refuse to sell, and to sue, a process that would have taken years to grind its way through the Ontario courts and consume money they didn't have for lawyers.

Clark and family even sat down with them, trying to figure out if they could afford to pay what the Hennings would need to survive, and buy the damn land.

"They're very wealthy people," Don says, "but they couldn't afford to flush that down the toilet."

Finally, two days after the premier had announced in the Legislature that there was a binding deal, the Hennings got a proper offer from the province at 8 P.M. It was, John's notes say, the day before the opening of bass season.

Still, the Hennings didn't sign. Instead, they sent the offer back to the government. Another flurry of calls and meetings ensued.

The brothers were looking for indemnification from the government, so that if any of those who had been involved in DCE—builders or buyers—decided to sue them, they would be protected. It was a real sticking point.

"You know what?" Don says. "The deal nearly fell apart over that."

But the government wanted something too: the Hennings, who had gone to court in the first place, almost five months earlier, to get the injunction, now had to agree to drop it. They did.

On Tuesday, July 4, they signed all the paperwork at the land registry office in Cayuga. The next day, at the hearing Judge Marshall had called, Michael Bruder duly brought a motion to set aside the injunction order; no one opposed it.

The judge, however, refused to release the matter, and ordered the parties back again on July 24 to make submissions on how he should deal with the outstanding contempt order.

For the Hennings, it was finally over. They took the Thursday off, though they were working on a new subdivision by now and were also trying to buy a building for an office.

"Our wives are sick of us being at home," Don says.

Don and Julie took the kids and went away for a few days to a lodge. "And I remember sitting there," he says. "I was afraid to walk away from my cell phone because I'd spent so much time on it that, you know, I didn't want to leave it because I figured something would happen. We had said all along that we were going to take them [the cells] and throw them up in the air and shoot them if [the government] finally paid."

"Are you good enough to shoot them?" I ask.

"Oh yeah," says Don.

Later, after the rest of the deal had been negotiated and closed on August 31 and they had paid back everything they owed and spent a week filling out credit applications, they took some holidays.

"We went to Argentina for a while," John says.

"Yeah," says Don, "and shot doves."

John estimates that when all was said and done—the government paid them another $3.5 million, for a total of $15.8 million—they still lost more than $10 million.

"I've said it before," Don says ruefully. "I would love to have had it on my gravestone that we brought down the McGuinty government."

———

Chris Diana, who so smarmily had warned Judge Marshall that what was spoken in a courtroom "reverberates" dangerously in the larger community, was lucky it wasn't so in his case. Had it been, Diana might have found himself with a gaping wound on his arse where his words had returned to bite him.

Indeed, for a town that had been presented in court as near-peaceable and briskly returning to normal, Caledonia was, in the summer of 2006, decidedly not. Nor was everything tickety-boo with the OPP, the force Diana represented.

In June, for instance, two out-of-town officers, not knowing their way around, mistakenly drove onto Six Nations along the Sixth Line. They were immediately surrounded by natives, of course, because the OPP wasn't allowed on Six Nations or DCE. The constables were essentially taken prisoner—forced to sit in the back of their cruiser, stripped of their gun belts, which were removed and put in the trunk of the car. They were then duly charged with trespassing by Six Nations officers. Finally, after the OPP negotiated for three hours, they were driven out of the area—a Six Nations officer at the wheel of their cruiser—and released.

The event was described the next day in a Haudenosaunee press release issued by spokesperson Hazel Hill as part of the occupiers' magnificent efforts at peaceful negotiations.

That was on June 4. Six days later—right after the explosive triple of June 9—officers sitting at the north end of the Thistlemoor subdivision saw a native man with a rifle pop his head up over the barricade. That evening, for the first time, the OPP strung police tape behind Thistlemoor Drive itself—the "no-go" zone or DMZ (demilitarized zone) had been marked off. Some time later, NO TRESPASSING signs were posted, but all on the Caledonia side, of course, meant for the residents of the subdivision. On the DCE side, there were no such signs.

As Dave Hartless says, "Well, the buffer zone, no one was allowed to enter it except for the natives. "And the natives would come up—all the NO TRESPASSING signs were all pointed at us."

People in the subdivision began stealing the signs, or folding them up and throwing them back. "Some of the things that happened here were very schoolyard," Hartless says, but these were folks who could exercise power only over the minor.

Hartless had developed a nifty little tic in his right eye. "I had [it] for about three months . . . drove me insane," he says. "Tic, tic, tic—it's stress-induced."

On July 31, shortly before midnight, there was the notorious train incident.

Two of the subdivision residents—the one I spoke to is one of those who wants his name kept out of it, so I will call him Paul Trickey in these pages—were standing outside the south-end Hortons having a coffee when they heard the train stop. It often did in those days. The tracks run just behind Trickey's home on Braemar Avenue, where the backyards basically end at the rail line. Behind the tracks is the Hydro One right-of-way, behind that the Highway 6 bypass, and then Six Nations. The occupiers had controlled this whole area since day one; they were living, camping, back there, and they patrolled the tracks. Trickey and the others by now were accustomed to the trains being stopped—the very ones that, the railway's lawyer had suggested to Judge Marshall, were running like clockwork again—and to seeing natives park their ATVs on the tracks and shine the lights at the sound of the train. Trickey had phoned several times to find out whether there were dangerous chemicals on board, because the occupiers so often jumped on the trains and stood atop them, smoking.

"Why would they do this?" I ask.

"Because they could," says Trickey.

In fact, the trains were, for a time, so often screeching to a halt, waking Trickey up, that he started phoning RaiLink executives whenever it happened so that they'd have to get out of bed at four in the morning too.

But this night, it was about 11 P.M. when Trickey and his friend heard the train stop. They raced back to his house.

"We go through [the yard] and look over the fence," he says, "and there's the train, and there's a female and a male [these were the engineers] over there, and I said, 'What's going on?' And the girl's crying. She said, 'We hit somebody!' And I said, 'Where is he?' And she pointed to the back of the train."

Trickey then grabbed a flashlight and went into the bush with his friend, and there they found Gilbert (Gibber) Hill. "He's wasted," Trickey says, "so he's not feeling anything. He's just dazed." But he had been grazed by the train—he had apparently been "patrolling" the tracks when it brushed by him and threw him into the woods— and had suffered, it turned out, a broken shoulder.

"I found him basically behind Hartless's house," Trickey says. "The natives were all standing on the tracks, and they're saying,

'Is he dead?' They were afraid to come down. There were about fifteen guys standing around, and they're on the tracks."

Trickey was furious, at the lack of help, the lack of interest, the whole darned shooting match. One of the Warriors, decked out in the de rigueur hat and the shirt and a bandana, approached him. "I said, 'Aren't you cute? You look like a fucking fairy. What are you doing—this isn't Hallowe'en, right?'"

The Warrior just laughed. "I said, 'You guys are wasted, you're stoned, what are you on?' I said, 'Why are you back here? This isn't DCE.'"

Clyde Powless showed up, and Trickey got him to clear a path in the bush with his ATV and to call an ambulance.

"So Clyde does all that," he says, "and the ambulance shows up, and so now, we had to come out at the very end of the court and up the hill."

There were two female paramedics, both young, and they took a look and said they couldn't lift Hill, so Trickey and his friend lifted him out, got him on the stretcher and took him back up the hill and put him in the ambulance. The OPP were there, at the court, where they always were, but by now there were about thirty of them, as well as some Six Nations police.

"And then the cop turned to [Trickey's friend] and said, 'What about the engineers? Can you go get them for us?' So he went back and got the engineers and brought them up" so they could be interviewed.

"The police even had civilians go and get the witnesses?" I ask.

"Yes," says Trickey.

He did extract a measure of, if not exactly justice, then vengeance: he stole Gibber Hill's radio, and thereafter was able to listen in to the occupiers' transmissions and get their frequencies. For months afterwards, he and the friend who'd helped him would sit in Trickey's garage, playing a few select tunes for the natives who were running the show and working the radios: Robin Williams's opening monologue from the film *Good Morning, Vietnam*; a few marching songs from the American South; and sometimes, his friend would affect a Pakistani accent and start talking on the air, telling the natives, "You're not an Indian!"

It was all they had.

For Dave Hartless, it was after the second nut-loosening incident that he stopped even calling the OPP, and really began writing letters to the editor.

As he says, "The best weapon I found against all of them was my poison pen. So I started writing."

During one of his regular checks, he discovered that the wheel nuts had been loosened on his wife's minivan—a second time. "I caught it in the driveway before she left," he says. "For almost two years, every day I would go out and check underneath the car, check the lug nuts."

Before he joined the Hamilton force, Hartless was a soldier, a military police officer. He spent six years in the Canadian Forces, leaving as a corporal. "I'm a big one for the rules," he says. "So I'm watching an entire police force lose credibility, and standing, in the eyes of the townspeople—and not just them, but myself. I'm a fellow officer.

"To this day, I see an OPP cruiser and I get a knot in my stomach."

Twice, he has sworn an oath to Canada, once as a soldier, once as a cop. He takes it very seriously. "I'm no longer a soldier, but that doesn't absolve me of the responsibilities of that oath I swore," he says. "I still carry that. And I swore as a police officer, and that just reinforces the oath I swore as a soldier. To safeguard the citizens of this country and anybody else in trouble. It's a simple, a very simple, ideal."

After June 9, he also began to act. He set up a "resident response plan" for Thistlemoor residents, a one-page sheet he delivered door-to-door after work.

"If the past 100-plus days have taught us nothing else," it began, "it is that the natives are extremely organized in their responses and that we are not. It is time we became organized."

A short preamble noted—politely, given all that had happened—that the OPP response "has been largely ineffectual and it is now apparent that in order to protect ourselves, our families and our homes we must do so collectively."

What followed was a six-step plan "in the event that a home or a resident comes under attack or act of intimidation." Residents in difficulty were to sound their car alarms or horns; others, hearing it, were to respond to the area and form "a community shield against the agitators"; people were not to chase anyone past the borderline; they were to stay there until the agitators left or the OPP responded.

"This is to only be a defensive act," the plan read. "Offensive acts will result in a reciprocal event from the natives and neither can be condoned or supported in any way. The goal is not to engage them [occupiers] in like behaviour. We are not vigilantes and we are not a replacement or substitute for law enforcement. This is to simply be a matter of organizing a defensive response to overt acts of aggression."

The letter ended with another caution: "This response plan is NOT a licence to fight, it is not a licence to engage in civil disobedience. It is to be an organized response to danger . . . it can only work if we stand together, united in the same purpose: To protect each other."

In his letters to local papers, Hartless never identified himself as a police officer; he would just sign his name and describe himself as a resident of Braemar Avenue. In fact, many of his neighbours didn't know he was a cop until after the occupation started, when someone accidentally outed him, not realizing how private and compartmentalized a man he is.

But it was his training that profoundly informed his distress. In police college, he was taught the famous "broken windows" theory, which he describes this way: "When you allow things to occur, broken windows in a neighbourhood, you end up taking steps back, and before you know it you've got a complete and total shithole that you're living in, and that's what they [the OPP] did here.

"Every time they drew a line in the sand, the natives would step over it. I shouldn't say 'natives'; really, it's a small percentage of thugs. But they'd step over it. And the police and the government would step back, and they'd draw another line, and they'd [the thugs] step over it again.

"And every time they stepped over it . . . hmmmm. Nothing

happened. 'Let's see how far we can push it.' And they keep pushing it and pushing it to the point now that the OPP and the government are leaning so far backwards, they're on their backs."

The police, in other words, by their inaction were actually enabling and encouraging the occupiers onto increasingly extreme behaviour.

In August, there were a couple of incidents that nearly saw Hartless's head explode. The first, on August 7, is known in Thistlemoor as the Night of the Rocks.

Something drew residents to the street that evening; Hartless isn't sure now, but thinks some of the occupiers had started a fire. It was a dry summer—the Goldilocks summer, remember—and residents started to gather, "and they're talking to the police [the cruiser always stationed there] and saying, 'How about we get the fucking fire department?' The natives start showing up, there's lots of yelling back and forth, threats, a bunch of pissing on trees, essentially. And then the next thing we hear, they're on Jack's lawn."

Jack Dancey, a Second World War veteran who has since moved to the seniors' home in town, was, at ninety, the oldest guy in the neighbourhood; his backyard, on Thistlemoor facing DCE, was one of the few that wasn't fenced. As Hartless says, "He's an easy target to get. Lived by himself."

Hartless and other residents raced over to Jack's, to find that the natives, on quads, were tearing up the backyard. The residents all joined up and created a wall of people at the rear of his property.

On the DCE side, there was now a crowd too, lots of people wearing masks. Suddenly, a bottle came sailing over the residents' heads and landed in the yard. "Okay, here we go," Hartless thought, and sure enough, "Bottles change to rocks and they're all throwing them. More and more, and now we've kind of retreated to the house, this little group of us, now they're using lacrosse sticks and they're throwing rocks the size of your fist, using lacrosse sticks to launch them. Just hugely dangerous. They're punching holes in the siding with the rocks, trying to hit people."

A vanload of OPP, in full riot gear, arrived.

"They refuse to come in," Hartless says, still astonished. "Parked around the corner. They refuse to come in. One of the sergeants says, 'You know, if you guys just leave, they'll get bored and they'll go away.'"

The victimized were being painted as provocateurs, urged to correct *their* behaviour.

"So now," Hartless says, "we got people swirling up, couple of supervisors there now, and they're [the residents] yelling at the police, 'Fucking *do* something!'

"They won't come in."

The rock-throwing went on, he says, for two or three hours; it started about 10 P.M. and didn't stop until one or two in the morning. "It's ongoing," he says. "We're getting pelted into the court here. We got a couple of people's cars get damaged. Sam down the road gets hit in the side of the head with a rock; Maria, who is pregnant at the time, she gets hit in the ankle with a rock."

Hartless could see a woman, a non-native Six Nations supporter, on a cell phone on the Thistlemoor side of the DMZ, "and she's directing fire. You know, they've moved back, adjusted" at her instruction. People overheard what she was doing and marched up to the OPP and said, "Get her the fuck out of here," and the police escorted her out of the subdivision.

In the midst of all that, one of the residents started whacking golf balls back at the occupiers. "After about two hours of being pelted with rocks, he comes out with a bucket of balls and starts firing off golf balls."

Hartless spoke to him, told him the smarter thing was to collect all the rocks as evidence, and the fellow stopped.

"He's furious, everybody's furious," Hartless says. "The OPP won't do a fucking thing."

Finally, as the natives wandered off and the police disappeared, it was over, but now Jack Dancey was too scared to go to bed. Hartless took his deck chair and his mag light and sat in Jack's backyard until 5 A.M., when a neighbour relieved him so he could go to work.

A brief OPP press release painted the encounter as one of regret-table mutual violence. "The situation escalated to the point where projectiles such as rocks and golf balls were thrown from both sides," the release said. "Police along with others from both sides were able to de-escalate the situation and ensure peace was kept throughout the remainder of the night."

It was an egregiously dishonest description of what had actually happened.

This was one of the most debilitating and Kafkaesque aspects of the policing in Caledonia: the citizens' own reality, which they saw with their own eyes, was so rarely acknowledged in any official way and often outright denied. They would hear gunshots (and know the difference between them and fireworks, for instance), but be told it had been fireworks. They would suffer considerable violence before responding in kind, but were treated as though they were perpetrators. They would report lawlessness or crimes, but never saw anyone being arrested, and government and police appeals for peace were always made to both sides, as though both were equally responsible.

On Sunday, August 27, Hartless's wife, Linda, had had enough. She had some friends from Newmarket visiting. She made up a Thermos of coffee, rounded up some of the women from the neigh-bourhood, including AnneMarie VanSickle, a local hero for having famously said at a rally of Dalton McGuinty, "You, sir, are a medical anomaly. The fact that you can stand when you don't have a spine will surely be discussed for generations." VanSickle left a dinner party to join her neighbours.

They took their lawn chairs and plonked them down in the no-go zone and had a coffee. There were about five of them. Hartless was watching, of course, from the house.

"So off they go and they sit down," he says, and the OPP in the cruiser that was always there began yelling at them to get out of there.

"And Linda's blowing them off—whatever, fuck off. So the natives start coming out. Skye [Brian Skye, the ostensible DCE security boss] is wheeling around at full speed in his white Jeep four-by-four there, and now I'm getting . . . I tried talking her out of it, probably not the best thing to be doing, saying, 'They're not going to care that you're women, and if someone touches you, I'm going to kill them.' By this point, I've got absolutely zero tolerance left.

"She goes out and does it anyway."

Fifty-three OPP officers showed up.

When Hartless first told me this, I thought perhaps he was laying it on a bit thick, but I later saw a video of the entire performance—after six months of hands-off policing with the occupiers, fifty-three officers actually did arrive. Every one of them was videotaped by one of the residents, and gave either a name or a badge number. Some had the grace to look ashamed.

"So they have 53 police officers on this," Hartless says. "Fifty-three show up for five women who are sitting there having coffee.

"So they form a line in front of us, facing us. The natives are fucking yelling and screaming, threatening death and everything else—it's nuts."

The police were yelling at the women to leave, telling them they would be arrested if they didn't. The other women backed off.

"Linda refuses to move," Hartless says. "Now it starts to rain. I come back in to grab an umbrella for her, because she's not going to listen to me. I grab an umbrella and a coat for her, and as I'm grabbing that, [someone] comes in and says, 'They're arresting your wife.'

"So I come back out and they're yelling at her, and one officer pulls out his handcuffs, and an older guy behind him yells, 'Put those fucking things away, you retard!' So he puts the cuffs away.

"So two officers pick her up, they tell her she's under arrest for breach of the peace, they pick her up and carry her off and they put her down, and now she's sending AnneMarie to get Super Glue. AnneMarie's like, 'Oh my God, she's going to glue her ass to the chair,' but she's [Linda] thinking she's gonna put it on her fingertips and make it hard for them to do their fingerprinting."

One of the officers then told her she was being arrested for breach of the peace. "And I tell him, 'I hate to burst your bubble, but it's an illegal arrest.' And the guy says she's breaching the peace, and I say, 'She's sitting there, having a fucking coffee—how is that breaching the peace?' The fucking natives are threatening death and driving the truck around her, and *they're* the ones breaching the peace. *That* would a lawful arrest; this is an illegal arrest."

"Oh no no no," he was told, "that's not the case."

Eventually, the sergeant approached and told Hartless that Linda was free to go, that they weren't going to take her in. "So we come back inside, and people are yelling and screaming at the fifty-three police officers who are still there," he says. Within minutes, his phone rang. It was OPP Inspector Dave McLean, the new Cayuga detachment commander.

"And he starts by saying, 'Is your wife okay?'" Hartless says. "He says, 'Perhaps we should get your wife some help.' Now I'm pissed. [McLean says,] 'We might get her some psychological help.' And I'm, 'She's not crazy, she's pissed off, and with good reason, and everybody else here is pissed off, because you guys are a bunch of fucking tools.'"

Hartless hung up on McLean then, and never spoke to him again except for one night, about six months later, when he was mowing the lawn and McLean stopped his cruiser, rolled down the window and asked how it was going.

"I kind of look at him. 'How about you play hide and go fuck yourself?' His face goes bright red and he goes, and those were the last words I ever spoke to him," Hartless says.

In 2008, McLean was named the OPP's Officer of the Year for his leadership in Caledonia.

———

Ten days after the lawyers told Judge Marshall how much better things were in Caledonia, Debbie Thompson was leaving for work. There are exact dates she forgets—there were so many incidents they all blend a bit together—but this one she remembers. It was June 25, 2006.

"I know," she says, "because it was my daughter's birthday. It was probably about seven-thirty in the morning. And a native with his camouflage and mask or whatever on, he walked right by my house, stopped, and he was carrying a rifle. And I thought, 'There's a pretty sight. This is lovely.'"

She regularly heard gunshots too. "It's not something we heard before," she says, "or it's not something I ever was aware of. Maybe I might have thought, 'Oh, a car backfiring.' Now I listen and I think, 'Oh no, that is a gun.' And for the longest time, my husband would say, 'No no, that's fireworks, it's firecrackers, and I'd be like yeah, yeah. Then, finally, he said, 'It is . . . yeah, it's guns.'"

In those days, the occupiers used to gather under the bridge for what she believes was target practice. One night, when Carl got home from work, Debbie told him she wanted a gun. "I said I want to go and take lessons, and he said, 'No, why do you want a gun?' And I said, 'Because the police aren't coming and I'm not calling them. Someone comes up here and threatens me, I'll blow them away.' That's how I felt. I don't feel that way now, because I don't believe in it. But that day, I did. And he was scared for me. He thought I would turn the gun on myself—that if someone came, 'I know you would never hurt anyone, you'd hurt yourself.'

"So he didn't want me to have it. And truthfully, now I've gotten over that day, the few days, and I wouldn't want one here."

On Hallowe'en night, there was another incident she can pin-point. She'd gone to the Canadian Tire to get switch plates, and though there had been no vehicle lights behind her on the way home, when she got to the driveway, suddenly, there were blinding full-beam lights behind her, "so close I couldn't see a licence plate."

"I didn't know what to do," she says. "Like, I didn't know who it was, but I figured if it was someone I knew, they'd probably get out. They didn't. I didn't want to phone him [Carl] because I thought he'll come out and start going nuts on them, so I didn't do that. So I got out and I went to the driver's side there, asked if there was a problem or if they needed anything. They said I was in trouble, and I needed to get a lawyer and that it was going to happen the next day."

She could smell liquor. "That doesn't mean they were drunk," she says. "I know. They looked to be native people, but maybe not, maybe they were Mexican. I don't really know."

She thought she could identify the vehicle, though—it was a dual-wheel truck. "So I went back down to the Canadian Tire, where the police sit—because, of course, you know they can't come right here." As she was telling them what happened, she saw lights coming off the Sixth Line, and as the vehicle got closer, she realized it looked like the same truck. She told the officer. "He said, 'Oh really?' He did not go and stop the vehicle, and had he stopped it, I could have identified the person [who had threatened her]. Nothing. He wouldn't do anything."

Gunshots, usually from the direction of Six Nations but some-times from DCE, were a regular occurrence. Chris Dudych, who lives with husband Myron and two children on the south side of the Sixth Line west of the Thompsons, began keeping a diary on April 20. It is peppered with references to days they heard shots ring out, many of them in the summer and fall that year, when things were supposed to have been so much quieter.

During this period, virtually none of the events Dudych noted ever made the news. Rather, they were the stuff of ordinary life for those on the Sixth Line: short-lived roadblocks that sprang up for no reason the residents ever understood, sometimes with the occupiers dragging the hydro tower briefly back into place; constant trespassing by natives in camouflage or wearing masks; reports of unmufflered ATVs tearing about the road in the wee hours; new fires on the site; helicopters flying over it; the appearance of new bunkers or makeshift shacks; the arrival of new signs (one, which appeared on August 14 on the Sixth Line bridge, read, JUDGE MARSHALL AND GENERAL CUSTER UPHOLDING THE RULE OF LAW), or more purple Haudenosaunee or red Warrior flags.

"We had a friend who counted forty-nine flags on and around the protest site," Dudych wrote on August 5. "And now they are erecting the flags off the site and along the Sixth Line. WHEN is this going to be all over?"

Faithfully, she reported all of it—to Mayor Trainer, to MP Diane Finley (who met Dudych in August), to MPP Toby Barrett, to the OPP and to Six Nations police. Trainer and Barrett, or their assistants, always took her calls and were attentive; the OPP was usually disinterested; Sergeant Dave Smoke of the Six Nations force was helpful and kind. Yet, regardless of the reception she got, nothing changed.

A couple of notes from the diary stand out. On September 15, the family saw a black pickup sitting in their driveway. Chris wrote down the licence plate number and her son phoned Six Nations Police and asked for Sergeant Smoke, who wasn't in. When her son asked if someone else could come, the dispatcher said, "That's not our jurisdiction" and told him to call the OPP in Cayuga. "No," he said, "we have to call Six Nations because OPP aren't allowed down our road."

The dispatcher replied that they were shorthanded, but she would try to send someone. Instead, she apparently phoned the OPP, because a few minutes later, the provincial police phoned the Dudych house. "We told the OPP that the truck had just pulled away," she wrote. "They [the OPP] said they would phone Six Nations and tell them. I'm so confused. I have spent the morning in tears. Most of all I would like to know WHO is patrolling us."

Then came the parade of dead deer.

On October 5, Dudych heard from a neighbour about two deer hanging from a light standard at the end of the Sixth Line. Shortly before 9 A.M., she went to see for herself.

"There are two deer hanging from the rented light that is at the first camp as you turn down the Sixth Line," she wrote. "There is an adult deer and a younger deer hanging by their hind feet. As well, both have been gutted and left wide open. It really is a disgusting sight to see . . . would this not be called animal abuse since there is no reasoning for this?"

She called Mayor Trainer, whose assistant phoned back to say the mayor had passed the message to one of the negotiators. By day's end, the deer were taken down. "Yes I know that the natives kill deer and take their meat," Dudych wrote. "The only difference here is that when I see this on the reserve, the deer are hanging amongst trees. Where these deer are, there is no nearby forest . . . they have purposefully hung these deer here just to upset us, and intimidate us."

On October 20, another deer appeared. Dudych phoned Mayor Trainer again, spoke to her assistant, and heard back from her again that the mayor had passed it on to the negotiators. Again, by day's end, the deer was down.

On October 29, another dead deer was on the light standard. The next day, Dudych's daughter called to say the school bus had just dropped off the kids: The deer was now skinned and beheaded. "Most of the kids on the bus thought they were going to be sick to the stomachs," her daughter told her.

The next day, the deer was removed.

But on November 27, Dudych wrote, "Another deer went up at the end of our road. This time the deer is not gutted. I would think this is a good case of animal abuse/cruelty." It took until December 14 before this deer was finally removed. "Is it coincidence or what that the deer should come down overnight after the local paper had put a picture in the paper?" she wrote.

Most telling was a plaintive note she made in the midst of the deer saga: "I also spoke to the mayor about the fact that I keep sending email, or she sends them for me, to various people who are dealing with the negotiations and that I never hear back from them." She still imagined that what was happening to her life mattered, that if only she found the right words, put things the right way, made the right call at the right time to the right person, someone would do something about it and things would change.

———

In fact, throughout 2006, residents of the Sixth Line, and Thistlemoor, and Dave Brown and Dana Chatwell all badgered the authorities and elected officials, every which way they could think of, begging for help. They phoned and wrote as individuals; every single resident I interviewed has a file folder or ten jammed with letters they sent their MP, MPP, Premier McGuinty, Prime Minister Harper, various ministers and municipal officials. Most were ignored, while some politely answered—sometimes by underlings, sometimes by form letter.

The residents tried acting collectively, shakily forming themselves into groups of the "concerned residents" of one or another of the affected areas or streets, and sent petitions. And they went to meetings—endless, interminable meetings that went on for hours, sometimes held once or twice a week that first summer.

The Caledonia Citizens Alliance was the earliest and most durable of the groups, and the only genuine grassroots organization that was not sanctioned by the province. Frank Stoneman was involved, from the beginning, right after the occupation started. For a time, he served as co-chair.

"I went up to the Chamber of Commerce and I said, 'Listen, we got an issue here. This is calm now, but you wait until they get the court orders to go in and move those people out—we're gonna have problems.'"

Stoneman was forty-five and had just opened up a business in the town he loved in October of 2005. Born and raised in the area, first on a farm and then in town after his father died when he was just nine, Stoneman always felt he owed Caledonia. "One of the things about this town growing up, because I didn't have a father," he says, "was that I got involved heavily in sports, and the guys like Merlyn Kinrade [a plumbing contractor who later became an activist with Gary McHale], and all of those guys who supported, coached and did everything for the minor hockey kids . . . because of the situation I was in, I could have turned out to be a very bad seed. It could have happened very easily. But because of efforts of guys like that, I went off to university, and when I went off to university, I always had in the back of my mind, 'I'm coming back here to operate my own business and do what those guys did, make the community better.'"

He went to Wilfrid Laurier University in Waterloo, Ontario, got his business degree and another in political science. And if his decision to open Caledonia Wireless on the downtown stretch of Argyle Street was all hard-nosed pragmatism—he prepared a business plan, read the Greenbelt legislation, saw that Caledonia was the place to be and knew that 450 new customers were coming to DCE—it was also sentimental.

His store not even open yet, he organized the town's Terry Fox Run in September, within two weeks. "We got it pulled off," he says, "and it was really great and I felt fabulous, because I'm doing what I set out to do from the moment I left this town in 1980: I'd come back, and now I'm contributing to the community in a positive way."

Everything went according to plan for the first five months, too. But he heard rumblings in the late fall that something was in the works, that some on Six Nations were claiming that Douglas Creek Estates was stolen land.

"But growing up here, like, we've heard this—I've heard this my whole life," he says. "There's been situations where little land claim things have popped up, and they were dealt with quickly and very effectively. Like, you hear about these things, growing up, and you kind of get immune to them, thinking, 'This will be over, this will be over.'"

As a political junkie, his biggest concern once it started was that Caledonia would be divided, either deliberately by government strategy, or by accident.

"So I kind of know how it's going to fall out," he says, "and I'm trying to get in front of it by going to the Chamber and saying we need . . . to unite this town, this town needs to be one lump."

The Chamber was supportive, he says, and they started making calls to prominent locals and trying to figure out how to keep the town together. This was when Ken Hewitt and Jamie McMaster held the big rally at the fairgrounds, and though it seemed such a success, Stoneman says it was also when two distinct factions emerged.

"There was a group that blamed the natives," he says, "and there was a group that blamed the government. I believed right from the beginning that our battle was with the government; it's not with the natives. My thing was, we've got to go after the government on this, because fighting with the Indians on this isn't going to get us anywhere, because when all is said and done, we're still their neighbours and vice-versa."

The resistance group, as they came to be called later by the Alliance people, were the ones who marched, after the rally, down to the barricades. Stoneman was worried: "That was my biggest fear, that people would say we're going to take this into our own hands and go deal with the Indians, and I didn't want that to happen because that looks bad on us . . . Sometimes it's great to be the only virgin in the whorehouse: You can sit there and go 'That's wrong' and 'That's wrong' . . . That's the kind of strategy I thought we could get going here and that's why the Alliance started to form."

The resistance group was never formally organized, but it was some of these folks who would go down to the Friday Night Fights.

"I can't deny them their feelings," Stoneman says. "I didn't live back there [close to DCE]."

In fact, though his business was in town, he didn't yet live in Caledonia, but near Hamilton. Moving back home as a resident was supposed to have been step two of his plan, and it was now on permanent hold because "Who knows who owns the land I'm going to be moving to?"

The first economic assistance from the province, announced May 1—it was awarded as a $50,000 contract on May 24 and swelled to more than $200,000 within a couple of weeks—was the "Close By, But A World Away" ad campaign.

"As I called it," Stoneman says, "it was an attempt to put a Band-Aid on a gaping head wound. It was obvious they [the government] were trying to do just the bare minimum to try and gloss it over, nothing of any substance. That way they could say, 'Oh, we gave you this, we gave you that.' Well, it really didn't do anything, because it's pretty hard to market a town when there's a native insurrection inside that town, scaring the living daylights out of people that are coming in."

Even then, the campaign generated its own little controversy. The contract had gone to Brian Torsney's ad agency, Play. Torsney is the brother of Paddy Torsney, a former federal Liberal MP and former special assistant to—guess who: David Peterson when he was premier.

The second initiative was a direct payout plan to residents and businesses as a result of the power outage on May 22—token sums, but as Stoneman says, "What are you going to do? I'm not going to refuse it." But the $800 he got didn't cover his loss of sales for the period.

It was when the government arbitrarily decided that Haldimand County wouldn't have a seat at the "main table" during negotiations that, only after much pressure from the Alliance, the community liaison group or table was also formed, allowing Caledonia a voice of sorts, albeit a faint and indirect one. Stoneman puts it like this: "You know how, at Christmas dinner, there's the adult table and the kiddie table? Well, we were the kiddie table; that's what we called it."

The "lias" table was distinct from the Community Advisory Group (or the Community Appearance Group, as it was known to some people). The CAG was chaired by Dianne Woods, but Woods was also a regular attendee at the lias.

These two groups were in addition to the four official side tables: land resolution (which dealt with Six Nations claims); archaeology and appearance (which dealt with how Douglas Creek Estates looked); public awareness and education (which promoted Haudenosaunee traditions); and the consultation issues side table, which was to study the impact of development on Haudenosaunee and Six Nations.

Stoneman was one of the Alliance's reps at the liaison table for the first year and a half. He quit because he couldn't stand it anymore, then went back after a year away. He walked into his first meeting of round two, he says, "and they're still talking about the same goddamn things that they were talking about three years ago.

"They wear people out," he says. "And people leave, and so more people go, and then they wear *them* out, and people leave and more people go. It's just a revolving door of attendees."

Dave Hartless went to some of the CAG meetings. He remembers one where Ottawa sent a newbie, "and he's going on about the same stupid fucking questions that everybody's asking. Every time you kind of bring them up to speed a little, they get replaced by someone else. And it's a never-ending cycle; you never get anything accomplished. They come in and they say, 'I'm kind of new to this file,' and I'm like, 'Well, why are you here?'"

At that meeting, Hartless got up and drew a quick map of Ontario, with Toronto, Windsor, Niagara—and a small circle for Caledonia. Then he erased it and said to the new federal guy, "We don't exist. We don't exist. You're here for nothing. You've got no input, you can't do anything, you won't do anything. You won't see any of the issues that are ongoing here. You refuse to believe that any of your 'mitigating factors' are actually acts of domestic terrorism . . . You've just wiped us off. We don't matter."

The CAG, Hartless says, functioned "as a kind of disclaimer" for the government, allowing them to say, "You know, 'We're actively talking to the citizens of Caledonia, trying to address their needs,' etc."

Only the Alliance kept its eye firmly on the ball: ending the occupation. And if what Clark and Luimes regularly reported back to the Alliance was a general lack of progress at the liaison table, their notes were insightful and often revealing.

The process was that each of the major players—the feds, the province, sometimes specific ministries and the OPP—would brief the group. It was at these meetings that the Alliance really pushed for a buyout of the homes in Thistlemoor and on the Sixth Line.

"The difficulty seems to be around real estate values," Clark wrote of the October 18 meeting. "To be honest, I can see why they're having problems. Where do you draw the line? What do you use as a bench mark for 'values prior to the occupation,' etc. etc." But Clark insisted: "I explained to them that the longer they [the government] wait, the better the chance of it not being well accepted and they agreed. I get the feeling this is real," he wrote. "I don't think we're being played, but having said that, we don't HAVE anything yet."

The Alliance reps also tried to push Ontario to act on a growing thorn in the community's side: the illegal spread of smoke shacks from Six Nations onto Highway 6 and the vacant Hydro One land. At one point, Clark wrote, the province seemed poised to at least crack down on the illegal signage on public roads. "I hadn't thought of this before," he wrote, "but it is illegal in the province to advertise cigarettes for sale." But the real sticking point, for action on smoke shacks as for much else, was "the potential negative reaction from removing the signs," Clark wrote. "My point to Nolan [John Nolan, a senior negotiator for Ontario] was that if the natives threaten retaliation, he should threaten the table, or the Burtch property or the feds should threaten their involvement. I have believed for some time that the province needs to get control over this process. It's been the other way around for too long."

Clark also confirmed with the federal representative, Monique Doiron, that Ottawa was firm that there was no validity to the Plank Road claim. While the feds felt they might have some "risk" with some of the other Six Nations claims, she told the table, Ottawa was confident the Plank Road piece "was properly surrendered by natives and it is defensible in court."

It was at this meeting that Clark broke the news that the Alliance had received legal advice that "Caledonia may have a claim for damages against a group or individual who was supporting the occupation financially.

"It was as if I hit everyone around the table with a Taser," he wrote. "No one said a word and some turned almost white." Within the next ten minutes, he said, all the government people became very attentive, arranged various meetings, and Doiron gave Clark her card and said he could "call her any time."

He was learning what his friends the Hennings had learned in their dealings with government: the only thing that worked at all was hardball. Clark was optimistic the Alliance may have found "the hammer" they needed.

There were also clues in the Clark–Luimes reports as to the dysfunction engendered by what Clark once politely called "the governance challenges on Six Nations." In a November 1 update, he said another advisory table had been set up for all the communities along the Grand River watershed, and as part of that, the Confederacy had asked for a presentation from the Grand River Conservation Authority. Staff had spent considerable time preparing it, but when they arrived at the meeting, they were greeted by a small group of protesters "who wouldn't allow the presenters to make their presentation and decided to taunt them with irrelevant questions while acting undignified through the entire meeting."

For all his ready goodwill, Clark was also growing frustrated. For instance, the goal of the archaeology and appearance side table was to remove the houses on DCE and clean up the site—a simple enough task. But everything seemed to move such at a glacial pace—for instance, the Dumpsters for the site cleanup weren't anticipated to arrive until the next spring. The Alliance, meantime, knew "we could get equipment and volunteers to clean up the site in a couple of weeks." At one point, Clark wryly advised the woman from the Ontario Realty Corporation that he knew "some contactors who would do it for nothing."

"As always," he wrote in one note, "government time is not our time."

By then, though, the Alliance, the government and the OPP had one thing in common: an enemy, Gary McHale, who was coming to town on October 15 with his "March for Freedom" rally.

———

That summer, the OPP was in turmoil, in all kinds of ways.

On June 15, Commissioner Boniface, in the midst of wrapping up two days of testimony at the Ipperwash inquiry, interrupted her

evidence to offer an apology to "the First Nations community" and
in particular to Sam George—Dudley George's brother—and his
family for their persistence in pushing for a full inquiry. She also
repeated condolences offered earlier, by former OPP boss O'Grady,
"for the loss of Dudley," and said, "I've done my best to move the
OPP to the forefront of policing in our ability to understand
Aboriginal issues."

Caledonia, the current crisis and, as was increasingly obvious, a
policing mess, got only passing mention in Boniface's testimony.
When inquiry counsel Derry Miller—one of five inquiry lawyers and
a total of forty-seven lawyers who were there that day—was asking
her about the efficacy of court injunctions, with the proviso that, as
he put it, "I don't want to get into Caledonia."

Boniface replied that the OPP had "really worked through the
framework document" ("A Framework for Police Preparedness for
Aboriginal Critical Incidents," the bible for the inquiry and the
OPP), then said, using the future conditional tense as though all this
actually had not happened yet, "We would have, particularly, the
Aboriginal liaison officer [Ron George] and the Aboriginal Relations
Team people on the site."

She then added something that was such utter bafflegab it was
meaningless: "Injunctions are quite nuanced. You . . . it can either . . .
I mean, it would have to be assessed in the process whether, in
fact, it is a way to get to the peaceful resolution that you need, is
one of the factors."

The "Framework" is held up within the OPP as the guiding document for all critical incidents involving natives. First formalized in
2000 as a result of Ipperwash, and updated in 2005, it is a slim bit
of work—eleven pages, much of it naked rhetoric: the ART teams
are to build trust with native partners, "while honouring each one's
uniqueness and the Creator's gifts with dignity and respect"; the
Aboriginal liaison officer is to facilitate communications and "foster
trusting relationships" with native communities; police are to use
the framework before a critical incident, and among the signs to look

for are "words and images used to describe an initiative or event [that] could generate negative emotions, dissension, disagreement or conflict," etc., etc. While perhaps a worthy statement of principle or organizational values, it is difficult to imagine the framework ever being of use in practical policing.

Boniface ended her remarks that day at the inquiry with a commitment to push for ever more change at the OPP; little more than six weeks later, on July 28, she suddenly announced she was resigning to take a job in Ireland. Her new gig was as a deputy chief inspector with the Inspectorate, a new independent oversight arm of Ireland's national police, the Garda Siochana. According to reports in the Irish press, she was one of sixty-seven international candidates who had applied for two positions. Though there were rumours she'd been pressured to leave, Monte Kwinter, then the minister of community safety and the man who actually made the announcement—Boniface was already in Ireland—said she had recently signed on to another three-year term. That would seem to indicate that the government was happy with her performance, and as the search for her successor began, Kwinter said he wanted to "replicate Gwen Boniface."

In fact, the government must have been exceedingly happy with her, or despite the fact she reportedly left of her own volition, she had a lucrative golden handshake—her salary jumped more than $100,000 from 2005 to 2006. The province's "sunshine law," which mandates disclosure of salaries above $100,000, shows that she earned $326,210 in her last year with the OPP, up from $220,378 the year before.

(Boniface refused an interview, albeit through her husband, Gary, whom I reached on May 5 at their home in Orillia. I introduced myself and explained I had sent her several notes, one of which I was assured by the University of Western Ontario's media relations director, Ann Hutchison—Boniface was then back in Canada and doing an investigation for the school—had been forwarded to her. Mr. Boniface said his wife wasn't home. I asked if he had another email address for her so that I could explain what the book was about. He said he doubted she was interested in speaking to me.

I asked if he could speak on her behalf, and said I'd prefer to hear it from her directly. "I would think she's not interested," he said, "and that's all we have to say.")

In any event, the fact was that, smack in the midst of an occupation that already had gone on far longer than Ipperwash, the beleaguered force was now looking for a new boss.

OPP Association boss Karl Walsh and his directors also had their hands full. With complaints from frontline members and union reps flooding the office, Walsh kept trying to find out "who was actually calling the shots in all this.

"The consistent message we were getting out of the upper echelon of the OPP was that this was a West Region issue."

So, in August that year, in advance of a meeting of West Region command and headquarters staff, the association asked twenty-two questions about Caledonia of the brass, thirteen of which dealt with the officers' confusion about why they were policing the way they were in Caledonia. The association specifically queried why officers were being asked if people in custody were white or non-white (the answer was that no such order had ever been made); why, when laws were being broken, they weren't allowed to enforce them (action doesn't always mean "taking immediate action," was the answer); and why natives were being treated differently (the answer was that the OPP "takes into consideration" the rights of Aboriginal peoples with respect to land claims).

Walsh didn't buy the notion that the West Region command in London was running the show.

"I beg to differ," he says. "I don't think there was a goddamn decision made on the ground there that wasn't being put past the commissioner at the time, who was Gwen."

Walsh actually went to Caledonia for few days himself, and was for a brief time allowed to sit in at the command post. He was there, sitting with Chief Superintendent Larry Beechey, the incident commander, when ERT officers complained about having been ordered to turn their backs to the occupiers at the barricades.

"I remember to saying to Larry, 'How can you *do* this? How is it that you're able to rationalize contravening your own training, your own policy, your own procedures?' And I basically said to him, 'If this happens again'—and this was post-incident, and I actually said to him, 'If this happens again, and one of our members gets hurt or killed, it's *you* that we're going to be dragging into a court of law and it's you that will held accountable for these decisions.'"

Soon after, Walsh notes dryly, "our extension of courtesy was run out" and the OPPA was given the boot from the command post.

What he calls "the logistical minutiae" of the OPP's biggest—and longest-lasting—operation in history began to consume the association.

"We got involved in all the day-to-day," Walsh says, recounting complaints from members: "'I can't take a piss'; 'I can't get a glass of water': 'I haven't eaten in two days.' And it just started ramping up from there—it was officer safety issue after officer safety issue."

Boniface, in his view, was "at the heart of everything. When everything started to decline, I think the sole responsibility rests on her shoulders."

It was only after he publicly criticized what he called the "two-tier justice system" and said it was endangering officers that he got a call from her. "She called me and she was just indignant. She said—I didn't really have an opportunity to respond to her—she just started yelling at me and telling me she had never placed the safety of anybody at risk. And I told her—I think my exact response to her was, 'You may not have directly done that, but you were responsible for everybody making the decisions down there.' And 'I beg to differ.'

"And then she hung up on me," he says, pounding the table, "and I have never, ever heard from her since."

He believes that OPPA criticism of "her inaction and her lack of leadership" was what "caused her to finally decide to step down." That fall, at the association's annual general meeting—one of two traditional times a year when the OPPA can question command staff—Caledonia was still the dominant issue. The association had even commissioned a poll about the occupation—among other things, it showed that most Ontarians believed a deadline should be imposed on the talks.

And frontline officers were still bewildered by their orders and felt enormous abandonment by their senior command. At one point, in July, senior commanders did go to Caledonia, ostensibly to talk to their people, but they "brought along a First Nations chief from British Columbia. Members felt hesitant about airing internal complaints," association minutes from the fall AGM note.

"I got numerous calls from members who will tell you that they were petrified of the repercussions of acting," Walsh says, "and this was over a sustained period of time. They were being told, 'This is a no-go zone.' What the hell is a no-go zone in Canada? I mean, if you're a provincial constable, that applies to the province, right? The whole damn thing, not willy-nilly as required. But these guys were being told, clearly . . . there was a clear demonstration that if they did something contrary to orders, that they were going to be hung out to dry."

Within the OPP, this is known as "disguised discipline"— unexpected transfers, stalled promotions and careers, small punishments meted out to officers who don't play ball. And already there were some examples of it happening in Caledonia: Dave Scott, banned from DCE and scolded for having created "a flashpoint"; Brian Haggith, who, after June 9, made it crystal clear he wanted to see arrests made when occupiers broke the law and who suddenly found himself transferred to Toronto late that summer (he launched a formal grievance over the move and won); and Detective Sergeant Dave Hillman, an experienced and well-respected unit supervisor who had his knuckles rapped a couple of times for having spoken out against the DCE style of policing.

"So," Walsh says, "they've got all these examples of people on the ground who have already been persecuted, disciplined, had repercussions career-wise. The only tether they had to hang onto was us [the union]; they knew we'd stand behind them. But who the hell wants to go through that [the process of grieving]?"

Walsh was also beginning to get disturbing reports about how the ART team was working—or rather, not working.

"It's almost like it's being operated like it's an intelligence team," he says, and as a former military policeman and intelligence officer in the Department of National Defence, he can speak with some authority.

He kept hearing that the ART members were "talking to, cavorting with, drinking with, eating with, getting subject to Stockholm syndrome with" the occupiers and their leaders. "So if I go back to the April incursion, when all this mess started, and you just think about the intelligence gathering that can take place before an operation is put together, the only conclusions that you can draw from that are two: either they didn't do significant intelligence gathering before they put that operational plan together, or they did, and just ignored the intelligence."

Walsh wasn't the only one who was worried about the kinds of relationships the ART members were forging on the site.

In a November 24, 2006, note to the Alliance, Ralph Luimes wrote, in a brief he categorized as "internal confidential," that after a recent meeting, he had a discussion with Cayuga detachment commander Dave McLean.

"I questioned [soft challenge] Dave on viewing the relationship between Ron George and Dick Hill as 'untouchable.' My point was that if it is left as it is, we will never resolve the 6th Line/DCE disengagement issue—even if there is no one on the site.

"Other people need to be a part of that conversation," Luimes wrote, "because at this point, Dick is calling the shots."

Hill and his wife, Hazel, who issued some of the most florid press releases during this period, were certainly key spokesmen for the occupiers. From the get-go, they were listed on native websites as leaders, their cell phone numbers freely available online. And Paul Barnsley of Windspeaker, which bills itself as Canada's Aboriginal news service, said this of Hill in July 2006: He "has been described as a Warrior Society member and has led occupations in the past."

OPP members were also hearing reports of the ART becoming too tight with some of the less savoury characters on DCE. Few people knew about an incident that occurred at the Unity Road command post sometime after the failed raid, but before the end of June that year. Constable Monty Kohoko of the ART had come into the old school. He sought out Inspector Haggith, then still the detachment commander. Kohoko said he had some intelligence to pass along about weapons on DCE. He and Haggith headed down the hall to fill in Junior Johnson, probably the best intelligence officer in the detachment and a native man himself, and Kohoko was about to do just that when, out of one of the old classrooms, burst a furious Ron George.

"Shut your mouth," he told Kohoko. "You don't tell them anything!"

If there might be a possible rationale for keeping a distance between the ART and the regular OPP—the former had a mandate to "build trust" with natives, the latter to police—surely it would not have extended to keeping secret information about weapons that could conceivably have been used against any one of them. The ART were the OPP's eyes and ears on the ground in Caledonia, the behind-the-lines guys for the frontline officers. "You don't tell them anything"? Us and them? Whose side were they on?

———

John Tory was on Caledonia like a dog on a bone.

He guesses he probably asked three hundred questions about it in the Legislature, and indeed, as researcher Stephanie Chambers found out when she reviewed Hansard, he did rise on seventeen occasions, with multiple questions each time, before the end of that year. Toby Barrett was on his feet twenty-five times.

The dog analogy is fitting, the former Conservative leader says, because whenever he raised the subject, he was invariably greeted from the government side with mutters of "Oh, there's another dog-whistle question."

Dog whistle is shorthand among MPPs for the silent or unspoken aspects of a question, the parts you can't hear but believe are there. With Caledonia, Tory says, what *dog whistle* meant was "that it was an anti-Aboriginal question," and that the guy asking it was anti-native, or racist.

"That's what they'd say," he says. "I'd hear 'the dog whistle,' which is they're saying of me, of all people, that I'm asking a question to stir people up, as opposed to because I care about the rule of law."

The Hansard review shows that there were often "interjections" after Tory's questions, which were usually directed to the premier but often offloaded to Aboriginal Affairs Minister David Ramsay.

Tory, who is widely believed to have lost the 2007 election because of his stubborn loyalty to his plan to extend public funding to Ontario faith-based schools, is almost as universally acknowledged to be ridiculously fair-minded. And so he was whenever he asked about Caledonia. Yet Premier McGuinty, who on numerous occasions denied outright that anyone in his Cabinet had directed the OPP, frequently accused Tory of "fanning the flames" and regularly hinted that, if Tory were in his shoes, he would tell the OPP to go marching onto DCE.

A lawyer by training, who worked as one for twelve years before joining Rogers Communication, Tory was most distressed by the rule-of-law aspect of Caledonia. "The greatest tragedy," he says, "and maybe it hasn't infected the rest of the province, but I think every time you let that kind of thing happen, where you have disrespect for the law, two apparent standards for different groups of people, all that stuff, you whittle away at what is the foundation of our democracy."

He understands the politics, though pragmatic compromises were hardly his signature. But after Dudley George was killed at Ipperwash, he says, "They [the Liberals] had a practice of asking a question every day. I think they had somebody every day get up and ask, 'When are you going to call an inquiry?' And they did that for a reason, and I think that, having done it, it put them in a position, and I would understand the politics of them saying in a room somewhere, 'Well, now that this thing [Caledonia] has arisen, the last thing we can ever afford to have happen is something like that, on our watch, so therefore we will do everything to stop it from happening,' basically papering it over and buying land and everything they've done."

Tory is convinced that this—the Liberals' decision to make Ipperwash a defining issue, one of those on which they rode to power—is at the root of what happened in Caledonia. Answering the why of Caledonia is the reason that, when he was in opposition, he pressed for a public inquiry, for all his reservations about the process and its cost.

"Why didn't they [the OPP] enforce the law?" he asks. "Did they just decide on their own, and if they did decide on their own, how does that work? I mean, what meetings did they have? Because I thought each officer was sworn to uphold the law, they have to use their discretion each time they do that, have reasonable and probable grounds and all that. So if it wasn't the government, who was it said, 'Don't do this'?"

Tory believes that, while it was perfectly reasonable for ministers to have had daily briefings with the OPP—"You're responsible, to a degree"—the police must be able to make independent operational decisions. He points to Tamil protests in Toronto in the spring of 2009 as an example. Tory was by then freshly out of politics and working as a host on radio station Newstalk 1010. He remembers that Torontonians, furious after days of seeing University Avenue closed for the protests, were calling in to say that then Mayor David Miller should be telling the police to get the Tamils off the streets.

"And I said no, no," Tory says. "David Miller doesn't instruct [police chief] Bill Blair what to do. Bill Blair makes his own decision about what to do, that's his job. And if you don't think he's doing a good job, fine—get a new police chief. But don't tell him what to do."

Had he been in the premier's office when Caledonia burst into the headlines, he says, "I would have been making sure someone was having a daily discussion about it too—not in the sense of giving instructions, though what happens, I think, and again I'm prepared to be much fairer than I probably should be about this, when two human beings are having a discussion, and one is the superior of the other, the body language, the tone, the words all give you the sense that you're getting instruction, even if you're not."

He isn't sure if what happened is that benign—the premier and ministers' staff saying, "Well, of course we don't want to see anyone hurt," "We don't want to see anything really go on down there," and "We just want to try to keep a lid on it"—or if the orders were more explicit. Either way, "I was always convinced, and I remain convinced, it was the government," he says. But, he adds, "Perhaps there will be no memo, I don't think."

A former Ontario government insider, whose ministry was one involved in Caledonia, agrees that concrete evidence might be hard to find. Aides and senior staff were discouraged from making notes, he says, and most decisions were made in conference calls among the ministers' senior communications people. But the former staffer, who contacted me after reading the government's published expenditure on the occupation in my column (I believe it was the $64-million figure) and realizing immediately it was years out of date, says it's not that the Liberals were opposed to giving the OPP direction. Rather, it's that "they just can't be seen to be providing direction to the OPP."

Tory admits ruefully that, though he handed the Liberals a better issue anyway—faith-based schools—as the 2007 election campaign began, he nonetheless believes that in that period, the government likely gave the OPP "even more instructions not to do anything that would allow me or anyone else to make this [Caledonia] more of an issue."

Tory didn't just thunder on in Question Period. He was the only non-local politician, federal or provincial, who regularly went to Caledonia. In fact, he went on thirteen separate occasions, six of them in 2006. He met Dave Brown and Dana Chatwell, talked to residents and businesspeople and knocked on doors with Toby Barrett. Tory also talked to OPP officers when he was in town, and "sort of within the bounds of propriety, nobody said, 'I got a memo.'

They all said, 'Look, we're just carrying out orders here. I hope you understand,' and I said, 'I always have.'"

He remembers having a press conference with some local residents, as six or seven OPP officers stood nearby. "The people were shouting at me about the police—not shouting at me, but to give me this message about how the police were not enforcing the law. The police were standing about twenty feet away, so they could hear it all. I felt badly for them, because I was convinced, and I certainly was after I went over and spoke to them, that the frontline officers were not making individual decisions not to enforce the law."

Another exchange he remembers vividly was with Ruby Montour, an older Six Nations woman who, with her husband, Floyd, was a fixture at protests throughout the area. This was at an occupation outside Caledonia. Tory approached her deliberately—he was always seeking opportunities to talk to natives, regretful that "the Aboriginal people wouldn't see me as often, because they came to see me as someone who was not their friend." He asked whether, if the premier were to promise to resolve the land claim by a certain date, she would agree to meet him with a view to ending the occupation.

"She looked at me and she said, 'No, because you don't understand, Mr. Tory.' And I said, 'What don't I understand?' She said, 'Your laws are not of application to us.' I said, 'Wait a minute— they're *our* laws, we're all in this together.' She said, 'Well, no, we don't recognize those laws.'

"So I said, 'I've seen that written before, but I guess I just don't accept it. I sort of figure every Canadian is subject to the laws.' And I said, 'Well, do you believe you have the Charter rights?' And she said, 'Oh yes.' And I said, 'And what about all those programs you're a part of? You recognize those programs?' And she said, 'Oh yes.' And I said, 'But you don't recognize you can't just take a piece of land and say, "It's ours"?'"

Tory remembers telling Ruby Montour, "Now, you may be right. It may be yours. But we have ways of deciding that—the courts and so on."

"Oh no, Mr. Tory," came the reply. "They're *your* courts."

He wishes the whole exchange had been televised. "Because if people had seen that, they would have said, 'Look—I respect their right to have that view, but we can't operate that way, because what if everybody decided that?' What if the Cabbagetown ratepayers said, 'Look, we just don't buy into these laws and we're going to do our own thing?' That's called anarchy."

During one of his visits, Tory even stayed overnight on Thistlemoor with AnneMarie VanSickle and her family. Nothing of particular note happened, Murphy's Law being what it is, but he got to see the police car stationed 24-7 outside their house.

"And I thought to myself—and I talked about this when I got back, and I said, 'How would you feel if somebody sat outside your house and was sort of recording your every movement?' That's a police state. And I know the police weren't trying to do that, to be a police state, but they're doing that."

The VanSickles insisted, of course, that Tory sleep in their bed.

"I was horrified," he says, blushing at the memory. "It was one of those horrifying things where I came to stay, and of course they treated it as though it were the Pope [coming] or something . . ."

No wonder the VanSickles were so excited; certainly, no other politician of Tory's stature was even remotely interested in their plight. Dalton McGuinty, though he travelled all around Caledonia, never set foot in town, and Stephen Harper was nowhere to be seen.

———

In August, as the OPP's search for a new commissioner was presumably underway, Gary McHale was busy assembling information to tell the Caledonia story on his website. He took and posted pictures (including shots used as a sort of "WANTED FOR SERVICES NOT RENDERED" poster, which showed the OPP standing by as occupiers pulled down the Hydro One tower), collected and posted documents (such as fact-finder Michael Coyle's report) where he could find them, and

wrote and reprinted news and opinion pieces. He also posted a petition asking for Gwen Boniface to be removed, and another one asking
that no amnesty be given to those who break the law.

The first news story about McHale and CaledoniaWakeUpCall.
com appears to have been Karen Best's July 13 piece in the Haldimand
Review. Best, who now works as an aide to Six Nations Chief Bill
Montour, distinguished herself with her extensive and even-handed
coverage of the occupation, and this story was no exception. The
piece was reprinted on the Six Nations Solidarity Network online,
with the usual disclaimer: "The following mainstream news article
is provided for reference only, as an example of how mainstream
media treats indigenous resistance to genocide. Mainstream media
often presents biased and distorted information, lacking pertinent
facts and/or context."

McHale was planning the "March for Freedom."

"It was based on Martin Luther King's concept of gathering people
together and simply marching down a road," he says. He has long been
an admirer of two groups—black Americans and Jews. "It's amazing
that the Jews, coming out of the Holocaust, don't have a hatred for
German people," he says. "They have a dislike for Nazis, will hunt them
down and prosecute them—not hunt them down and kill them, not
hunt them down and beat the crap out of them in a dark alley. Even
that in itself is amazing testimony to the character of Jewish people."

That collective response to evil, to stay within the confines of the
law, is what also impresses McHale about Dr. King. "You have a comparison between the Black Panthers and King," he says. "Both leaders,
Malcolm X and Martin Luther King, both obviously clearly witness
violence against black people. They experienced it themselves, they've
seen the corruption with the police, the governors, and yet one makes
the choice that the solution is to have a revolution, to tear down the
white man in order to raise up blacks, and the other one comes up
with a vision—what we want to do is lift ourselves up to be equal.

"And it's very impressive," McHale continues. "There must have
been many times he [King] felt temped to pick up a bat and beat the

crap out of some cop who was doing something. It must have been incredible for him to resist that. And yet he changed the nation. So there's some lessons there: if you're faced with absolute racism, with injustice of any kind, do you really want to change the nation, or do you just want to vent your anger?"

He knew, by August, he had to focus Caledonians' rage. "If you give people no option to speak—they can't speak to police, they can't speak to the government, their own politicians won't listen to them, nobody's paying attention—all you're going to get is violence. So I provided an outlet: let's have a rally . . . let's have speeches and build everyone up towards that."

He had a standard message: "We're having a rally. There's no swearing, no racial slurs, no violence allowed, no criminal behaviour." Yet, in short order, McHale had managed to offend just about everyone—every level of government, natives and their supporters, the OPP and the OPPA.

He began renting, or trying to rent, Lions halls in the area—Brantford, Waterloo, Deseronto, Cayuga, Caledonia.

Some of the rentals, in Brantford and Deseronto for instance, were cancelled after the OPP paid whoever was in charge of the hall a little visit; McHale knows this happened because the Cayuga Lions Club president told him about it, though, as Christine says, "He basically told them [the OPP] to take a flying leap."

But the idea was to tell people about the upcoming rally, about the rules of the rally, and get some media attention. After all, McHale points out, "the natives had already had information seminars and all that, so if you're a native person you can go into a town and 'educate the public,' but if you're non-native, and you want to go and speak about the exact same issues, you'll be shut down."

And the OPP *was* keeping a wary eye on McHale and his plans. Even in the Clark/Luimes report back to the Alliance from the "liaison" table on October 4, fully half of the update from the OPP is devoted to McHale. The Alliance rep noted that "the OPP is following promotional material about the October 15 march/rally very closely . . . The county reported it has not received a request for permit. People in general are increasingly finding the promoter [McHale] regularly makes inflated reports . . . There is a concerted effort by many business leaders, residents, community leaders, county councillors and others are all onto him. They are not putting up with the promotion of activity seemingly intent on disturbing the peace."

Furthermore, in the three days immediately leading to the rally, the OPP issued three press releases, all under the authority of acting Commissioner Jay Hope. The October 11 release warned, "Because of increased rhetoric and mounting tensions, the OPP does not support people attending this planned protest," and Hope "strongly urged" anyone planning to reconsider. The next day's release said flatly, "This weekend's proposed rally is not supported by the majority of local people," an absurd statement given that, by now, the police were so alienated from their community they would be the last to know. All the OPP could be certain of at this point was that the only thing most of the locals didn't support was the OPP.

The release also warned, "The OPP will not tolerate disturbances that may set back negotiations."

And on October 13, the notice said primly, "Rallies fuelled by negative emotions generally result in injuries and criminal charges." (Who ever heard of a protest based on positive emotions?) Again, Hope directly urged people not to go.

No one seemed to ask the obvious question, which was: In Canada, since when is it up to the police to bless a rally or protest? Isn't their task, rather, merely to police it?

In April of 2009, Dave Hartless, the outspoken Hamilton Police officer, was called to testify by Gary McHale, who was defending himself against the bizarre charge of "counselling mischief not committed." In the course of his evidence, Hartless described the six duties, under the Police Services Act, of any Ontario police officer: preserving the peace; preventing crime and providing assistance and encouragement to others in their prevention; assisting victims of crime;

apprehending criminals and other offenders; and laying charges and participating in prosecutions.

Wide-ranging as those responsibilities are, none would seem to include spreading propaganda against a protest advertised as, and intended to be, lawful and peaceful.

Still, if McHale the newly minted activist was doing all right, all was not so sublime on the home front in Richmond Hill. In early August, the McHales came home from Caledonia to find a notice on their door—they were behind in their monthly condo fees. They had become obsessed with Caledonia at the expense of earning income, and now the evidence was staring them in the face.

McHale sent out a group email on August 26, "saying, 'Look, it's been nice, but I have to get back to my job. I have to make a decision to provide for my family.'" But some of the McHales' supporters, including Hartless, who wrote Mayor Trainer to suggest that the county cover the couple's expenses, begged them to stay on. People offered donations. What brought them back was a note they received from VanSickle on August 27, the night of the sit-in led by Linda Hartless, saying their "little event was for you guys."

"It was because people were willing to stand up and be arrested that we decided to continue," McHale says.

In September, McHale announced the March for Freedom would take place on October 15. And so it did—uneventful and peaceful for the most part, the most complete coverage, as usual, provided by Karen Best in the Haldimand *Review*. She reported that a crowd of two thousand had turned up, policed by hundreds of OPP and London officers; she quoted from AnneMarie VanSickle's moving speech and another given by Mary-Lou LaPratte, an Ipperwash resident who said the OPP was still not enforcing the law there and urged Caledonians to speak up; she interviewed a handful of townspeople in attendance who were furious at the OPP, and described how, "against his [McHale's] wishes," a smaller group broke away from the crowd, approached DCE from the Thistlemoor side and then walked down to the Argyle Street entrance, where more than a thousand occupiers had gathered. There were but a handful of arrests, for intoxication and breach of the peace, from that smaller group.

At the liaison table three days later, Jason Clark reported the OPP was "happy with community support against march," said they estimated "two hundred people involved were from Caledonia," and noted that AnneMarie VanSickle "was very vocal throughout . . . I was told she wasn't asked to join the advisory group because the province learned she was the resident who taped Jane Stewart and forwarded the info to McHale for the website."

(Actually, it wasn't VanSickle who taped Stewart, McHale says, but another Thistlemoor resident, the man who rescued the native injured by the train and who is known in these pages as Paul Trickey. So, not only was Big Brother keeping tabs on who said what, he was also getting it wrong.)

The McHales were struggling to hang on financially—by December they'd started to get notices from the bank about their mortgage payments—but now they were fully committed. On December 2, a local group headed by Rick and Valerie Vanderwyk and Dana Chatwell organized a rally for residents to hang Canadian flags, decorated with yellow ribbons, throughout Caledonia in honour of Canadian troops. They were stopped as they came down Argyle Street to put up flags near DCE, where red Mohawk Warrior flags flew from every other utility pole.

This was not a rally organized by McHale. In fact, he says, "Val made a point of telling me I was not invited." He found out where and when it was taking place only from a friend, and "just showed up myself to take photos." It was at this event that a local resident, Bo Chausse, was arrested; he later sued the OPP for wrongful arrest and settled out of court. But McHale instantly recognized the genius of the idea.

"As soon as I saw Bo being arrested," he says, "I knew the issue: I'm holding these flag-raising events until we put up a flag.

"It had nothing to do with the military. Matter of fact, I made it absolutely clear: It was just to put up a Canadian flag. It was just to prove that in Caledonia you can't put up a Canadian flag. And where to put up the Canadian flag was determined by where the police stopped the first people (the Vanderwyks]. Wasn't going to be any other flagpole but that one. You stopped them on December 2, 2006, we are going to keep going until a flag goes up on that pole. You can offer up any other pole in the province, that's not the one we want."

He picked a date: December 16.

———

In the way that reporters know the public figures we cover, and perhaps a little better than that, I'd known Julian Fantino—who officially started work in his new job on October 30—for about twenty-five years.

I've always done at least some crime reporting, sometimes a lot. I don't recall having any dealings with Fantino in his first incarnation as a homicide investigator and cop with the former Metro Toronto Police, but I was certainly aware of him when he was the police chief in London, Ontario, and then in York Region—the area north of Toronto, where he lives—and finally when he returned to Toronto to head the force in 2000 after a bitter and unsuccessful try for the job six years earlier.

He was always a bit of a lightning rod for controversy. In London, he drew the ire of the gay community, there and elsewhere, for Project Guardian, an investigation into the gay teen sex business. And in Toronto, he was in the hot seat as corruption scandals broke out. He left the Toronto police in 2005 on a sour note, after he made it known he wanted his contract extended and the police board refused to reappoint him.

Born in Italy to hard-working parents who emigrated to Canada when he was eleven, Fantino is a practising Roman Catholic, moralistic and sometimes almost prissy in his sensibilities, conservative (and one of those perpetually rumoured to be a sought-after candidate for the Conservative party), and a man who sees things in stark black and white.

In his various incarnations as a chief, he was combative, shrewd with the press (feeding bits of information to those he could trust, the way most in public life do), a reasonable if often hackneyed quote, and accessible. I had his cell and home numbers, though I guarded them and used them judiciously.

I couldn't remember a time when I didn't defend him, in fact, but I had researcher Stephanie Chambers check the old files, just to be sure. I was remembering correctly: of thirty-eight stories from the four newspapers where I've worked and where I discussed Fantino's leadership, I was always on his side, usually without qualification.

In February 2005, he surfaced at Queen's Park as the commissioner of emergency management, a Dalton McGuinty appointee. It was a big job, though a quiet one, and Fantino was uncharacteristically out of the news for a short time. But when Gwen Boniface announced her resignation in June, speculation quickly arose that Fantino—who, after all, was already working in a senior spot in the same ministry for the same minister, Monte Kwinter—might end up on top.

The speculation went public in *The Toronto Sun* in mid-August and culminated in a thundering column by my friend Joe Warmington. Under a headline that read, "The Caledonia situation is a mess. Who better to clean it up than a tough, straight-talking cop named Fantino?" Warmington argued that Fantino's appointment would mean instant credibility for the McGuinty government. "Tough decisions are needed in Caledonia," he wrote. "Hell, any decisions are needed down there."

I was in Afghanistan for much of 2006, but if I'd thought about it, I probably would have guessed Fantino was the right man for the OPP job, too.

Almost everyone on the law-and-order side of the Caledonia equation did. Karl Walsh, who was elected in the fall of 2005, says Boniface was "just knee-deep, living and breathing the Ipperwash inquiry. That was her sole focus in life when I got this job. She was just coming up to the end of that [the inquiry]; this [Caledonia] was the first major incident after that. She'd done all kinds of ground work to try to rebuild, or build [a relationship] with First Nations people in this province, then, when this [Caledonia] happened, quite frankly, I think she had Stockholm syndrome, she had absolutely *no* idea what to do at this point.

"And I think she was petrified what would happen if she had taken proactive, OPP policing action as she was mandated to do through her office as commissioner, and failed to do it. And it just got progressively worse.

"Obviously, we all know how it fleshed itself out," Walsh says. "It eventually just fell flat on its face. People started getting hurt; she didn't know how to react to that, either. We were breathing up— actually, we were barking up—her ass, and then she was gone.

"Julian," he says. "We needed Julian at the time. We needed somebody at the time. The three things that we complained about was that nobody knew who the commissioner of the OPP was, right, outside of [the press]; we had no voice. We had no face. And we had no backbone. And we thought we were getting all three with Julian." He adds that at first, "I would say, we got all three. I mean, he picked morale up, started becoming the face of the OPP, started talking tough."

Yet on the ground in Caledonia, the approach remained the same. "I have no idea what happened," Walsh says. "I don't know why the traditional, what you would call the Fantino approach to things, got so watered down." He suspects now that the OPP's senior command was so wedded to the Boniface and government path, and so skittish about the coming inquiry report, that "in fairness to him, I don't think he knew where to turn."

At the time, though, the OPPA believed that their saviour had arrived.

I'd like to have asked Commissioner Fantino himself about all this, but he declined my request for an interview. His spokesman, Inspector Dave Ross, told me in an April 13, 2010, email that he and Fantino "feel it would be inappropriate to provide an interview due to the ongoing civil and criminal cases" related to Caledonia. I then offered to provide a written undertaking that I wouldn't ask Fantino about those cases, most of which involve Gary McHale, and invited the commissioner to have his lawyer sit in on the interview. By then, of course, through my coverage of the Brown/Chatwell lawsuit, I was well on the record about the OPP and the government's handling of Caledonia.

I had also committed what counts as a cardinal sin in the Fantino book of rules. I had mentioned in a column—it was about a court case involving McHale and Fantino and the appearance of fairness—that Fantino's son Gregory had recently been appointed by the McGuinty government as a justice of the peace, a job that pays $114,000 a year. Fantino was furious; he regards his family as sacrosanct, apparently even when they accept juicy public appointments and earn decent public salaries, and it was evident to me that our previously good working relationship was over.

The OPP press release of December 3, 2006, which appeared to quote the new commissioner in his trademark lurid language (he has always had a penchant for the histrionic), showed he was surely making his mark.

"The OPP will not tolerate the actions of those willing to put their own self-motivated agendas ahead of the betterment of the community," the release said. "The OPP remains committed to keeping the peace and wish to remind everyone that there will be serious consequences for these types of selfish and juvenile actions."

Fantino's name didn't appear in the release, but the phrases were familiar to those who had followed his long career, and would soon become more so.

If it was an odd way to characterize ordinary citizens like the Vanderwyks, who were merely exercising freedoms of assembly and speech, it was nothing compared to what happened to McHale's rally almost two weeks later.

McHale and Christine had just come off Highway 403 and turned onto Highway 6 south, heading for Caledonia, when they were approached by an OPP cruiser with lights flashing. It was about ten-thirty in the morning.

One of the officers got out of the cruiser, walked up to McHale's open window, assured him he'd done nothing wrong and said the purpose of the stop was to advise him that if he attempted to raise a Canadian flag at the rally, he would be arrested.

The officer, Detective Sergeant Bernie Cowan (he is normally attached to the behavioural sciences bureau in Orillia, but was seconded to Caledonia duty), and his partner, Detective Sergeant Doug Cousens (who was then in the anti-rackets squad but also seconded), had attended a "special briefing" about the planned McHale stop earlier that morning, where they were directed by Detective Sergeant Greg Walton to tell McHale that "raising flags in a certain location would be considered a breach of the peace because of the situation."

In any case, Cowan introduced himself and said, "We've been sitting there pretty much most of the morning looking for ya, just because we wanted to have a couple words with ya." He added that police had "some concerns today for you and the safety of the community," and "it's our belief that if you or anybody else attempts to erect flags or ribbons directly across from Douglas Creek Estates, that it may cause a confrontation, and we can't let that happen, and we won't let that happen.

"We will allow you to raise flags and ribbons, just not across from the Douglas Creek Estates. Okay, and anybody that—anybody that attempts to do that, to raise those flags and ribbons in that restricted area, will be arrested for breach of the peace."

McHale, of course, asked, "So have the natives been arrested for putting up their flags?"

"They have not," Cowan replied.

"Why?" McHale asked. "You said 'anyone.' Your words were 'Anyone who tries to put up flags will be arrested for breach of the peace.'"

"That's today I'm talking about," Cowan replied.

Around and around they went, with McHale pressing his point

and Cowan's only answer for it that, when natives put up their flags, it was "a long time ago."

"And I'm not here to comment on that," Cowan said. "I'm just telling you what our plan is today, and that's what my purpose is."

"Well," McHale said, "you know what my plan is."

"What is your plan?" Cowan asked.

"My plan is to make you guys look like a bunch of assholes," McHale said, "and you've done a great job [of helping achieve that]. The media will be here, and it will be quite clear to all Canadians across this country, because they will see the native flag. The cameras will show the native flag. And you'll be there, and your officers will be there, saying, 'If you put up a Canadian flag, we will arrest you.'"

He continued: "You guys are looking more ridiculous as time goes by. You do nothing when the power station was destroyed, you did nothing when the bridge was burned down, and now we're talking about a simple flag, and the natives have their flags up and there was no violence."

"Well," Cowan said, "we just believe that today, if you guys attempt to do that in that area, there's a confrontation. We just don't want a confrontation today, and that's what I'm talking about."

Round and round they went for a little longer, then Cowan said again, "And your intent today is to . . . what? I don't know."

"Well," said McHale, "I already told you my intent: to make you guys look like assholes, and you've done a great job."

The conversation lasted a little over four minutes, and as he continued on his way to town for the rally, the OPP prepared a transcript of the chat, sent it up the chain of command for approval and worked on a press release.

As promised, McHale was arrested that day and charged with breach of the peace, though in fact, at the time of his arrest, he was standing on Argyle Street, a flag in his hand, waiting to hear from the OPP if, as he had requested, someone senior would come and speak to him. "You show me him coming here," McHale had told them, "and I will speak to him and will tell everyone to leave."

Instead, he was handcuffed, put in a paddy wagon and taken to Cayuga.

Fully expecting he might be arrested, McHale had given Christine his keys and wallet, so he had no identification on him. Officers kept coming in, he says, and asking, "Are you Gary McHale?" To which he replied, "I was the guy holding the Canadian flag." Every ten minutes, someone would come and ask the same question, and he'd reply the same way.

"So I had made a decision," McHale says, "and I said to the officers, 'This is all mind games. You're trying to intimidate me, so here's going to be my response.'

"And I had purposely worn boxer shorts," he says, "so they throw me in jail, first thing I did, within seconds, was strip down to my boxer shorts. This is December 16. It is cold. It's a steel bed—you probably haven't been in jail—there's no blankets, there's no pillow. So you're on a steel bed, cement walls: it was cold, cold, cold, cold."

They brought in dinner; he wouldn't touch it. He refused to sleep. They began asking if he wanted a blanket, or his clothes back. Now, worried he'd get sick, the police began cranking up the heat in the cells; they were now responding to McHale.

"Within about an hour and a half," he says, "I'm really toasty." He was sitting with his hands clasped behind his head, happy as a clam. "I really was quite comfortable; it was getting to be quite warm."

One of his friends, fellow protester Mark Vandermaas, had also been arrested and was in the next cell. He hadn't stripped down, so he was cooking. Vandermaas is a former Canadian peacekeeper and real estate agent who co-founded CANACE, Canadian Advocates for Charter Equality, with McHale. He was released after several hours, but McHale was held overnight.

The 17th was a Sunday, and there was no court in Cayuga, so McHale was taken to Hamilton, where assistant Crown attorney Andrew Goodman stood up and said he had no information on McHale, no paperwork.

Only later, in one of his various court actions, did McHale receive a statement from Goodman, in which he confirmed that he had been under some pressure to impose a peace bond with conditions upon McHale before releasing him. Goodman refused, pointing out that under Section 31 of the Criminal Code, once the purported "danger" has passed, "there is an obligation to release" an accused charged with breach of the peace.

Goodman said that, before court, he had spoken to Detective Sergeant Walton and perhaps one other person, and that there was more than one conversation. "There were some strong views provided to me suggesting that the Crown take a certain course of action which I did feel was appropriate," he said. "I cannot, at this juncture, quantify the degree of any pressure or influence placed upon me by the OPP, other than to state it was present."

The OPP issued a press release after the rally, and this time, Fantino was quoted. The release, first of all, said the rally "was organized under the pretext it was in 'Support of Our Troops,'" but that was the one earlier in the month organized by the Vanderwyks, not McHale. Then, without naming McHale, who was identified only as "a male party from outside of Caledonia," the release said the rally leader "said to police that his intent was 'just to make you guys look like a bunch of assholes like you already do.'"

McHale still giggles about it: "They just thought the community would be [aghast]. They've had some native women say every swear word in the book to their faces, and they think, 'Oh, Gary called us assholes.'"

In fact, McHale rarely swears; I have seen him cringe at my language. It's a measure of how angry he must have been to be stopped that morning that he did.

"They never brought it up again," he says. "The OPP, after six months of investigation, the best they got on me is that I'm making them look like assholes."

He wasn't the only person in town who had caught the OPP's— and, in particular, Fantino's—attention.

By now, Dave Hartless had two signs on his front lawn, one quoting Judge Marshall on the rule of law applying to all ("Yes even you," it concluded) and another that read:

NO CONFIDENCE,
BRING IN THE ARMY!
EJECT THE TERRORISTS ATTACKING CALEDONIA.
OPP = 2 TIER POLICING
NO PROTECTION 4 US.

He was writing letters at a furious clip—never identifying himself as a police officer, only as an enraged Caledonia resident. And after the Vanderwyks' flag rally, during which Bo Chausse was arrested, Hartless posted an editorial on CaledoniaWakeUpCall.com.

He was infuriated that the OPP had stopped the townspeople from raising a Canadian flag at the same location where "the OPP sat back and watched the natives erect Warrior flags, Six Nations flags and unity flags without so much as a 'Hey, what are you doing?'" He called the force ineffective, impotent and "nothing short of traitors to the country as a whole." He demanded that Haldimand council remove the OPP, asked the province to investigate the force's practices and urged Ottawa to bring in the Royal Canadian Mounted Police and the army.

On December 5, senior Ontario negotiator John Nolan forwarded a copy to a handful of people, including Inspector McLean. Within three hours, McLean was writing to his superiors, Chief Superintendent Bill Dennis and Acting Superintendent Doug Babbit.

"As you are aware, the OPP in the past has been victim to Hamilton Police Service Officer David Hartless and his direct verbal aggression as well as written slander by signs on his lawn and articles in the website of Gary McHale. We have in the past contacted his chief, Brian Mullen, and on several occasions he [Hartless] has been spoken to by their senior command."

McLean suggested Hartless was violating the code of conduct under the Police Services Act, noted he has "a contact who also openly discredits the attempts of the OPP to maintain peace in a fragile environment" (this was McHale, of course) and suggested this mere "association" with McHale was also a breach.

McLean asked that Chief Mullan be sent the Hartless article and that Hartless "be held accountable for his actions and comments."

Dennis duly passed the article to Mullan, who sent it to Hamilton deputy chief Ken Leendertse, who reported back that "the OPP was not willing to formally complain about Hartless' activity at that time."

But Mullan instructed Leendertse to speak to Hartless, and on December 13 Leendertse duly called him in "and I discussed the issues in Caledonia and I told him that his actions, even though off duty, reflected on him as a police officer. I advised him to be careful of his actions and words in the future."

Fantino's name didn't appear in the email chain, but, as developments in the new year would soon reveal, he was keeping tabs on Hartless.

"The OPP, the county, the government, the natives have all worked together," McHale says now, "and I mean worked together, to silence any resident" who wouldn't play well with others.

As my former government insider puts it, "You could get mugged, and the first reaction from most of the people in the bureaucracy was to assume you had done something to provoke it." He was "really surprised at how the entire focus was on containment. The whole thing [at government meetings] was about not letting this flare up, keeping everybody's temperature and blood pressure down, and quite frankly, marginalizing anybody who made a scene."

McHale, Dave Hartless, the Vanderwyks, AnneMarie VanSickle, Bo Chausse—anyone who criticized the government or the OPP had become the enemy.

"Solzhenitsyn's rule," says Pat Woolley, the land surveyor. "Silence dissent. Attack people personally—anyone who says anything, attack them personally. Make them too afraid. We kind of feel that in this town."

Woolley spoke up, mildly for the most part, in letters and occasional articles in the local papers, and estimates he lost $40,000 in billings that first year, "and some of those were clients who didn't give us work" because, he suspects, he was vocal.

He is not sorry.

"Every citizen has an obligation to speak up," he says. "We have an obligation to participate, not to be a radical. You don't have to go to a protest. But you know, it's more than just voting, which a lot of people don't take the time to do.

"If you see something wrong, you have to say something."

———

December was a turning point, not only because the likes of Chausse, Vandermaas and McHale were arrested at protests, not only because Dave Hartless was cautioned to watch his mouth, not only because the OPP as an organization had thrown down the gauntlet at the feet of the citizenry—and then demanded, in the name of peace, that they not pick it up. It was also a significant month because, on December 14, the Ontario Court of Appeal released its decision on the appeal of Judge Marshall's August 8 ruling, in which he had suggested (though didn't order outright) that all negotiations should be suspended until the rule of law was restored to Douglas Creek Estates and refused to unconditionally dissolve the Henco injunction.

The Attorney General of Ontario immediately appealed the order and asked for a stay pending the hearing of the appeal; on August 22, the Court of Appeal heard the motion and told the parties they were "free to continue to negotiate," and reserved judgment on the other questions. Three days later, when the court released its reasons, it noted that Ontario now owned DCE and was content to let the native occupiers remain.

"We see no reason why it should not be permitted to do so," the three-member panel said. "If the protesters cause a nuisance or other disturbance affecting neighbouring lands or residents of Caledonia, then action may be required. But no evidence was presented to us of any current incident requiring the intervention of the Attorney General, the Ontario Provincial Police or the courts." The judges quoted themselves on this point in their December 16 decision.

In another section of the thirty-four-page ruling, they also noted, "Ontario has complied with its legal obligations. The record does not show that by permitting the protesters to remain, the government has breached any municipal requirements, created a nuisance or adversely affected public safety."

The judges also said, "On the record before us, by July 5 all cars and barricades preventing access to the property had been removed."

No evidence of any current incident? Nothing on the record that the protesters had created a nuisance or adversely affected public safety; all barricades removed?

The barricade across Surrey Street, the main entrance to DCE, remains to this day.

The appeal court found that Judge Marshall was within his discretion to have kept calling the parties back to his court for updates, and to have asked the OPP and the government to report publicly on the exercise of their respective operational and prosecutorial authority. But, the judges said, Marshall had gone "further than he should have" in reviewing both OPP and government conduct.

"This is especially so in a case like the present one," the court said, "where the alleged widespread and ongoing defiance of an injunction occurs outside the face of the court. In this kind of case, the police and the Crown, not the court, are in the best position to assess whether a serious breach of the injunction has occurred and if so, by whom."

The appeal court had no way of knowing that the state—the government and police—had evidence up the ying-yang about incidents that, to put it at its mildest, "affected neighbouring lands and residents," endangered public safety and had occurred both before Ontario bought DCE and long afterwards.

As one of the lawyers for Ontario once told Judge Marshall, "Almost everyone you've heard from has asked that you leave the matter with those that are responsible for dealing with the rule of law"—meaning, of course, the government and the OPP.

But what if the government and the police didn't care about the rule of law? What if the very agencies of the state that had the evidence didn't bring it forward?

"It is clear that the police and the Crown have wide powers of discretion in when, and how to act," Judge Marshall wrote. "The police and the Crown each have important roles in maintaining the peace. But that discretion should not be used to advance a particular policy," he said.

Was that what the government and OPP were doing? Had the appeal court been misled?

Judge Marshall had a poster on his library wall, at his home along the Grand River, with a quote attributed to Pastor Martin Niemoeller. "He made each of the kids read this statement aloud and asked us to explain it," his son Albert, also a lawyer, remembers. "The page he cut out is still stuck on the wall today. It reads: 'In Germany, they came first for the Communists, and I didn't speak up because I wasn't a Communist. Then they came for the Jews, and I didn't speak up because I wasn't a Jew. Then they came for the trade unionists, and I didn't speak up because I wasn't a trade unionist.

"Then they came for the Catholics, and I didn't speak up because I was a Protestant. Then they came for me, and by that time no one was left to speak up.'

"This quote really struck me as a boy," Marshall says, "and I have tried to live by it. I believe my father lived by this as well . . . When this matter in Caledonia came before him, he had a choice. He could take the easy road and [accede] to the Crown's requests and ignore the rights of a few. If he had done this, no one would have faulted him. The day in court would have been short, and he could have gone home early to his family.

"Instead, he chose to stand up for what he believed was right. When he did this, he was very much alone.

"There were few in power who supported his position in the beginning. He did not mind standing alone on an issue he believed right."

But on December 14, the last and most vigorous defender of the rule of law was overturned and effectively silenced. Now, there was almost no one left, as Pastor Niemoeller famously said, to speak up in its defence.

After

———

Police discretion is fundamental to reducing the potential for
violence at Aboriginal occupations and protests. Discretion
may involve whether, when or how enforcement action is
taken to address alleged breaches of the law.
This concept is easily misunderstood.
It does not mean that anyone is above the law or that police
services should have different standards for Aboriginal people.
Nor does it mean that the rule of law and public order are
somehow subservient to Aboriginal interests.

— COMMISSIONER SIDNEY LINDEN,
IN THE FINAL IPPERWASH INQUIRY REPORT

ON JANUARY 12, 2007, Dave Brown was holding court in his kitchen. Jeff Bird, his OPP officer friend, was hanging around; Bill Anderson, a local real estate agent, was over because Brownie and Dana were going to put the house up for sale.

As Anderson drew up the listing agreement, there was a lull in the conversation. Then, they could hear a sound coming from somewhere. "You hear *click, brrrrrrr,*" Bird remembers. "It was loud enough that I looked up; everyone noticed."

"Brownie," Bird said, "there's something fucked up with your icemaker."

"I don't *have* an icemaker," Brown replied. He pulled a chair over towards the source of the sound—like something rewinding—climbed up on it, and reached up to a cabinet over the fridge.

"Holy fuck, boys," Brownie said. "We're on *Candid Camera.*"

Hot-glued to a terracotta pot planted with greenery was a tiny camera—one inch by one inch by four inches. Behind it was a video-cassette recorder and a power cord. As they examined the setup, they could hear the lens moving, trying to focus. It was a surveillance camera, and it was pointed directly at Dave Brown's kitchen table.

Bird later had a look at the tape, which showed, he says, "Us sitting at the table . . . Brownie in his underwear, eating a bowl of cereal . . . It was ridiculous."

Dave Hillman, the sergeant in charge of the crime unit, had phoned Brown earlier that morning. He'd heard Brown was thinking about trying.to sell the house; he'd also been told the OPP had put a camera in the basement. Hillman had the unenviable task of breaking that news to Brownie. The conversation had ended by the time Bird arrived, and Brownie was steamed, ranting about the OPP having betrayed him by installing the camera in the house. After the three men discovered the unit in the kitchen, Brownie called Hillman and told him where they'd actually found the damn thing. Then Anderson vamoosed to stash the camera and VCR in a safe place.

On January 23, the OPP came looking for their property, and Brown and Chatwell handed over the VCR, the power cable, the camera and the piece of pottery to which it was attached.

The background to all this is that the month previous, just before Christmas of 2006, the Brown/Chatwell house had been trashed— the place vandalized, walls strewn with terrible graffiti such as PIGS; RACISTS!; WHITE TRASH; and worse. Brown and Chatwell had been out at a couple of holiday parties. When, with a friend, they arrived home shortly after 1 A.M., they claimed to have seen intruders leaving, and called the OPP.

Over the next few days, Brown himself became the leading suspect; on one occasion, he was asked directly by the OPP if he had paid someone to break in, which he denied furiously (though some on Six Nations still believe he did); Dax Chatwell, fifteen at the time, was also interviewed at length without either parent present.

The OPP never interviewed, let alone investigated, anybody on DCE, as Superintendent Cain testified in discovery for the Brown/Chatwell lawsuit.

He also acknowledged that the only information the OPP had that might implicate Brown in the vandalism of his own house came from Superintendent George and the ART team, who claimed to have "received information that Dave Brown had been spotted at the back of his property on the night of the B&E—meaning break and enter—pointing a flashlight towards the Douglas Creek Estates."

"Brown had been approached by some of the occupiers who asked him what was wrong," Cain said. "Brown stated nothing."

"Was there any other information that would cause the investigation to be directed at the plaintiffs?" lawyer John Evans asked.

"I'm not aware of any other information," Cain said, "and I will check."

Cain testified he was "not aware of any First Nations people being interviewed as suspects," though he agreed that "the evidence that was presented, it would cause one to start in that direction." Neither did the OPP ever arrest anyone in the break-in.

But the upshot of the incident was that the OPP approached the family and asked permission to install an alarm system and security cameras at the house, purportedly for their own protection. In part because they were going away for a short vacation to Roatan, an island off the coast of Honduras, Brown agreed, but made it absolutely clear there were to be no cameras *in* the house. What he understood was that motion detectors would be installed outside, which in turn would trigger the cameras and lights, as well as an alarm system. He gave the OPP a key to the house and the alarm code. Brown also signed an authorization allowing Chatwell's uncle, and only him, to check on things while they were away.

And now here he was, just a few days after returning from Roatan, and what did he find but a camera, clearly aimed not at potential vandals or trespassers, but at him and his family.

When Hillman got to the house, he seemed genuinely shaken by what Brown had discovered. He even showed Brown where, in his notes, he'd recorded what he'd been told earlier by other officers: that the camera was in the basement but focused on the doors to Dana's long-since-disused hair salon. Though this still breached Brown's specific instructions, it was at least defensible, as this was the least visible entrance to the house and thus a logical place to break in.

Hillman immediately went down to the basement and tore it apart, looking for the camera he'd been told was there. He emerged, empty-handed, about twenty minutes later, covered in bits of fibre-glass insulation, his face red.

"Where's the camera?" he asked Brown.

Brownie, by now wild with rage, snarled, "If you [the OPP] didn't put it here, I guess it's not yours." He had already called Mayor Trainer, the family's most reliable and trusted point of contact, to tell her.

Trainer confirms the call, and that it was followed a little later by one from Dave Hillman, who asked her "not to tell anyone, as he thought the press would make a big deal about it."

For Bird, the situation was profoundly awkward: he'd just been visiting his friend when the discovery was made, so he also put on his police hat and duly made notes in his memo book. He was then ordered by Hillman to stay with Brown and Chatwell all day, to keep them calm. The OPP used Bird this way several times, assigning him to watch over the couple and keep them out of trouble, forcing him to use his friendship with Brownie to the force's advantage.

During Brown's lawsuit in Hamilton in the fall of 2009, what was revealing was that, when David Feliciant, the lawyer representing the government and the OPP, cross-examined Brown, he never attempted to deny that the OPP had put the camera there. Rather, Feliciant suggested that Brown and Chatwell had no intention to return to their vandalized home after their vacation, so the OPP would have assumed they could put cameras wherever they liked.

Brown just snorted in disbelief. Dana's uncle and cousin had moved in bunk beds and furniture while they were gone, he said, to replace their ruined furniture and "so we had somewhere to sleep."

"Make no mistake," he told Feliciant, "I really didn't want to go back to that house again," but he and Dana had never discussed not returning—and certainly hadn't done so with the OPP—nor did they have an alternative.

As a friend remembers, "Dave said specifically, because they smoked dope and walk around the house naked, 'Under no circum-stances are there to be cameras in my house.'"

One OPP officer, Jeff Bird, was present when the camera was discovered and saw where it was pointed. Another, Dave Hillman, had been told there was a camera in Brown's basement, showed Brown his notes to that effect, and then went looking for it. The OPP had a key to the house, had installed the alarm system and had the code. Except for Dana's beloved uncle, the police were the only ones with such unfettered exclusive access to the house. And at trial, the government's own lawyer never disputed that the OPP had installed the camera aimed squarely at Dave Brown's kitchen table. Rather, Feliciant merely suggested that Brown must have either agreed to it or that it wouldn't matter to him as he wouldn't be living there anymore.

The evidence was compelling, the case as clear as it could be that, almost a year after the occupation of DCE started, the OPP had been spying on the family whose only crime was to have the bad luck to be living cheek by jowl to the site and the bad manners to complain about it.

They weren't the only ones.

Dave Hartless, for instance, knows "I was marketed to area officers as a zero-tolerance enforcement target."

"What's that mean?" I ask.

"It means if I roll through a stop sign, they want me ticketed—any traffic infraction, whatever.

"The majority of officers wouldn't enforce it," he says, "but I also know I've been followed, several times, by a spin team. You know, whoever it was the first two times wasn't very good. I do that [surveillance] for my job. By that point, I'd been in the gang unit, and that was all we were doing."

Hartless found a tracking device—a magnetized GPS-like unit, six inches by four—on his truck.

"Could have been the OPP's," he says. "Could have been Hamilton's. Could have been fucking Six Nations police. Could have been the government.

"It's a complete violation of everything that we're sworn to do," he says. "So I don't know who the tracking device belonged to; when I found it, I drove it out to Dunnville and I fed it to the fish, and they can go track it down."

That was in 2007.

"I still check every so often," he says, "see if I get another one."

Far less opaque is what happened to Hartless in February that year. On February 17, he wrote "An Open Letter to the Government of Premier Dalton McGuinty," which he sent as an email to about fifteen people, including members of Haldimand County council, Mayor Trainer, the prime minister, Opposition leader John Tory, Aboriginal Affairs Minister Ramsay and Community Safety Minister Kwinter—and, probably most critically, a handful of newspapers and the CaledoniaWakeUpCall website.

In it, Hartless accused the premier of allowing "the OPP to operate outside of not only their mandate but the laws of this country" and called him "a coward who hides from his responsibilities and avoids his duties as a leader."

He pointed out that Mr. McGuinty had been repeatedly asked by residents and local politicians to come to Caledonia, "yet you refused."

"You have disparaged and downplayed the people of this community and that of the Six Nations of the Grand River." In fact, Hartless said, "your presence here once requested by all is now no longer welcome." He promised to "celebrate the demise of your party and your cowardice in the upcoming months [as the October 10 Ontario election approached] as I would the arrival of Christmas Day."

He signed it, as always he did, simply "David Hartless," with his address.

As with Hartless's earlier email, the "reporting" chain went like this. Senior Ontario negotiator John Nolan fired it off the same day to detachment commander Dave McLean, who within less than twenty-five minutes had sent it to John Cain with a note that read, "I could be wrong but perhaps Chief Mullin [sic] might like a heads up should the Premier's office or the minister of CS [community safety] who also got this email want to discuss it with the officer's chief.

"Just a thought, as I know you would like a heads up if I or any of your officers called the Premier a coward directly in an email to so many politicians and press including *The Hamilton Spectator*, which the chief likely reads.

"Again just a thought."

By the next afternoon, Julian Fantino clearly had been told about, but not read, the offending email, because the ever-helpful McLean emailed him a copy just before 6 P.M., with an apology: "Commissioner: Sorry so long getting back to you. Here you go."

Within three hours, Fantino was firing off a missive of his own. He sent it directly to Hartless's boss, Hamilton chief Brian Mullan, and copied McLean, Chief Superintendent Mike Armstrong, Deputy Commissioner Chris Lewis—and, for good measure, Karl Walsh of the OPPA.

> Brian,
>
> Not again! I am afraid that we, the OPP, have had enough of this nonsense.
>
> Your man Hartless has gone over the top this time.
>
> I realize that he is also a private citizen and quite entitled to exercise freedom of speech; however, as a police officer, on or off duty, he is also held to a higher standard of accountability which is where I am coming from on his latest vicious public rant.
>
> I am formally taking exception to his latest mean-spirited and totally false accusations directed at the OPP that are very serious and about which I take exception.
>
> Bad enough that he slams the men and women of the OPP, refers to the Premier as being a coward on several occasions, but then scatters his venemous [sic] email far and wide.

If this isn't conduct unbecoming, I don't know
what is.

Please let me know what action the Hamilton
Police Service is prepared to take respecting
Hartless' conduct.

Regards, JF.

A copy of the email chain, later made public, shows that someone signing himself as "B" (presumably Mullan) wrote "D/C has
been alerted for action," and by February 19, another handwritten
note, signed by Deputy Chief Ken Leendertse, read, "Professional
Standards: I am ordering an investigation into the actions of
Dave Hartless."

That day, Leendertse also sent Hartless an email, telling him
the force has "now received an official complaint of discreditable
conduct from the Commissioner of the OPP" and that he had forwarded the matter to the professional standards bureau. Leendertse
added, "I am ordering you to cease and desist any further emails
concerning the situation in Caledonia. Don't send any further email
about this situation until this matter can be properly investigated."

"Fantino fires off the complaint," Hartless says, "and the deputy
chief throws a gag order on me, and I'm not allowed to speak to
anyone, no letters, blah blah blah.

"I tell him, 'You can't do that. It's actually against the law—thou
shalt not.'"

He sought advice from his police association, which basically
told him to "let it wash out through the investigation, and I said, 'No,
I'm not standing for it.'

"I've got a reputation for being a bit of a mouthpiece, but when
something's wrong, I challenge. It's what I'm supposed to do. So the
association tries to talk me out of launching the civil action—no
one's ever won. So what?"

Hartless hired John Findlay, the lawyer for a then-fledgling class-
action suit brought by residents and business owners in Caledonia,

and filed a motion in Ontario Superior Court, alleging that the gag order infringed on his freedom of speech as a private citizen. The mere filing of the motion won that battle for Hartless pretty quickly; by April 10, Leendertse was writing him, formally rescinding the illegal gag order.

Hartless was never after money. He always said, from the get-go, "I want an apology and I want my court fees. I don't need their money; I make my own."

By July 7, *The Hamilton Spectator* was reporting that Hartless—who had given an interview before he realized the details were supposed to remain confidential—had been completely cleared by Halton Regional Police, the force that did the investigation. His legal costs were covered. That day, he told *Spec* reporter Dan Nolan, "It feels pretty good."

But in truth, he says, "I think when I ended up having to sue my own department, that broke my heart."

———

On April 5 that year, Haldimand councillor Craig Grice wrote a note to a constituent named Jason Smith. He was replying to a letter from Smith, complaining that council was trying to discourage Gary McHale from coming to Caledonia.

McHale had briefly taken down his website for a couple of days. He was genuinely tired of the constant effort to paint him as an outsider and troublemaker—by the OPP; the OPP Association, which had issued an "extreme caution" press release before the January flag-raising in which it condemned "these people not from the area"; and even Haldimand County, which in a press release issued the day before his January 20 rally joined the fray and denounced him. Still, it was also a considered move. McHale suspected the backlash from regular readers of the website would be real, and that councillors would be deluged with complaints. He was right, as Smith's letter to Grice demonstrated.

"I have never once stopped Mr. McHale from coming to Caledonia," Grice replied. "I have never spoken to Council about not letting Gary come to town. In fact, the opposite is true. I do believe Gary brings media attention to our situation and I do support his stance on two-tier justice. I do not know why he would suggest to anyone otherwise as he knows this to be true."

But Grice also made it clear he was no McHale booster. "On the flip side of this," he wrote Smith, "every positive has a negative and I've talked to Gary about it. Honestly, I know of people who are the most affected by this who want nothing to do with him, and countless others who leave town, send their children away and simply pray that no one gets hurt. Do I commend Gary for some of [his] actions and standing up? Yes I do. Do I have concerns on how Caledonia is seen and how others I represent feel when he comes [to] town? Yes I do.

"It is unfortunate that he [has] chosen this route, as I fear no matter what myself or Marie [Mayor Trainer] may or may not say will divide our community even further. Freedom of speech, the right to associate, I'll never take away from anyone. If Mr. McHale wants to give up, that will [be] his choice, not mine."

The note was a classic example of equivocation, not merely a political answer but the genuine response of a man who was firmly caught in the middle of the DCE debacle. Grice lives on Braemar Avenue, in the Thistlemoor subdivision next to the site, and could empathize both with those who wholeheartedly embraced McHale as well as those who just wished he would go away.

Whatever else his reply was, it was hardly a ringing endorsement of Gary McHale. Smith forwarded the correspondence to McHale, who promptly put the CaledoniaWakeUpCall site website back up and posted the letter there, with the comment that at least one councillor had had something positive to say about him. Two days later, a furious Julian Fantino saddled up his high horse.

In a two-page letter sent to Mayor Trainer and Haldimand councillors—and, revealingly, copied to Premier McGuinty's then chief of staff Peter Wilkinson, press secretary Chris Morley (now the premier's chief of staff) and Tony Dean, then secretary of Cabinet—the OPP commissioner let loose. He called Grice's tepid email "a deeply disturbing communication," accused him of commending McHale "on his efforts in Caledonia" and said, "In fact, the comments are perceived to actually encourage McHale."

Fantino said he wouldn't enter into a debate with Grice about Charter-guaranteed rights, but railed, "My primary concern is solely focused on preserving the peace in Caledonia and nothing more, a concern that very much includes preventing provocations that could lead to renewed violence such as has happened in the past." He then praised his officers and said, "It may not be apparent to our critics and those with special agendas of their own that the OPP, all of us, have worked tirelessly on the front lines and beyond to simply maintain order in an otherwise chaotic and very turbulent situation, made especially difficult every time McHale and his followers come to town."

(By this point, McHale had staged exactly two rallies in Caledonia: the one on December 16, 2006, for which he was arrested and jailed overnight, and the second, on January 20, 2007. Except for his and Mark Vandermaas's arrests for breach of the peace at the first one, both rallies were completely nonviolent.)

But Fantino highlighted "the extraordinary policing costs that are borne by Ontario taxpayers every time the situation in Caledonia escalates" and said "now, apparently, we have Councillor Grice commending someone that he knows is a lightening [sic] rod for confrontation and potential violence."

Fantino then issued a four-point ultimatum "in the event any of my officers are injured as a result of further forays into the community by McHale and his followers." He would (and all the emphasis is his) "publicly hold accountable Councillor Grice AND Haldimand County along with McHale"; "support any injured officer" in a lawsuit; "forward the ensuing related costs of policing to Haldimand County; and "strongly recommend to my Minister that the OPP contract with Haldimand County NOT be renewed once the current contract expires.

"As much as we, the OPP, sympathize with the Citizens of Caledonia and the difficult political position you face, we believe that in the context of the situation that prevails in Caledonia, comments such as those attributed to Councillor Grice are gravely detrimental to the morale and safety of my officers and much more. When I appeared before you several months back, I came away believing that we had a mutual understanding about the detrimental effect that McHale and his followers were having on Caledonia.

"I know that Councillor Grice has some personal issues that he finds particularly aggravating; however, we never expected that he would fall prey to McHale's propaganda and it is now up to you as a Council to deal with the fall-out."

It was an absolutely astonishing response to a careful, if not outright milquetoast, note from a small-town politician.

Ten days later, on April 17, McHale, Vandermaas and Caledonia resident Merlyn Kinrade all filed separate formal complaints with community safety minister and solicitor general Monte Kwinter, alleging that Fantino had tried to intimidate Haldimand Council. They held a press conference at Queen's Park, then walked over to hand-deliver their complaints to Kwinter's office.

Fantino was undeterred. First, as Trainer has since testified under oath in court, though she could say nothing about it, he had an in-camera meeting with the mayor and council about the email. Trainer also testified that she found Fantino's email threatening, that she believes the OPP failed in Caledonia, that council had investigated—in vain—other policing options and that the OPP had in fact provided council with the draft of the January 19 press release that was issued in council's name.

Over the ensuing weeks, Fantino badgered Trainer sufficiently that, on June 26, she finally wrote Rod McLeod, the outside lawyer hired by Kwinter after McHale, Vandermaas and Kinrade filed their complaints, and said wearily of the OPP commissioner, "This man does not stop."

What had caught Fantino's attention this time was that, in an interview with a Canadian Press reporter two weeks earlier, in mid-June, the mayor said residents had lost faith in the OPP. That was all she said, and it was hardly a revelation to anyone who was remotely in touch with either the community or the story. But Fantino emailed her the same day the story appeared, saying, "Here we go again. Did you say the comments attributed to you? Did you actually say these things about the OPP?" When she failed to answer quickly enough, he wrote her again to ask if he "might expect your response any time soon?"

When Trainer wrote back, explaining she had been reflecting remarks she'd heard from Caledonia residents, Fantino demanded to know if she was speaking "on behalf of ALL the citizens of Haldimand County" and reprimanded her with a snarled, "Also, I thought we had agreed to tone down the inflammatory rhetoric?"

In the new Caledonia world order, mere remarks by the mayor that her constituents had no confidence in the OPP now qualified as "inflammatory rhetoric."

McLeod, a former senior Crown by then in private practice with the firm of Miller Thomson in Toronto, wasn't hired by Kwinter to investigate whether Fantino had acted improperly by issuing the ultimatum to council; rather, he was solely to advise the minister on what to do with the complaints. It was, at least in anyone's memory, the first time that citizens had complained to the minister about a commissioner of the OPP. McLeod confirmed in a brief telephone interview in June of 2010 that his instruction was simply to "assist the SG in deciding what to do." In short, there was no investigation at all of the commissioner's conduct, merely a review of the government's options.

Trainer testified that she spoke to McLeod the morning of June 28. He'd phoned her to go over a few things as he finalized his report, and told her, she said, "he wanted to soften the report a little bit so that Commissioner Fantino wouldn't look too bad." McLeod said they'd talk again, and that he'd call her back a bit later.

Instead, Mayor Trainer was called by a reporter from the Canadian Press, asking for her comment on the news, just announced by Kwinter, that Fantino had been cleared. Kwinter told the CP that he had reviewed the complaints and that they didn't have any substance—by any measure, a distortion of Rod McLeod's assignment.

Trainer was stunned, she testified, and told the reporter, "Pardon me? The report isn't even written yet. I just talked to the fellow who's writing it."

She was also furious, and told the CP that the decision was "100 per cent wrong" and that Fantino at least should have been disciplined.

The hiring of McLeod gave credence to the prescient remarks made by Ontario Ombudsman André Marin just the week before about the government's practice of using outside lawyers. Marin said that in cases such as the Fantino complaints, where the government finds itself in a conflict of interest, it often prefers to hire private lawyers so it can dictate the scope of any investigation and control the results.

"The government is queasy in these kinds of cases to relinquish control over the issue," Marin said at the time.

"You don't have that when you come to the ombudsman's office. You don't know where the ball's going to land because we don't accept scripted mandates.

"The government . . . wants to be in the driver's seat," he said. "From the government's perspective, the risk is much more contained when you go out and hire a contractor."

But Fantino wasn't the only man who, in Trainer's words, "doesn't stop."

McHale was now on a mission, though it would take two years to unfold.

———

The "Three Musky Steers," as they call themselves in private, didn't coalesce as Julian Fantino's axis of evil until 2007.

Merlyn Kinrade and Doug Fleming knew one another from around town and liked what they saw, but until the occupation turned ugly, and both got involved in various local protests, that was about it.

Gary McHale was a perfect stranger to them both. Kinrade had met him for the first time after the second flag-raising event in Caledonia, on January 20, shortly after he met Mark Vandermaas. Vandermaas was standing on the bank of Argyle Street—just past the Canadian Tire, where the OPP stopped the marchers shy of DCE—asking if one of the officers would hold his Canadian flag so he could give his speech. The police were shrugging, Kinrade remembers, "So I walked over there and said, 'You guys are all fuck-ing assholes, why don't you hold his flag?'

"They wouldn't respond. So I clambered up the bank and I grabbed a hold of this bloody steel flagpole."

Kinrade was bare-handed on this frigid day, a measure of what a tough SOB he is. "And I said [to Vandermaas], 'I notice you've got that blue beret on,' and I said, 'I served under that flag on a couple of occasions.'"

Kinrade, who was with the Canadian navy for about five years, served with the first United Nations peacekeeping mission, during the Suez crisis in 1956 (it was this historic effort that won Prime Minister Lester B. Pearson the Nobel Peace Prize in 1957); Vandermaas was there as a UN peacekeeper twenty-two years later. Kinrade adds, "And I said, 'Well, I was really effective, wasn't I?'"

Vandermaas gave his speech in the bitter cold, while the OPP chopper hovered above, and the two of them—the seventy-one-year-old senior citizen and the fifty-year-old real estate broker—got a fit of the giggles and were shrieking with laughter, Kinrade says, at the thought "of that asshole [Fantino] up here cruising around."

"When it was all said and done," Kinrade says, "I invited them all back to the house," and thus was born a friendship with McHale and Vandermaas (who is, for all practical purposes, the fourth Musky Steer, though, unlike the others, he didn't run in the fall 2010 municipal elections in Caledonia). The group has met often at the house ever since.

Kinrade is related to Dana Chatwell—their mothers were sisters— so he was drawn into things early on by virtue of blood as well as location. His house is on the Thistlemoor side of DCE, close enough that, on the day of the OPP raid, he says, "I see all these SUVs come down here, all muddy and shitty, and it was the OPP. They'd got their ass kicked. They'd come off the back end of Douglas Creek Estate and come up here.

"Well, I thought they'd been successful. And I'm giving these assholes a thumbs-up and they're going like this [nodding glumly] and I'm, 'What are you shaking your heads for?'"

He was one of those who went to the barricades, as well as to Alliance meetings. But, he says, "each and every time we'd have a meeting and they'd tell us what was going on, they were also preaching 'Be patient,' just like the government was." Kinrade is disinclined towards patience, spin and the like.

Wiry, fit, magnificently profane yet possessed of a curious courtliness, Kinrade in his prime worked four jobs at the same time. He worked full time as a plumber at Dofasco even as he started up Kinrade Plumbing, and ran a small dairy as well as concession stands in the Caledonia Arena and Kinsmen Park. He was, as he says, "busier than a one-legged soccer player in an ass-kicking contest."

He has tried it all, playing nice and not. He has gone to Queen's Park, dolled up in a nice white sweater and a fresh haircut, to give speeches; made presentations at the local Rotary Club (he and Vandermaas thought it had gone terribly well, but in the end, they raised not a penny for the cause); attended just about every rally and protest in town; and reached into his own pocket to help the McHales, who were slowly going broke.

Once, Kinrade tried to rent the Lions Hall for a McHale rally. "They passed a resolution in the club they wouldn't rent to anyone controversial," he says, practically thrumming with outrage. "I'm for law and order—is that controversial? I said, 'Your fucking town is going down the sewer . . . Is that all you can do?'"

He even phoned Six Nations Chief David General once, to invite him and his wife to dinner. "I said, 'You don't know me, I don't know you, but maybe you and I should meet,' and he said that sounds like a good plan. I said, 'I want you and your wife to come and break bread; my wife puts on a mean meal, but we do have cocktails here. He said, 'I'm going to take you up on that.'"

The next day, Kinrade came home to find a voice message from General, saying, "I can't meet with you." He called General, who told him it was because of his connection to McHale. Kinrade was regretful, but undaunted. "I tell those guys [McHale and Vandermaas] all the time, I'm so thankful they came to my town."

As long as he stays in Caledonia, Kinrade will fight. He wanted to get out, he says, and would have but for his little daughter, Olivia, who is eight. "We want some continuity in Olivia's life. Don't want her bouncing around like a rubber ball. She's got all her little friends from school, and that's because of continuity." He and Patricia, his second wife of more than twenty years, won't even move across the river, because it would mean Olivia would have to change schools.

One time, he says, a pair of OPP officers came to his house; they wanted to talk about an upcoming rally. As it happened, Olivia was home sick from school that day, and Kinrade refused to invite the officers in, believing his daughter already had been exposed to too much heated talk about Caledonia, the OPP and the like.

"They kept insisting," he says. "And I said, 'Do you not understand that I'm trying to teach her so that she feels safe in going to you? I'm trying not to get that [suspicion of police] ingrained in my child. I want her to think of you as I used to, as an incredible police force with morals and scruples.'"

———

Doug Fleming says that if he'd met Gary McHale ten years before he did, "I'd have thought, 'Get a job.' But I'm wiser now than I was then, and when it's in your own backyard, it makes a difference."

He first laid eyes on McHale at the Caledonia Lions Hall (before the club got nervous about renting to him) in the fall of 2006, when McHale was trying to spread the word. Fleming handed over the $20 price of admission, had "a gut feeling, and it turned out to be correct, that he was genuine" and thereafter attended any public event McHale organized. But he had had no face time with McHale until that January 20 flag-raising; he was one of those who went back to Merlyn Kinrade's house.

Fleming had never taken part in a protest in his life, and he stayed out of things in the early days of the occupation. What got his attention was the night Dave Brown got arrested after the Blue Jays game, just for trying to go to his own house. "'You have got to be kidding me,'" Fleming says of his reaction to the news. "It was a violent, very unreasonable incident. I thought, 'This is just wrong.' It was after that for the first time I went out."

He started with meetings at Rick and Val Vanderwyk's place. "We used to go to their house, just a group of concerned citizens, to discuss our options—what can we do? And you know, we were so naive. We were so naive. We thought if we just went to Queen's Park and just made them realize, face to face, just how unhappy we were about this, if we sent letters to politicians and stamped our feet and held our breath, something would get done. We had no idea.

"And it's only after you start to test the waters—or peel away the layers, if you will—that you begin to realize just how deep-seated and ridiculously complicated this is, because even back then, it was never an issue of just simply enforcing the law. All this other political bullshit would come up.

"Just enforce the law!"

By that fall, Fleming, then forty-five, had branched out and found a sideline all his own—Doug's Smokes. That summer, smoke shacks—basically, makeshift lean-tos selling bags of rollies—had spread off the Six Nations reserve and begun popping up on public land in and around Caledonia. After the second shack opened, Fleming was driving out of town when he noticed a kid riding a bike heading the other way. The kid looked to be about fourteen, and he had a bag full of smokes on his handlebars.

"I told an OPP officer what I had seen," he says, "and asked what he could do about it. He didn't seem terribly interested."

Fleming went next to the land registry office to search the titles; he got lucky and ran into lawyer Ed McCarthy. "It took him about five minutes to find what would have taken me five days," he says.

What they found was that the two farms in question had been purchased by the Six Nations several years before; the properties aren't considered reserve land, but are deeded land, thus legally subject to Haldimand County bylaws. Fleming marched over to the county office to see what permits had been issued; none had. He said he wanted to file a complaint, and was told the properties were "in limbo" and that the county had no jurisdiction.

(At one time, there were seven of these illegally located on one sort of publicly owned land or another—Hydro One land, county land, Six Nations deeded land. At this writing, there are four, Six Nations having shut down the two on its land.)

As Fleming put it once in a speech at Queen's Park, "Growing impatient with the indecisiveness of people in positions of authority, I attempted to light a fire under them—I went into the business of selling smokes!"

He began selling cigarettes from the back of his well-used truck, which is decorated with stickers of cartoon figures relieving themselves upon OPP figures. He got permission to set up on a vacant lot. He had a little table and a sign, and if you bought one bag of smokes, you got a free coffee; two, you got the coffee and a copy of *The Toronto Sun*; three, you got the coffee, a *Toronto Sun* and a pumpkin.

Fleming was careful to break only the same laws that the operators of the new off-reserve native smoke shacks were breaking without repercussion. As the native operators were making a point—that they could do this, unmolested—so was Fleming trying to make one about the double standard of policing.

"I told the cops, 'You can arrest me, but you gotta go out on the road and arrest them.'" But even when he set up in the little plaza, right outside the Caledonia substation, the OPP refused to take the bait. They didn't move, either against him or the native smoke shacks.

Foiled, Fleming then decided to organize rallies against the smoke shacks. And as he supported Gary McHale-led events, so did McHale support his. The first smoke shack protest was set for the Plank Road 1 Stop at the end of Argyle Street on December 1, 2007.

———

The Ipperwash Inquiry report was finally released, to enormous media attention, on May 31—Day 458 of the Caledonia occupation.

Inside the community centre in Forest, Ontario, where the inquiry was held, David Ramsay, the minister of natural resources and Aboriginal affairs, apologized for the death of thirty-eight-year-old Dudley George. In the Legislature, Premier McGuinty rose to offer another solemn apology "for the events that led to the loss of life," and he apologized privately to George's brother, Sam.

The massive report—it is as long as the inquiry was expensive: 1,433 pages for $25.6 million—was scathingly critical of the OPP, particularly for the botched communications and flawed intelligence that led to the TRU team overestimating the threat of native occupiers in the park that night, and of the former Conservative government, with Mr. Justice Sidney Linden, the commissioner of the inquiry, finding that former premier Mike Harris had indeed said that he "wanted the fucking Indians out of the park." With that incendiary remark, Linden said, Harris had "created the risk of placing political pressure on the police," though he nonetheless found that the former premier "did not inappropriately direct" the OPP.

Mentioned in virtually none of the stories that day was what could have been called the Caledonia effect upon the inquiry commissioner, who seemed to have at least one gnawing concern about the new and ostensibly much-improved post-Ipperwash OPP.

While, in the report, Linden still held out the Framework for Aboriginal Critical Incidents as a "best practice" and noted that the force "has been applying the Framework at Caledonia," he acknowledged its efficacy was being severely tested.

"Events there [in Caledonia] have raised important questions about whether the Framework can be sustained in the face of considerable opposition from a sizeable proportion of local non-Aboriginal residents, criticism from members of the provincial Legislature and the media, apparent opposition within the rank and file of the OPP, and the sheer endurance and resources necessary to sustain this approach over many months."

Linden said the merits of the Framework, and of its associated programs developed after Ipperwash—notably, the ART and the aboriginal liaison operations officer, the job held by Ron George—were such that they shouldn't be dependent "on the outcome of Caledonia." But he said the DCE occupation "raises important political, financial and operational questions about the sustainability of this approach, whether it is a best practice or not."

The Framework should be subject to independent, third-party evaluation, Linden said, noting that "the reaction of many Ontarians to the policing at Caledonia" demonstrated the need for "transparent and publicly accessible policies and with explanations for police decision-making." He rued the fact that "it is not clear whether the provincial government or the OPP intend to issue a detailed, public report describing their decision-making and strategy for this incident [Caledonia]."

(Three years after Linden wrote that, it is evident that the government has no intention of doing any such thing. Queen's Park remains as tight-lipped as ever on the subject. Premier McGuinty declined to be interviewed for this book.)

It is unclear how much the Ipperwash commissioner knew about the actual state of the ART, and it is unlikely he knew much, given that virtually all his information would have come from the OPP itself, which was still strongly singing its praises and pushing him to heartily endorse the Framework and related Aboriginal policies.

Shockingly, though it garnered no attention, the report also managed, without a shred of evidence, to tar those who opposed the Caledonia occupation and the so-called "measured response" policing of the OPP as racist. On page 210 of his report, Linden quoted from the OPP's written submission to Part 2 (the policy and research portion) of the inquiry. Linden wrote that OPP lawyer Mark Sandler had been reflecting "on the nature of some of the opposition in Caledonia," when he characterized such opposition as "sometimes deeply offensive and at times hateful and racist. Intemperate opposition often obtains a disproportionate voice in the media. It may be articulated, for example, in stereotypes about Aboriginal peoples and the assertion of their rights. Intemperate, aggressive, hateful or racist expressions inflame any incident, make the peaceful resolution more difficult and leave scars in the community that are not easily healed."

Sandler's remarks were duly footnoted in Linden's report—page 21 of the submission. There, in paragraph 52, Sandler prefaced what Linden had quoted with the following: "Opposition to the Framework's approach is not unexpected. People are entitled to their opinions. However, in the OPP's experience (reaffirmed by recent events), this opposition is sometimes deeply offensive, and at times hateful and racist."

Sandler didn't mention Caledonia specifically, but the reference to "recent events" makes the inference unmistakable.

Sandler's submission also contained a footnote that referred to Wayne Wawryk's "The Collection and Use of Intelligence in Policing Public Order Events," a research paper that had been commissioned for the inquiry. The footnote reads, "The author states that anonymous critics of measured response can 'contribute to the demonization of the protesters (indeed of the police) and skew public opinion.'" Alas, the paper produced by Wawryk, a retired RCMP deputy commissioner, is dated April 20, 2005—almost a year *before* the

Caledonia occupation even began. Obviously, he could not have been talking about DCE, let alone characterizing its critics in any way. And he didn't. Yet Wawryk's general observation about "demonization" was used to endorse the OPP suggestion that those opposing the occupation in Caledonia were racists.

In court, such a practice is disparagingly called "bootstrapping."

In the spring and summer of 2007, the ART was, in fact, in crisis. On the weekend of March 17–18, the OPP senior officers' association held its annual conference at the Ontario Fire College in Gravenhurst, just thirty-five kilometres north of OPP headquarters in Orillia. It was the first such conference under Commissioner Julian Fantino, who had been on the job for about five months.

Because the college has accommodation on campus, with rooms for everyone to stay overnight, it had been determined that it would be fine to serve alcohol. Shortly before two o'clock that Monday morning, a citizen called 911 to report a suspected impaired driver. The driver refused to pull over, and Rama First Nations police followed the car to a driveway in Orillia, where the vehicle hit another car that was parked there.

The driver was Superintendent Ron George, the OPP's top Aboriginal operations officer, the man who had been directing the ART in Caledonia and who had once been described by one of his colleagues as "the fucking king" of DCE.

George was charged with impaired care and control of a motor vehicle. The story of his arrest appeared on the front page of the local paper, the Orillia *Packet and Times*, on March 21, then completely disappeared. Researcher Chambers could find no further mention of the case in any Ontario newspaper over the next three years.

But on November 12, 2008, George was found guilty of "care or control—over eighty milligrams" under section 253(b) of the Criminal Code, and was sentenced to a $750 fine and a one-year licence suspension. Two years later, on April 14, 2010, he pleaded guilty in front of an adjudicator to one count of discreditable conduct under the Police Services Act. On May 26, the adjudicator released his decision: "In light of the seriousness of the allegation and bearing in mind all the evidence," George was demoted from superintendent to inspector for fifteen months "upon his return to work with the OPP."

According to the force's media boss, Inspector Dave Ross, George "is currently on leave from the OPP."

He also appears to have gone to ground. At the Kettle Point council office, where he once sat as a councillor, he is no longer known. The receptionist had no contact information for him at all. Though he was listed as the coach of the University of Windsor's team in the Kawaskimhon Moot—an annual Aboriginal forum where law students debate a given legal problem, which in March 2010 was held at the University of Ottawa—emails sent to the university, where he is a "special lecturer," went unanswered.

In a final effort to make sure Ron George knew I wanted to speak to him, I called his brother Vince, a retired OPP officer who lives in Sarnia, and explained the situation. He promised he would be able to get the message to him, but said, "I don't know where he lives. I'm his brother, but . . ."

George's unravelling wasn't the only sign of trouble within the ART. An Alliance report from the liaison table, dated February 21, noted under the OPP section that "people seem more open about their suggestions to cut back on MELT [Major Events Liaison Team] and ART people" and said there was a "reduced dependency on Ron [George], who built relations with Dick [Hill] . . . based on our prior conversations with different OPP members breaking the relationship with Dick and Ron is a very good thing." This reflects what one well-regarded OPP officer says: that George and the ART team, whose primary job was to build relationships with the occupiers and develop sources they could rely on, had, in effect, fallen for the wrong people and then got too close to them.

According to this officer, from the moment George first met Hill, he fell into a posture of trying to please or appease him. This may have been sparked by Hill's reported greeting at that first meeting.

He is alleged to have made a disparaging remark about his tribe having routed George's, and said, "We kicked your ass hundreds of years ago, and I'll be fucked if I negotiate with you."

In any case, this officer says that, during the original ART's stint on DCE, they only ever reported four "contacts": Hill, Clyde (Bullet) Powless, Jesse Porter and Janie Jamieson. Only when Superintendent Gentle reviewed the ART within the past year, essentially ripping it apart and assigning two new leads (ironically, one of them, a fellow very well thought of, is related to Ron George), did the team actually build a list of more than 150 names of people they could call upon in the event of another crisis—and this within the first six months of doing business.

In the first years, every single time the OPP was planning any sort of DCE-related operation—whether it was a planned arrest, how they would police a citizen protest or where protesters would be allowed—the force would first run their plan by George and the ART, who in turn would run it by Dick Hill, who would condemn it. In other words, the OPP was essentially seeking the permission of the occupiers before taking any law-enforcement action.

"The answer was always the same: 'If we do this, there will be a huge backlash, rising tensions and the natives will have two hundred men here at sunrise blocking roads,'" this officer says. "So every operation was stood down." He calls it unmitigated nonsense.

What's more, given the emphasis on "intelligence-led policing" in the Ipperwash report, bets are that Linden would have been astonished to hear what this officer, who was present at the time, says George told OPP officers at an early briefing: "I don't want any pictures taken, and no [licence] plates run. We don't need intelligence; this is a peaceful protest."

———

On the morning of September 13, native protesters took over another Caledonia subdivision under construction.

This was Stirling Woods, about half a klick north through the Thistlemoor area from DCE. About four of forty-nine houses in the new development were then close to construction. One of them was the place Sam Gualtieri was building as a wedding present for his daughter Michelle and her fiancé. He had a bricklayer who was supposed to be working on the arched entrance to the house, so he dropped by to check on him. Instead, he was stopped by the OPP, who had a barrier across Stirling Street, and told him he couldn't enter the site.

But Gualtieri saw a man climbing the scaffolding at the front of his house and walked in anyway; as he did so, he could hear an officer beside him on a walkie-talkie, saying, "The shit's going to hit the fan."

Gualtieri yelled at the protester to get down, telling him he didn't want to see anyone hurt at his daughter's house. "They said, 'It's our land, not your daughter's,'" he says, and he got mad and climbed up onto the scaffolding just as the protester was about to plant flags on the roof. He tossed the native flags into the mud below, "and they went nuts," Gualtieri says, so he decided it would be wiser just to lock the house up and leave.

At about four o'clock that afternoon, on his way back from other job sites with two nephews and another labourer, Gualtieri decided to stop by quickly and make sure the house was okay. Several OPP officers were still there, with a clear view of Gualtieri's house. All seemed in order, and they were about to leave when one of his nephews said, "There's a bunch of natives walking in the house." Gualtieri looked up and could see them walking on the catwalk inside.

The nephew suggested they go in the back way, but Gualtieri says he told him, "No, it's my house. Why should I sneak into my house?"

The front door had been obviously forced open; Gualtieri walked in—the others, it turns out, were allegedly jumped—and yelled upstairs, "This is my house, get the hell out!"

A voice yelled back, "It's our house!"

It was the last thing he remembers.

His nephews and the other worker found him unconscious in a pool of blood on the floor by the stairs; as one of the nephews came in through the back door, he saw someone swinging a section of four-inch solid oak handrail at Gualtieri's head. The assailants didn't even bother to run from the house—emboldened, the Gualtieris believe, from years of seeing others break the law with impunity.

"We are a lost people here," Gualtieri's brother Joe told me, about a year after the attack, for a story I wrote for *The Globe and Mail*.

Sam Gualtieri was badly beaten to the face and head; he suffered a swollen jaw and ear; his blackened eyes were almost swollen shut; he sustained three facial fractures and, most seriously, head trauma. The fifty-two-year-old framer and builder was in intensive care for two days, and in hospital for a total of five.

More than that, he was no longer the nimble man who could scramble up and down ladders, read blueprints on a dime and walk as surely as a cat upon rooftops. He needed new glasses; he began to move carefully, his head down, to watch his footing; he was often dizzy. When I met him—at the time he and his wife, Sandra, had filed a lawsuit alleging OPP negligence—he was attending an acquired-brain-injury clinic as an outpatient. More profound was his loss of faith: "I don't think the officers did their job," he said. "I have the right to be protected."

As his brother Joe said at the time, "His whole life has been defined by what he did. He loved this, he's been doing it since he was sixteen; he left school at Grade 10 to do it."

On September 19, as Sam Gualtieri was being discharged from West Haldimand Regional Hospital, the OPP, supported by Hamilton Police, entered Stirling Woods and arrested the nine protesters remaining there. Except for one man from Akwesasne, one from Hagersville and two of no fixed address, all were from Ohsweken on Six Nations. Half were hardly spring chickens—among them were a forty-seven-year-old woman, a forty-two-year-old man, a forty-one-year-old woman and a thirty-one-year-old man.

One of the younger ones, twenty-four-year-old Skyler Williams, was already facing charges in the attack on the two CHCH camera-men at the Canadian Tire on June 9 the year before. In October of 2008, the Crown dropped the charges against Williams and three others arrested in the occupation of Stirling Woods. In the spring of 2010, Williams pleaded guilty to the theft of the CHCH camera and was sentenced to the fifty-six days he'd already spent in jail and fined fifty dollars.

The three people arrested in the actual attack on Gualtieri were all young: two eighteen-year-olds (charges were quickly dropped against one of them) and a fifteen-year-old male. The province announced, through a press release issued by the Aboriginal affairs ministry, that the "confrontation" was "unacceptable," that "violence is never a solution to any dispute" and that the government was temporarily stepping away from the negotiating table in order to register its disapproval.

The attack was also condemned by the Six Nations' elected chief, David General, and Confederacy chief Allen MacNaughton.

"They [protesters] are certainly not there with the blessing of the elected chief," General said. "We have no idea who those people are and we condemn the violence." MacNaughton also expressed regrets, offered prayers for Gualtieri's speedy recovery and said the protesters were "on their own." It was a little late in the day for all that tsk-tsking.

Still, no one in officialdom appeared to make the links—and certainly no one publicly acknowledged them—that were so obvious to the Gualtieris and Caledonia residents: that violence unrestrained, or subjected to delayed policing, may empower those who commit it, and that young people are like sponges, soaking up lessons from the adults in their lives.

Julian Fantino, meanwhile, was quoted in the OPP press release issued when the police cleared Stirling Woods of protesters.

"Our job is to ensure that the rule of law prevails and this is what we are doing," he said, "strictly and absolutely enforcing the law to maintain public peace and order."

———

Less than a month before Doug Fleming's smoke shop rally, *The Hamilton Spectator* published a wide-ranging interview by columnist Susan Clairmont with the OPP commissioner.

Much of the lengthy interview was about Caledonia. But it was Fantino who introduced the subject of Gary McHale, remarking—unprompted—that "as long as we don't have those interlopers that come in creating problems, things are not all that bad."

Clairmont immediately followed up, observing that Fantino didn't mince words about McHale.

"And I don't still," Fantino replied. "Any Canadian can do whatever he wants, I suppose, but that's all mischief-making." He explained that there wasn't two-tiered justice, merely a misunderstanding of the OPP's role—oh yes, "and a lot of mischief-making."

When Clairmont pressed the point, reminding him that even OPP officers were saying they were enforcing two standards in town, Fantino disagreed. "You must have a different source of information than what I do because I spent a lot of time with my officers both on the front lines and meetings . . . I don't get that feedback at all."

But, he said, if they do see things that way, it's because "he or she would not have the bigger picture. Caledonia is not an isolated, stand-alone issue. Caledonia is connected with all these other First Nations issues not only across the province, but country-wide. Everyone's watching what goes on in Caledonia and one misstep in Caledonia will result in a flare-up right across this country of conflict and confrontation."

He pronounced himself unhappy with "the kind of attention the media have given these interlopers who come in to cause trouble," cautioned the press about making "heroes out of villains," and concluded, "The other thing we have to realize is there's many agendas in play. We have an agenda, right? When you get these interlopers coming in, the media should be asking the question about how is this in the greater good? I mean, I just told you how much the taxpayers

of this province are spending and how much of a sacrifice it is for us
to keep the peace when these people come in there.

"They're like throwing a bomb in the community and having everyone live in the ashes. Even the sensational play that was given to my
email to Haldimand Council. That's such an innocuous . . . That's just
me expressing concern about some of the very inflammatory rhetoric
that was being perpetrated by people who should know better . . .
How did people characterize it? As a threat. That wasn't a threat. Not
legally, not morally, and not ethically. I would write it again."

Even when he purported to offer sympathy to those living next door
to the site, he managed to work in a veiled reference to McHale ("I
can't bring relief to their situation beyond just trying to keep the peace
and keep the parties separated and troublemakers out of there and
keep things from flaring up") and could not restrain himself from
praising the "awful lot of work done on the part of Six Nations people."

Reading the interview reminded me of something Fantino said
in testimony given in discovery for the Brown/Chatwell lawsuit. The
couple's lawyer, John Evans, had asked him about a tour around
DCE he took in early 2007—with a couple of natives as guides, of
course. Evans asked what he learned from the tour.

"Well," Fantino said, "my visual was that it's an expanse of property, obviously that there was construction happening there. Just
highlighted the difficulties that I know about, which is basically how
this property was basically construction-frustrated, delayed or unable
to continue."

What struck him, he added, was "the vulnerability of the railway
tracks."

Only when Evans asked about "the vulnerability of Brown's property to the occupation" did Fantino mention it. As Brown later put
it, "What about the fucking vulnerability of my house?"

Fantino's praising of Six Nations people exemplified one of the
most extraordinary aspects of the occupation: the inability of people
to actually see, let alone credit, the remarkable, long-suffering patience
of Caledonia's townspeople. Similarly, in virtually all official public

pronouncements on the issue—whether from government, OPP, Haldimand County or the OPP Association—only McHale was ever castigated as an "outsider" with an "agenda." Akwesasne's Michael Laughing and the dozens of DCE occupiers who hailed from British Columbia, New York, Toronto and far-flung reserves were never so cheaply dismissed.

Still, surely Fantino's most outrageous comment in the *Spectator* interview was his suggestion that "McHale and company" wanted to see civil war in Caledonia.

"You can't call in the army and deal with this issue," Fantino said. "I mean, that's crazy. These things have to be resolved. We're a sophisticated society. We're a democratic society. Look what's happening in Pakistan, for goodness sakes. And that's what the expectation is that a lot of people have, including McHale and company. But you know they want to see this thing escalate to a violent outcome, and for what? For a piece of land."

Clairmont asked him if there should be an inquiry into Caledonia. Fantino answered by speaking about the "quantum leap" the force had made since Ipperwash.

"We've come a long way . . . But to the most critical thing, the communications thing, I do totally agree, absolutely agree that that is our insurance. And developing that trust, that dialogue, that face-to-face relationship with people. And that's why I'm spending the kind of personal time that I am, because I want to know these people and I want them to know me, personally. I want to know them by first name. I want to be able to call them on their cell phone number as they're able to call me. I want to be on the front end of any potential flare-up and that's worked very, very well for us. So the degree that communications are critical, I absolutely agree and to me that is our insurance.

"The other thing I should tell you too is that I've actually been on the land in areas where no other white person has gone since the occupation.

"Why? Because of trust. I'm not threatening, I'm not judging, I'm not condescending."

Clairmont did not reply, as I would have, "Well, not to natives."

The last question the columnist asked was about the camera Dave Brown found in his house: "Is that an OPP camera?"

"There's extenuating circumstances there," Fantino said, "and I wish I could elaborate more, but there's a lawsuit, as you know, that's been filed."

By the time I asked for an interview, that lawsuit had been settled, and so was the question. It *was* an OPP camera.

———

The OPP briefing on the cold, clear day that was December 1, the day of Doug Fleming's smoke shop protest, made things seem very simple. Officers at the Unity Road command post were told that a large crowd wasn't anticipated. They were told to expect a peaceful protest.

It was a curious approach, if only because Fleming had advertised the rally well in advance in the local papers, as he always did, including the fact that the plan was to march to the end of Argyle Street, past DCE, to the Plank Road shack.

By this stage in the occupation, there was a predictable quality to these things, almost a choreography, and a few hard truths: the mere presence of non-natives anywhere near DCE was considered a provocation by both natives and police; the closer to the site the protesters went or planned to go, the greater the size of the crowd of natives showing up to object; and the OPP's chief task was to keep the two sides apart, preferably at a distance.

As McHale says, at such events, "The police actually act as a private security force for the natives."

Normally, for a well-publicized rally like this, the OPP would have a minimum of 100 and usually 250 officers on duty—four public order units, each with about thirty-five members; intelligence and identification officers; TRU; a canine unit; and sometimes the OPP chopper, with reinforcements on standby or staged elsewhere in town. But this time, they called out only a fraction of that number:

about twenty uniformed officers and only seven ERT, or public order, members.

Gary McHale wasn't even mentioned in the briefing.

But behind the scenes, within the senior ranks of the OPP, it was a very different story. Shortly after the rally started at 10 A.M., a flurry of emails began among the brass, every single one of them focused on McHale—and, more important, how to arrest him. The discussion lasted well into the evening and continued over the next week.

These emails—at least twenty-seven of which were sent by Fantino to underlings—were so numerous that at one point, fully two days after the rally, Superintendent Ron Gentle, director of the OPP's criminal investigation bureau, pointedly asked one of his detectives, "Would you please tell me why you are submitting these updates? I am confident that you will keep Dave [McLean, the detachment commander] and I informed as needed. If there is someone else who has asked you for these, I'd like to know what the purpose is and why they tasked one of my members with this duty without discussing the matter with me.

"If I had every CIB member giving three updates a day on every case they were assigned, all we'd be doing is typing and reading," Gentle concluded.

Gentle was also the only one smart enough to realize that the email traffic, with its clear fixation upon McHale, had what he called "implications in relation to disclosure, evidence, and leaves one wondering who is the manager of the case—you, or is someone else directing the investigation from afar?"

Of course, that is precisely how McHale obtained the emails— through a disclosure request he made while preparing his defence against the bizarre charge the OPP later ended up laying against him.

Gentle's questions were prompted by the receipt of a note from Detective Inspector Bill Renton, apologizing for being late with his 2 P.M. update. The answer came forty-seven minutes later from Inspector John Stephens: "The deputy commissioner [Chris Lewis] has requested these reports to keep the commissioner briefed."

In all the traffic, only Gentle sounded a note of caution. At one point, when Lewis asked if the McHale arrest plan could be rushed (Lewis was at dinner with Fantino, he said, "and he's enquiring about the timing of the charges"), Gentle replied, "I fully understand the commissioner's concerns and the need for this to be expedited. However, he, you and I are crime fighters from way back and we all know the importance of doing the right thing here, keeping in mind our responsibilities to all involved and to ensure what we do sticks, rather than give more news bites to the detractors we have."

It was the diplomatic and deferential reply of an officer who was trying to put the brakes on the full-court press aimed at stopping not a dangerous thug, but a rotund, middle-aged man whose only weapon was his mouth.

———

About a hundred townspeople showed up for the rally, the first of them arriving before the police. The first call for ERT reinforcements went out shortly after 10 A.M.

It was clear the OPP didn't have anywhere near the numbers they needed to control the two sides, who already were jawing at one another. But still, by noon, police had made only one arrest: Kyle Hagan, a Caledonia resident who was charged with obstructing police and then released. This arrest was the last straw for Kyle's mother, Gail, who is Dana Chatwell's aunt; she was standing in front of her vehicle, near tears, and refusing to move.

"I can't take it anymore," she told officers. "I've had enough."

Fleming himself had his white truck parked across the road for a time. He was sitting in it, asking various OPP officers if he could speak to someone senior "about the reason why we're here." He was genial, relaxed and frequently bemused. At one point, he opened the rear door of the truck and appeared to "sell" some of his smokes, joking, "It seems to be the thing to do in this neighbourhood." Natives were blocking the road too—first with a truck, and for some time with the ubiquitous hydro tower that was once again dragged across it. Then, with officers in a loose line facing the Caledonia residents—a few nervously checking over their shoulders at the occupiers, some of whom were wearing bandanas or balaclavas—came the shoving, pushing and yelling that was by this point pro forma at such events.

McHale was in the thick of it, walking about, his mere presence seeming to enrage some of the occupiers, particularly DCE spokesman Clyde Powless. This was a little odd, because less than two months earlier, when Powless showed up at McHale's "Remember Us March"—held on October 8, the eve of the provincial election— he had been allowed to speak.

"We stand for law, yes," Powless had told the crowd that day, "and we don't support violence." No one heckled him or attempted to shout him down, and he even shook McHale's outstretched hand afterwards. But as the extensive video footage shot on December 1 shows, two things happened at the rally, though the timing isn't clear. First, a sturdy native woman—this was Powless's sister Camille—approached McHale, and as she drew close she suddenly shrieked, "Don't you fucking push me!" It is crystal clear from all the video that he had done nothing of the sort.

Some time later, Powless accosted McHale, furiously pointing a finger in his face and shouting, "It's all on you, McHale. You stupid fuck, you stupid, arrogant fuck. How stupid are you?" McHale looked—and physically turned—away from the forty-year-old ironworker, and was trying to *move* away from him, his hands in his pockets, when from behind, Powless reached over and around several OPP officers, grabbed McHale and began punching him in the face. McHale fell to the ground, his glasses breaking.

OPP officers who were there told Powless to back off, noting that as McHale lay there, other occupiers were kicking him.

There was a brief glimpse of Fleming going to McHale's assistance.

McHale was taken away by ambulance; he had a blackened eye and bruised ribs.

What was evident from video footage, and certainly to those OPP who were present, was that, while people from both sides were engaged in unpleasant verbal exchanges (at one point, McHale can be heard admonishing a Caledonia man for swearing), virtually all the physical violence and most of the verbal aggression came from the occupiers' camp.

Yet in cyberspace, where Fantino was getting his regular updates, the picture was entirely different. At 4.22 P.M., Fantino wrote Chief Superintendent Bob Goodall.

> Bob:
>   Today we had another flare-up in Caledonia spearheaded by McHale.
>   As the event unfolded things turned ugly and some violence erupted. McHale and a few others continue to converge on Caledonia to basically create mischief . . . All in all, but for McHale and his few supporters Caledonia is a relatively peaceful place.

Fantino ordered Goodall to assign an inspector to oversee the investigation and said, "I want every avenue explored by which we now can bring McHale into court seeking a Court Order to prevent him from continuing his agenda of inciting people to violence in Caledonia. We should be able to prove to the Court that McHale's forays into Caledonia have been planned and executed for purposes of breaching the peace which today also resulted in violence.

"I don't want us to get sidetracked by Crown lawyers on this," the OPP boss warned. "We need to be guided by the long established RPG [reasonable and probable grounds] criteria and not be constantly frustrated by timid Crowns who seem to only get charged up when they have a sure prospect of conviction."

Little more than an hour later, Fantino emailed a press release in his trademark cartoonish language. It appears that the release was not actually sent to the press or made public. It read, in part: "Today at approximately 10 A.M., a small group of protesters known to pursue their own agendas approached a smoke shack on Plank Road taunting and provoking those present. A confrontation broke out as police struggled to maintain order and peace . . . Commissioner Fantino expressed his outrage at the interlopers. 'The OPP will seek every legal remedy possible to end this madness and to bring them to justice . . . These incidents, where interlopers put their own personal agendas over those who are striving for a permanent and lasting resolution will not be tolerated.'"

The next day, Fantino was at it again, telling Lewis in one note, "The reason I waited to get back to you was simply to cool off.

"What are we doing in Caledonia? We seem to be in an almost state of paralysis when it comes to proactively doing anything respecting McHale et al. If it isn't us being told what to do by feeble Crowns, it's our own lack of fire . . . Ahh, I can't believe this!!!!!"

That evening, Fantino wrote Lewis again, saying the OPP was "falling short on exploiting every possible proactive investigative strategy that would curtail the activities of McHale et al . . . Did we have a plan to deal with him on the basis of any breach he may have committed regarding his bail conditions [McHale had no bail conditions then]? Did we assign an arrest team dedicated to McHale if/when the opportunity presented itself to take him out, etc?" Again, Fantino railed against Crown attorneys and concluded, "I want us to take McHale to court to seek a Court Order to keep him out of Caledonia . . . And even if we are unsuccessful, we will be able to publicly expose him for the mischief-maker that he is and whose activities if not stopped will surely result in more violence."

On December 3, Fantino sent a note to Chris Lewis and Detective Inspector Angie Howe, wailing, "I feel like doing what LA Police Chief Darryl Gates [did] go out and arrest the goof myself!"

(This was a reference to the late Daryl Gates, who, while still the chief of the Los Angeles Police Department, leaped out of bed and personally arrested Damian Williams, one of four men charged in the vicious beating of truck driver Reginald Denny during the 1992 riots.)

The next day, McHale, Fleming, Merlyn Kinrade and Brian Hagan (father of Kyle Hagan, the man who was the first to be arrested on December 1) held a press conference at Queen's Park to call for charges to be laid in the attack on McHale and denounce the OPP's handling of the rally. But even before they got there, at 7:40 that morning, Fantino was on the email horn, ordering Howe to prepare "a canned strongly worded rebuttal" to the group's "diatribe."

By month's end, another eight people were arrested in relation for the December 1 rally. Among them were Fleming, charged with mischief; Clyde Powless, assault and mischief; his sister Camille for public mischief in connection with her false complaint that McHale had assaulted her; and one Brian Jesse Porter, another DCE spokesman and regular ART contact, who was charged with mischief for dragging the hydro tower across the road.

(Brian Jesse Porter is the same B. Jesse Porter who, according to the Ontario ministry of finance's public accounts document, was paid $131,240 by the Aboriginal affairs ministry in 2006–07. I made this discovery inadvertently. I was searching the public accounts records to see what negotiator Jane Stewart had been paid after the government refused to disclose the information—$171,783 in 2006–07 and $77,766 in 2007–08, as it turns out—and recognized Porter's name. Why the Ontario government would have been paying an occupier anything—let alone that enormous sum—remains a mystery. According to ministry spokesman Greg Flood, the information is private and can't be disclosed publicly.)

Gary McHale was charged with "counselling mischief not committed," purportedly for having encouraged protesters to block the road.

The charge was so unusual both a senior Crown attorney and a judge later remarked that they'd never even heard of it. But it was nonetheless used to impose extraordinarily restrictive conditions upon McHale. For twenty-nine months until the spring of 2010, when the Crown formally stayed the charge, McHale was prohibited from even entering Caledonia—or Cayuga, near the village of Binbrook, where the McHales had in fact been living for almost two years at the time and where both of them now had friends and ordinary business dealings.

Most outrageously, when Clyde Powless's assault charge came before the courts in the fall of 2008, he had several letters of reference. One, from the Haudenosaunee Confederacy, simply confirmed that Powless and Porter "were delegated the responsibilities of maintaining peace and order on the site of Douglas Creek Lands of the Six Nations. They also have the responsibility of acting as liaison representatives." But two letters were from senior OPP officials.

Superintendent Cain's note was straightforward, and merely said "the OPP continue to work with Clyde Powless and Jesse Porter in their roles and responsibilities as liaison representatives." It was Julian Fantino who, in a December 4, 2008, email to Powless's defence lawyer, gave Powless a ringing endorsement.

"Much of the conflict, confrontation and provocation has occurred during the times that Mr. Gary McHale and his followers have converged on Caledonia that invariably resulted in heightened tensions and conflict that required an extraordinary deployment of police resources in our efforts to preserve the peace," Fantino wrote. "Although I am not in a position to address the specific circumstances that resulted in criminal charges being brought against Mr. Powless, I do feel that but for Mr. McHale's mischief-making forays into Caledonia, the very volatile situation that exists there would not have escalated time and again as it has virtually every time Mr. McHale came to town.

"I am not making excuses or apologies for Mr. Powless's actions about which he is accused, however, and with respect, the Honourable Court may wish to consider the volatility of the situation and provocation that simply could have been avoided but for the presence of Mr. McHale and his like-minded followers.

"As well, I wish to advise the Honourable Court that on a number of occasions Mr. Powless has been instrumental in diffusing [defusing] serious conflict and confrontation during which times he has actually been the peacemaker."

He signed it, "J. Fantino, Commissioner, Ontario Provincial Police."

It was extraordinary, and it was now official: Ontario's senior law officer and the head of the second-biggest police force in Canada was not only privately targeting and publicly denouncing the victim of an assault, he was also telling a judge it was the victim's fault and singing the praises of the assailant.

Powless formally pleaded guilty to assault in Oakville court on December 8, 2008. He received a conditional discharge.

———

The McHales lost their Richmond Hill condominium—the bank wanted to sell it through a power of sale, but the couple sold it themselves in February of 2008 for $232,000, emerging, after extra legal fees and debts, with very little. In March, they moved to Binbrook, an intersection-cum-village near Hamilton, where they rent a townhouse, and where they are regularly behind on the rent and are grateful for an understanding landlord.

They admit that the impecuniousness engendered by their Caledonia adventure has been hard on their relationship. "When you think of any marriage," McHale says, "that's the biggest source of problems. We have probably received four to six eviction notices since living here."

They are dependent on donations, and though, as self-employed entrepreneurs, they were used to having money coming in sporadically in chunks, for two people who have been remarkably, if quirkily, self-sufficient since they were youngsters, the adjustment has been tough.

McHale was born in Kingston, the youngest of six boys, and grew up there until his mother, Lucy, was killed in a car accident when he was about ten years old.

(As it turns out, as McHale learned only after getting hooked on Caledonia, his brother Brian was actually born there; he even has a newspaper picture of Brian as a little boy, blowing out his birthday candles.)

The family moved through a couple of small towns in eastern Ontario—Odessa and Violet—with the McHale boys referring to themselves as the "Kingstonian Raiders" because, with their hands-off father, Leo, often away, they ran wild and even had contests to see who could steal the most chocolate bars in one trip to the local store.

"At seven," McHale says, giggling, "I used to have the record—on one trip, I stole twenty-seven chocolate bars."

As several of his older brothers began to get into more serious kinds of trouble—notably drugs—McHale asked to move in with an aunt and uncle who ran a much tighter ship. "I probably put them through a lot of grief they didn't deserve," he says. "They experienced a lot of my anger toward my father, and society." It was while he was living with them that McHale, who had never tried drugs before, gave acid a brief whirl. "I used more than I sold," he says. "I loved it. *Loved* it."

His oldest brother, Greg—a Christian and easily the most stable in the family at the time, was working for IBM and living in St. Catharines—rode to his rescue, and McHale moved in with him and his wife, Donna, to finish high school. At Laura Secord High, he met Christine, who was, of necessity, as independent—if considerably more law-abiding—as he was.

Within a few months, he proposed to her.

Christine grew up in Val d'Or, a gold-mining town in northwestern Quebec (weirdly, just a stone's throw from Rouyn-Noranda, where I was born and raised) and St. Catharines, after her parents split up when she was six. Her late mother was, she says, physically and emotionally abusive, so much so that in her last year of high school, Christine's teacher and guidance counsellor actually encouraged her to move out on her own.

Christine and Gary lived together—McHale, who is a year younger and was a grade behind, finishing Grade 13 while working full-time at night, as Christine held down three part-time jobs—until they got married in 1981 and moved back to Kingston, where McHale says he briefly reverted to some of his old ways. Hired by a cash register company, "The very first day on the job I make copies of all the keys, because that's what you do when you're a McHale." Eight months later, when he was fired, the company was refusing to give him his last pay, so "I decide to go over and *get* my two weeks' pay," he says. He was charged with theft, then charged with shoplifting at a Kingston Canadian Tire.

"Just to show you how the legal system works," he says, his lawyer arranged for both cases to be heard on the same day in different courtrooms, then was accurately able to tell both judges that each was a first offence. "So I got a conditional discharge on one, probation on the other," McHale says.

Still, the experience shook some sense into him, and he began to straighten himself out. Then, in the guise of something perfectly ordinary—his brother Greg criticized him harshly for some of his shortcomings, then phoned him up afterwards to apologize— McHale decided that God exists. He became a Christian, just like that, at the age of twenty-one.

"In my mind," he says, "it's because McHales don't apologize for anything, for him to seek forgiveness for something I would have overlooked . . .

"Before," he says, "I believed in evolution. Evolution doesn't look at the moral issues, doesn't look at a lion stealing another lion's food and say it's wrong. My fundamental belief, before being a Christian, is that if evolution's true, if *you* want to work all week to get enough money to buy a stereo, and it only takes me ten minutes to break in and steal it, one of us is better evolved than the other."

He went whole hog, of course, and attended the Central Baptist Seminary in Toronto (it amalgamated with two other seminaries years later, and is now known as Heritage Theological Seminary), where he immediately raised hackles by objecting to the ban on drinking.

"I said I would agree to it, I would live by it, but I would work to change it," he says. "I'm not much of a drinker. The no-drinking rule would have been the easiest thing for me; I was in my thirties before I even realized beer stores were cold."

His point was that such artificial rules—that, for instance, "true Christians won't dance, drink, watch movies"—have nothing to do with the real values of Christianity. The Christian principles he is devoted to, he says, are the great abstract concepts, chiefly truth. "Truth is vital. If you don't have truth, you have nothing. Justice . . . There's people who have died for these things in the past. It's very important. Freedom of speech, that we take for granted, but that people have laid down their lives for . . . the things we think are, what, not worth talking about?"

He is quietly enraged at how no church took a role in Caledonia.

"Where's the church? Did anyone, any minister, any pastor, any deacon, ever walk into Dave and Dana's home and say, 'I want to pray with you, I want to deliver you some food'? Did anyone with any guts, with any true Christian beliefs, walk through the barricades and listen to all the crap they would have heard just to deliver a casserole?

"I'm not talking about whether they organized protests," he says. "I'm talking about the very fundamental basis of what Christianity's supposed to be. Did they walk down the Sixth Line? Did they go to Braemar-Thistlemoor?

"The answer's no, four years later."

Grinning, he says, "I believe God looks at Caledonia and says, 'There's not one I can find to step forward, so I've gotta bring a guy from Richmond Hill.'"

McHale is as unconventional a Christian as he is an activist. "I come from a family that's violent," he says, "that's involved in crime. So I have to wrestle with 'Is there right and wrong? Are there absolutes?' And is the concept of letting someone slap you on the cheek and turn the cheek—does that concept work? Does it make sense?

"True Christianity isn't this thing where we oppress people," he says. "You want to prove you're a Christian, then pay a price for your neighbour, whatever that means. I'd be considered a liberal because I don't believe the government should interfere with things like same-sex marriage, I really don't.

"I was going to start a website, before I got involved in Caledonia, about this oxymoron where Christian churches make a stand for moral issues that the Bible doesn't really make a stand for. Christian principles are what I live by; I don't tell you that you have to live by my beliefs. That's where the church is wrong."

The McHales' lives have changed dramatically because of Caledonia. Where they used to travel, for their wildlife photography, now they can't.

"A lot of times, now, I can't put gas in my car until someone gives me twenty dollars to put gas in my car," McHale says. "That all comes straight from donations, so we make decisions all the time based on what cash is available. We cannot say, 'Let's go for a Sunday drive.' We can't do that."

He says it took him more than a year—when the institutional criticism coming from the OPP, OPP Association and government was at its height, and supporters were falling away as though he was the plague—to come to the conclusion "that God wants me in Caledonia, come hell or high water. Not that we've done such a good job, but really, we're so unqualified to do what we're doing. We look around . . . I barely can read or write, most of the time, and yet I write these reports, I do these interviews, I've got a column in the paper [*The Regional*]. I'm not the person that you put before a committee and say, 'Here are the qualifications.' You wouldn't come up with me.

"And yet, for some bizarre reason, people with real power in this country are concerned with what I'm saying. I put something on my website one day and it creates news stories."

Obviously still amazed, he says, "I have to think it's something more going on than my efforts, when powerful people are concerned with what some fat guy says, sitting in Richmond Hill."

Christine is supportive, though she was badly wounded when supporters jumped ship. "I keep saying to myself, 'Why are we still helping when so many people would rather sit at home?' But we're not helping because other people are going to come and stand beside you, but because [it's right]."

When McHale enrolled in the seminary, she says, "He was committed to that. Everything he does, he's very diligent about. Long story short, here we are, involved in Caledonia. I knew it didn't matter what I would say—he'd be involved. I went along. I still have some reservations, but I'm going to be right beside him. That's the decision I made."

In front of her husband, Christine says, "As much as I hated to go from owning to renting, it is liberating. If I never own again, it's not going to bother me." But later, when we are alone in my car, en route to a rally, she allows wistfully that it would be nice, one day, to have a place of their own again.

———

On Friday, April 25, 2008, natives gathered at the overpass on Highway 6 in town and set up a barricade in a show of solidarity with Mohawk demonstrators in Deseronto, a small town on the Bay of Quinte in eastern Ontario. There, about 330 kilometres from Caledonia, protesters from the nearby Tyendinaga Mohawk Territory were occupying a gravel quarry considered to be part of a simmering land dispute. The Caledonia bypass ended up being closed for four or five days.

Nothing had changed: ART was still dealing with Dick Hill, albeit this time by BlackBerry; Hill and the natives were still issuing ultimatums to the OPP; the OPP was still marching to the natives' drum.

Debbie Thompson went out on the Saturday night to buy a lottery ticket. "I wasn't stopped by the protesters," she says, "but there were so many there I couldn't get through.

"So I'm on top of the bridge and I can see the OPP coming in, and I can hear, obviously, these protesters: 'Gonna kill them gonna kill them gonna kill them.' That's a constant, what they're going to do. You heard a lot that way. And I'm sitting there [in her car] thinking, 'Oh my God.' So finally I get into town, I get my lottery ticket, I use my cell phone, I call Phil Carter [OPP Staff Sergeant].

I tell him what I heard, how upset I was. And that things were *not* quiet here, 'even though you idiots'—and I used the word *idiots*— 'there's got to be a hundred cars down here and protesters all over this bypass.'

"And I said, 'Fantino makes a press release about how calm things are in Caledonia and we're not allowed to speak to him.' It's like, 'Hey fool, go down to the Sixth Line, look at the hundreds of cars, look at the . . . they've built a road at eleven at night till four in the morning, onto the bypass!'

"They had trucks in here. I mean, we listened to it all night. It's quiet, it's peaceful, nothing's happening? No, you're wrong."

Thompson made it home safely.

"Then Sunday comes," she says, "and Monday comes, and everyone's outta here, [out of the house, for] work, school, whatever, and I'm sitting at the kitchen table there thinking I can't believe what I saw. Can't believe what I saw. Wanting to kill them.

"All of a sudden," she says, "all I saw was my son, dead. I saw it. My eyes saw. And I thought, 'Holy shit, I can't live this way anymore.' And I vowed I would never, ever call a police officer again. And I haven't. And I never will. Someone could come up [the road] right now, Christie, and I would not phone the police. I don't want to be responsible for one of them being killed. And I believe that these people would kill them."

That's when, she says, "I was put on what I call 'make-me-fucking-happy pills.' And I take 'em. And this is me, happy. I don't think they work. My kids say they do, so I'm still on them. Remain on them."

They tried selling the house. "Nobody called about it, nor come to see it," Debbie says. Then—she is shyly, tentatively, apologizing for her perfectly nice house—she adds, "Now, I mean, even outside it's just your average house, but it's not a house that people would go, 'Omigod, I'm not looking there!' It's average. It's not like it's falling apart and 'I don't even want to look.' It presents itself okay. You would think people would come in and at least have a look. Not one. Not one. Not one."

The house was listed for six months and, Carl says, "the realtor never even had a call on it, and it isn't a shithole, it isn't the best in the world but—"

"Now this house is worthless," Debbie says, "and it's just a house, but it's *our* house, and you know. . ."

"For all of us, it's our biggest investment," I say.

"Yeah, it is," she says. "And we don't have that anymore; it's gone. So for us to go anywhere at this stage, we're not that young . . . So what do you do? Suck it up."

She wonders now if, perhaps, when Carl's dad was still alive but getting on and Carl wanted to move in with him, she made the wrong decision.

"I mean, I know I'm not responsible," she says. "I think we made the wrong decision moving here. I went along with it, I knew my husband wanted it. He knew I wasn't keen on coming here, and I didn't want to say I forced him to come, but I said, 'It's okay, we'll go.'

"I would do anything for his dad, you know, especially while he was still alive. Maybe I should never have said that."

On March 10, 2010, a Wednesday, Staff Sergeant Carter phoned Debbie and asked if he could come and see her. "He said, 'Don't panic, nothing's wrong, I just wanna come and see you.' So he come, and he could tell by the look on my face because I've been arguing this point for the whole forty-seven months, and he said, 'We're back on the road.'"

One month shy of four years after they stopped, the OPP was back patrolling the Sixth Line. The news was broken to the residents by phone or in person; there was no public announcement.

Debbie was happy, grateful. "But then, I do wonder," she says. "I think, 'Okay, that's today.' But maybe next week . . . they'll throw up a barricade and police will not be allowed in here. How safe are we if we can't announce this to the world?"

———

In the spring of 2008, at its semi-annual board meeting held on this occasion at the Nottawasaga Inn in the resort country north of Toronto, the OPP Association finally got an answer or two from the OPP brass. By this time, it had been more than two years since the occupation of DCE had started.

According to the minutes of the meeting, Detective Sergeant Roger Geysons, president of No. 3 Branch, which takes in Haldimand County, said the following, in part:

> Our members have experienced several occur-rences over the last few months involving First Nations persons observed committing a criminal act and subsequently fleeing onto the Douglas Creek Estates in their vehicles. Many of these members are unaware of the status of current agreements put in place regarding policing the DCE and the Sixth Line.
>
> To date, our members have not followed per-sons on these lands in order to apprehend.
>
> Given that the DCE is owned by the Province of Ontario and is not, as of yet, part of the Six Nations Reserve, what *written* order are our mem-bers to follow? Has there been a written agreement between the OPP and Six Nations as well as an SOP [standard operating procedure] in dealing with occurrences on these lands?
>
> Are OPP members allowed on DCE?
>
> Can you provide to our members written direction?

OPP Deputy Chief Chris Lewis answered.

"We'll address that," he said. "This is actually news to me that this was still an issue. There is obviously a communication issue." Then Lewis delivered a bombshell: "Short of somebody having a kid kidnapped and running onto the DCE, we're not going to go onto that property. It's just a recipe for disaster, and it will set things back there."

Lewis also confirmed that the ART was still calling the shots—which meant, to those in the know, that Dick Hill and the occupiers were still running the show.

"There may be times that we have to go on there," Lewis said, "but at the same time, we'll do it and negotiate that through ART [to] the leaders in the First Nations community."

He also said that the OPP would respond to calls—meaning emergencies—on the Sixth and Seventh lines, but general patrols would not take place in that area because "they [Six Nations] can't control all the people in their community . . . So it's a common-sense issue, and certainly, we're not saying we will never go on there, but we really have to be very selective of when we do and how we go about it."

Commissioner Fantino chimed in at this point, saying, "So enforce the law absolutely. We don't stand by and allow violence and that to occur, but at the end of the day, if we can do it in a more strategic way, that's the way to go." Fantino also acknowledged the earlier incidents "when officers have either accidentally or otherwise gone on there [DCE]. It's pretty difficult to extricate them once they get in there and they are surrounded and we've got hundreds of people on speed dial that converge on the area."

Lewis, unable to resist describing what sounds like a little boys-will-be-boys hot-dogging then said, "Just for the record, the Commissioner and I went on the DCE and that was quite a day."

"We were swarmed," Fantino said.

"Yes," Lewis added. "We were swarmed. We were driving by in uniform and the Commissioner told the driver, 'Pull in there,' and he said, 'Like on the DCE?' And the Commissioner said, 'Yeah, I want to talk to those people.' So in we went.

"Well, you can imagine all the roadblocks radioing in to the command post saying the Commissioner and the Deputy are on the DCE, they are out of the car, talking to people with guns on."

When first I read this, I wondered who was wearing the guns, but it was apparently clear that Lewis was referring to himself and Fantino. Still, since Fantino didn't take over until the end of October of 2006, it means that at some point between late in 2006 and April of 2008, the two most senior officials of the OPP had gone onto the DCE and been swarmed by native occupiers, just like everyone else. That ought to really comfort the residents of Caledonia, particularly those on the Sixth Line, and in the Thistlemoor subdivision.

And nothing can remove the shock of the bottom line of Lewis's message: short of what cops call a "fresh" kidnapping, the OPP were not to venture upon DCE.

"Do your guys boo when they hear this BS?" I ask OPP Association boss Karl Walsh.

"No, they don't," Walsh says, "because they're good soldiers. We've got a whole group—even though policing, by far, is a group of type A personalities, very strong personalities—there's also a very strong paramilitary ribbon that runs through the OPP. So when the deputy commissioner stands up and says, 'Okay, guys, if it's a homicide or a sexual assault and you're in fresh pursuit, you can go there. Otherwise, stay the fuck away,' they stay the fuck away.

"They all leave the meeting, and then they all yell at me, right, and then I go and yell at them [the brass], and they go, 'Too bad. This is an operational decision, the association has no business in the operations of the OPP, so butt the fuck out.'"

Still, the belated acknowledgement is the first and only official admission on the part of the OPP that, ninety minutes from Toronto, there is a slice of Ontario where their officers dare not and do not go.

"And just think about that," Walsh rages. "The only clarity they get on it [the DCE question] is through their union. What the fuck is that?"

Of course, neither Lewis nor Fantino ever answered Geysons' other questions: Were there written agreements? Was there an SOP? The only clarity the association got was that the OPP is not allowed on DCE.

And it took more than two yeas to get *that*.

"That's how long it took to get a succinct answer to a pointed question," Walsh says. "And that wasn't until the branch president—and that's the branch president who's responsible for that area, so Roger Geysons would have spent a significant amount of time on the ground, dealing with all the members and the issues down there—and then he finally came to the meeting and somebody asked the pointed question."

So, it was something; it was more than the OPPA had ever had before. But it didn't provide the rationale for how the force handled Caledonia.

"I still don't understand why we took different approaches to law enforcement in Caledonia," Walsh says. "I don't think I ever will understand it. I've never been given an adequate explanation as to why that occurred."

He is still furious. "I can't forgive them for a lot of the approaches they took to this," he says, "and I think numerous officers got unnecessarily injured, I think people from the general public got unnecessarily injured, I think everybody that was involved in this suffered injuries that could have been avoid had they just stuck to their training, stuck to their policies and stuck to the law. You know, the law doesn't discern colour of skin or ethnic background, and it's not supposed to. Justice is supposed to be blind."

Walsh describes the Caledonia approach as "a policy stance that had never been taken before, so nobody could say, 'Well, we've done an extensive study of this,' or 'We've consulted the ministry of the attorney general,' or 'We've consulted with the federal ministry of the attorney general.' Nobody was pointing to that.

"And what you found was that, unnecessarily, unfairly, frontline officers by and large were being held accountable for the actions they were being *directed* to do, which is completely something that should never happen. There should never be any incident of this magnitude where a frontline officer is called to speak as to why they decided to do A or B, knowing that A or B has been dictated by extremely high levels."

Ipperwash, he is convinced in his bones, has much to do with the Caledonia approach.

"It is huge," he says, "and it's got so many concentric circles of fallout that are happening now, it's just bizarre. It's almost like the government is just [he makes a hand-washing motion], doesn't have any more responsibilities.

"I disagree. I think they do have a responsibility to step in. Especially if you've got the minister of the attorney general in your cabinet, and that minister recognizes that the police are just way off-side—just think about policy, training and procedures and all that—then somebody has to step in and right the wrong.

"When the ship starts wandering off course," he says, "somebody's got to get it back on course."

Before he joined the OPP, Walsh spent fourteen years in the Canadian Forces, the first six as a navy diver and sonarman, the next eight as a military policeman. And from September of 1999 until July of 2000, while on leave from the OPP, he served with the United Nations civilian policing contingent in Kosovo.

"This [the lawlessness of Caledonia] doesn't happen anywhere else," he says. "I'd like somebody to say, 'Oh, here's a similar incident where we reacted the same.' Anywhere!" Even in Kosovo, Walsh says, "Just at the end of hostilities, when the Albanians and the Serbs were all killing each other, we had about twenty-two murders a day. I was the police chief in the northern city, right on the dividing line. And we'd have riots every day—five thousand people would come out of the woodwork, just on a text message, show up with guns, they'd riot.

"But I tell you, if they fucked with us, we'd have at them," he says. "It's not that we were placing ourselves in jeopardy. It's that, some-where along the line, you have to draw that line and say, 'Look, I understand that you're pissed off. I understand that you're protest-ing. I understand that you don't agree with what's happening here in your homeland.' But if you're gonna fuck with us, we're not just going to sit there and take it.

"That was the most disturbing thing about all this [Caledonia]," he says. "Coming from there, a United Nations mission in what was, at the time, almost a Third World country, no rule of law. But somehow, the rule of law *was* able to be established there. There was a line drawn, and the line that was drawn was, 'Look, there's law and order here. That's what we're here for, that's what we're paid for, this is what we're going to do. Go ahead and break windows, all that shit. That's not going to hurt anybody. [But if you're] going to hurt one of us, or somebody who's under our protection, then we're going to act.'

"That was fine. Everybody was okay with that. So I completely understand all this—people on the ground, wanting to do their jobs, being told that they have to stand up and put their hand on a Bible and swear to uphold law and order, uphold their office, and then, all of sudden, they're told, 'Well, not in this particular circumstance. You're not going to do it here.'

"With no reason why, no explanation given."

The day I interviewed Walsh at the OPPA offices in Barrie, there was a meeting of potential retirees going on the building. Walsh makes a habit of attending these, and invited me to sit in. He talked to the group a bit, then took questions from the floor. Most were about pensions and the like, but someone noted that it was public knowledge that Commissioner Fantino's contract was set to expire shortly after the G8 and G20 summits in Ontario in June of 2010, and asked Walsh who he thought would be the new commissioner.

(Walsh was concerned at the time that the integrated security unit, of which the OPP was a part and which was in charge of policing the G20 summit in Toronto, might bring Caledonia-style tactics to the protests. "It would be disastrous," he said. But although the unit, led by the Toronto Police, certainly took the modern, "measured response" approach—particularly early on, before anarchists seized control of a peaceful rally, torched police cars and ran wild through the downtown streets—they had also arrested five hundred people by the end of the first night.)

Walsh's answer was that he believed the new OPP boss had to be an outsider. (At the time, though Walsh didn't say this, Chris Lewis, Fantino's handmaiden in the pursuit of Gary McHale, was a leading contender for the job. Lewis was named Commissioner in July, 2010.) Afterwards, back in Walsh's office, I asked him about it. "It's not just the generational piece," he said, meaning that he thinks the current senior command is too tainted by Caledonia. "It's the operational approach. I think there's a severe lack of understanding of how much politics plays into the OPP." He believes the blow the OPP has suffered was significant and the organization will take a long time to recover.

"I can't imagine being more upset about it," he said. When he left the military, "the only place I wanted to go was the OPP, because I always had reverence for the OPP. And my reverence was solid up until Caledonia, and I was like, 'Man, I can't believe this has happened to the OPP.' This was just abysmal."

He didn't sound forty-seven then, but as crushed as a boy.

———

On the CaledoniaWakeUpCall website, Gary McHale calls 2006 the Year of Terrorism, 2007 the Year of Resistance and 2008 the Year of the Courts—the last being a reference to various legal actions he instigated that year as a private citizen. The title fits for another reason: In early December of 2007, but mostly in 2008, the criminal charges against Albert Douglas began winding their way through the system.

OPP officers who were there for some of Douglas's early appearances were appalled by what they saw unfolding in Courtroom No. 3 of the graceful old Cayuga courthouse—angry supporters sitting, and sometimes standing, in the body of the court, yelling out "Who is the army can arrest this judge?" and "Why don't you let him [Douglas] the fuck out?" There was audible hissing and swearing, and hostility so naked that the complete lack of security precautions genuinely began to worry the police.

These concerns were brought to the attention of several Crown attorneys and senior court officials and, indirectly, even to a couple of judges, none of whom took any action.

To appreciate how huge a breach of protocol all this is, you have to understand that Canadian courtrooms may be the last bastion of old-fashioned decorum in the country. No one is allowed to stand, ever; if there are no seats, you don't get to stay. And, generally speaking, court officers make Green Hornet parking-enforcement officers seem like easy-going slackers and utterly reasonable by comparison.

Court officers take their jobs *very* seriously. They routinely admonish people for slouching, wearing hats, talking, reading (even during breaks), placing coats or sweaters on a seat in such a way that the judge might be able to see them from the bench, note-passing, and gum-chewing (they will often make a public show of handing the offender a tissue as a receptacle for the vile substance).

I have had my cell phone ring in the Sistine Chapel at the Vatican in Rome, while the Pope's private choir was singing, and I have had it ring in Ontario Superior Court in mid-trial. While both experiences were mortifying, I think that, on the whole, the Sistine Chapel was slightly less so.

On December 19, 2007, one of the spectators in court was Trevor Miller, Douglas's co-accused in the June 9 incidents. He was sitting in the front row, near Mitch Hoffman, then a Crown attorney and, as of the fall of 2009, an Ontario Provincial Court judge. One of the OPP officers, Constable Graham Ebert, heard Miller say, as he was leaving that day, "That fucking Crown, I could take his fucking head off!" With a crowd of Douglas supporters standing just outside the doors to the courthouse, Hoffman emerged from the courtroom, obviously looking for someone, when he was approached by a native man, who asked, "Can I help you with something?"

Hoffman, preoccupied, replied, "I don't know. Who are you?"

"I'm someone who knows everyone. You'd be surprised who we know; we have pictures and we know where they live."

At that point, Miller was walking quickly towards Hoffman, who had just spotted the woman he had been trying to find and was turning towards her. Constable Kevin York stepped in front of Miller and said, "That's not a good idea."

"What you think is not a good idea," Miller replied, "I may think is a good idea. I'm not intimidated by you."

"Likewise," York replied.

The officers immediately told Hoffman what they'd seen and heard and that they considered it a threat; Hoffman expressed concern and said he'd be informing his superiors.

Towards the end of 2007, the OPP again approached court officials, who again refused to take any action. But by the new year, word of what was happening in his courthouse reached the ears of Judge David Marshall. Constable Jeff Bird, heartsick and alarmed by what he had seen, approached the judge informally at a New Year's levee.

Though Marshall had no jurisdiction to tell other judges how to conduct business in their courtrooms, he was the senior judge, and thus in charge of courthouse security. He told court officials to invoke the Public Works Protection Act, a statute that, two years later, won a bit of notoriety when, during the G20 Summit, Toronto Police used it to designate the high-security fence surrounding the conference site an Ontario "building." At its most basic, the statute allows police to ask people for identification and require them to submit to a search before entering certain public buildings—courthouses being chief among them.

Sure enough, when Douglas made his next court appearance on January 9, 2008, the PWPA was in effect, sort of: contravening the spirit of Judge Marshall's instructions, only parts of the act were being enforced, and those half-heartedly. Bags, coats, briefcases and the like were searched, but some observers not properly frisked (they refused to raise their arms, for instance), and Trevor Miller and the unknown native man who had threatened Hoffman were still allowed into the courtroom. Once there, they and other Douglas supporters remained unmolested as they stood, loudly muttering curses and epithets such as "You racist" in Hoffman's direction.

Douglas was remanded again, and as he was led out, his supporters clapped and cheered for him. A teenager standing at the very front of the courtroom looked directly at Judge Joe Nadel and shouted, in a clear voice, "You fucking piece of shit!" To the OPP in the room, there appeared to be no chance that the judge hadn't heard the remark. Constable Steve Lorch was at the front of the room, and he heard it; Constable Bird was at the back and did too. Lorch kept looking hopefully towards the judge, waiting for a nod or a signal to do something.

The judge, writing busily in a notebook, didn't lift his eyes.

———

When the Dave Brown/Dana Chatwell lawsuit began in November of 2009, there were only a few of us from what is now commonly called the mainstream media—Al Sweeney from CHCH-TV in Hamilton, who had covered so much of the Caledonia story as it unfolded; Barb Brown, *The Hamilton Spectator*'s great court reporter; and me—in attendance.

Another terrific reporter, Adrian Humphreys from *The National Post*, joined our ranks a day or so later. The Canadian Press wire service sent reporters from time to time, but our little core group never grew.

Certainly, with the exception of Sweeney and CH, television steadfastly avoided the story, and if anyone from the major national networks, CTV or CBC, ever made the trek to the courthouse, I don't remember it.

There are bigger press turnouts in Toronto for routine government announcements, let alone run-of-the-mill trials, but then, as I always tell Gary McHale, reporters are just like everyone else. What looks to him like a conspiracy of silence is, in part, attributable to television's need for "visuals," the luck of the news draw on any given day, and collective laziness.

As oxymoronic as it may seem for a group whose job has been famously described as afflicting the comfortable and comforting the afflicted, the media sometimes follows the path of least resistance, and Hamilton, like Caledonia, is just far enough from Toronto to be an irritating commute.

But what I suspect was a significant factor at play in the media coverage of the Brown trial, and of Caledonia more generally, is this: In Canada, First Nations are usually seen as the afflicted, if not as victims. It is certainly the dominant and conventional view.

Doug Fleming isn't one of those who subscribes to it. He refuses to see native Canadians through this particular prism.

"I refuse to feel sympathy for the Indians who are alive today," he says. "And I don't feel sorry for them and I won't be shamed into feeling sorry for them or feeling guilty or responsible for residential schools, for example. I won't be.

"I tell people, I say, 'I'm no more responsible for Nazi concentration camps than I am for residential schools; why would I feel bad about it?'"

Fleming's view is that soft-heartedness masks condescension.

"I actually knew a guy who survived a concentration camp," he says. "He was a Polish Jew who survived. But his kids, who were born in Canada, I got to know them. I've known people of Cambodian descent, whose ancestors were persecuted, in some cases massacred, by the Pol Pot regime. I've known Russian people whose ancestors suffered under Stalin. It never occurred to me to feel sorry for any of those people, because now they're living in a country where officially they'll never be persecuted because of their ethnic background. They have all the same opportunities as I have. It never occurred to me to feel sorry for them, and it has never occurred to me to feel sorry for the Indians."

It was on day one of the Brown trial that I clamped eyes for the first time upon McHale, who would never be described, as we called it in Rouyn-Noranda when I was a teenager, as "a good dresser," and whose girth lends him a certain bellicose posture.

Like many, I'd heard some of what Julian Fantino had said about him, thought I knew his reputation, and was keeping my distance.

But even that first day, McHale earned his chops. He wanted to be able to tape-record the proceedings—a practice allowed in Ontario courtrooms only if the presiding judge okays it—and stood up to address Ontario Superior Court Thomas Bielby.

McHale explained that he was covering the trial for his website and *The Regional*, that Christine would sometimes have to sit in for him, and so he would need a reliable record of some sort, particularly on the days he was away.

He was polite, informed and good on his feet, and Bielby allowed him to use a tape recorder.

It may have been, if not the beginning, then the early days of, the career of one of the greatest jailhouse lawyers in Canadian history. As he got deeper into the Caledonia story, McHale began filing dozens of private prosecutions—against lawbreaking occupiers the OPP had failed to charge; against senior OPP officers who had failed to act and, most famously, against OPP boss Julian Fantino himself (on a charge of influencing or attempting to influence a municipal official through his notorious email to Mayor Trainer and Haldimand Council).

The very first charge was filed by Jeff Parkinson, who, with McHale, Kinrade, Vandermaas and Ipperwash activist Mary-Lou LaPratte, founded CANACE, Canadian Advocates for Charter Equality, whose central belief is that the rule of law is the foundation of democracy. Parkinson laid a private complaint of assault against Haldimand councillor Buck Sloat in connection with an incident that happened on August 7, 2007.

The charge was eventually stayed, or stopped, by the Crown, as were many of the others subsequently laid by McHale, including the one he pressed against Fantino. But winning in court was never the point of the exercise, McHale says, though he has been remarkably successful. Rather, the purpose was "to create the paper trail for the day an inquiry [into Caledonia] is held.

"I never believed, nor do I now believe, that the Crown would ever prosecute a single case." But an inquiry, he says, "needs real evidence, courtroom-type evidence. Everything we file [in court cases] forces the government to respond in writing in a court. You can't ask for better evidence."

Still, in the thirty months leading up to June of 2010, McHale was in Ontario courtrooms about eighty times, winning a number of significant decisions, mostly in Ontario Superior Court, but once at the Ontario Court of Appeal, without a lawyer at his side. Many of the rulings pertain to a citizen's right to lay private charges, to the openness of such proceedings and to limits on the Crown's authority to withdraw charges. Most notably, he successfully defended himself on the bizarre charge of "counselling mischief not committed" the OPP laid against him on December 7, 2007.

On April 21, 2010, in Hamilton, Crown attorney Brent Bentham stood and read a short prepared statement to Judge Bernd Zabel, explaining that the Crown was staying the charge against McHale. It had been twenty-nine months since McHale was charged, and until the preceding month, when some of his bail restrictions were eased, his freedom was grossly restricted.

Outside court, Christine at his side, McHale said, "The state used all of its power to silence a citizen," and indeed, for more than two years, it had been somewhat successful. Yet in the course of defending himself, McHale managed to do what no one else— including the government, the OPP Association, the provincial opposition parties and the mainstream press—had managed to do, and that was publicly call Commissioner Fantino and a handful of other senior OPP officers to account for their actions in Caledonia.

McHale actually got Fantino to court for three days of sworn testimony, in November of 2008 and April of 2009, at his preliminary hearing on the counselling charge. There were some informative exchanges.

Once, for instance, McHale played the video of Clyde Powless decking him. He asked if Fantino could identify the assailant.

"I believe that's Clyde Powless," Fantino said.

"And how do you know him?" McHale asked.

"From contact that I've had with him directly," Fantino replied.

"So you've had face-to-face meetings with him?"

"Yes, I have," Fantino said.

At this point, Judge Zabel interrupted and asked innocently, "Well, wasn't he the one on the video clip where he looks like he's hitting Mr. McHale?"

McHale then asked several questions about whether that was appropriate conduct for a protester ("I don't know all the circumstances," Fantino said) or if Powless wasn't inciting violence.

"I don't know all the circumstances," the commissioner insisted, though if he didn't, it was not for lack of trying, given that he had been receiving hourly, contemporaneous updates that day.

"He's [Powless] obviously somewhat agitated," Fantino said, "but I don't know what provoked all that other than the fact that had you not been there, it wouldn't have happened."

He repeated constantly that, but for McHale's "agitating," Caledonia would have been a quiet and peaceful place.

In April of 2009, McHale questioned Fantino about the people in Premier McGuinty's office to whom he'd copied the email to Mayor Trainer and council.

"So," McHale said, "in an email to Haldimand council regarding a policing issue, could you explain why you attached people directly in McGuinty's office to the email?"

By way of explanation, Fantino said at one point, "This was not solely, and never has been, solely a policing issue. The matter of land claim disputes, the issues in Caledonia, have not been solely a police issue. Some people try to make it so."

Yet, when McHale asked how often he would have emailed "those same people in the government," Fantino said he couldn't say.

"Would this be just the only time, or would there be at least more than just this only time?"

"There may have been other times, yes," Fantino said. But he insisted it was "a rare example" and that none of the three to whom he'd copied the note—Tony Dean, the secretary of cabinet; Peter Wilkinson, then the premier's chief of staff; and Chris Morley, then McGuinty's press secretary—ever replied to the note.

There seemed only two plausible explanations for Fantino having copied three well-placed officials in the Premier's Office and in Cabinet on that note, with its focus on McHale and the inside-baseball minutiae of the workings of Haldimand council.

One is that the OPP boss was in such regular contact with those officials that this was just another piece of information in the flood that he was passing along, to which they felt no particular need to reply. The other is that Fantino felt the matter to be of such significance that he took the unusual step of copying these senior officials, in which case it might have been expected that they would have answered him or made inquiries.

Yet, according to Fantino, bits of both scenarios were true: he communicated with these officials rarely, he testified; but when, according to his testimony, he copied them on the bizarre note to council right out of the blue, none of them ever asked about it.

———

Shortly after Christmas of 2009, the Ontario government quietly and suddenly settled the Brown/Chatwell lawsuit for an undisclosed amount of money and no admission of liability. The attorney general's office made the announcement on Tuesday, December 29, in a terse four-line news release. A case the government had fought tooth and nail every step of the way had ended, not with a bang, but with a whimper.

On the day the trial was supposed to start, government lawyers tried to argue that Judge Bielby should recuse himself—withdraw— because of an aged, minor and fleeting business relationship between him and Brown's lawyer, John Evans.

Fourteen years before, when Bielby was himself a lawyer, the company that insures lawyers had hired Evans's firm to represent him on a professional negligence claim. The two men actually met just once over the three-year duration of that case, and the matter was resolved in Bielby's favour before trial.

Government lawyer Dennis Brown argued that the relationship nonetheless raised "a reasonable apprehension of bias" and that the judge should step aside. "It is important in this case that the Aboriginal community sees this process as being impartial, absolutely impartial," Brown said. It was clear from that remark and others, and from the government's factum, that Ontario was completely preoccupied with how the lawsuit was seen by native groups, particularly the Six Nations.

When Bielby ruled the next morning that he wasn't going to withdraw, Dennis Brown immediately stood up to announce that he had instructions to appeal. It was only after Evans made an impassioned plea to the government's lawyer to first consult his clients that the government's lawyer agreed. Court reconvened several times, only to be told by Dennis Brown that he hadn't yet received direction on how to proceed; the inference was clear that he was taking his marching orders from at least several quarters within Queen's Park.

Finally, with his ducks in a line, he returned to tell the judge the government had reconsidered and would not appeal at that time.

Lawyer David Feliciant took over once the trial proper began, and if he stuck to the government mantra that the OPP treated Caledonia as a land claims issue, not a law-and-order matter, his secondary tactic was to aggressively suggest that Brown and Chatwell had provoked native misbehavior with their own actions. The record is replete with examples of this approach, but a few will suffice.

One day, while cross-examining Brown about his arrest after the Blue Jays game in May of 2006, Feliciant noted with something akin to outrage in his voice that Brown had "squealed his tires" as he drove through the barricade and that, once at his house, he had not gone inside but instead dared to confront the protesters who had—trespassing all the while—followed him there.

Another day, with Brown still in the witness box, Feliciant played a section of the family's homemade videotape from that first summer. Brown and Chatwell were outside, talking about whether they should call the OPP; there were natives, in a couple of trucks, shining spotlights into their home. It was to capture this act—to prove it had happened—that Brown got out the camera. Suddenly, a native woman could be heard on the tape, shrieking, "Stop harassing us! Put your camera away! You're violating our rights!"

Brown can then be heard saying, "Yeah, okay . . . unbelievable."

"Did you hear that?" Feliciant asked him.

"Yes, I heard that," Brown replied.

"You continued to film?" Feliciant asked.

Brown agreed.

"Why wouldn't you have put your camera down?" Feliciant asked. "Clearly, you've agitated them."

Brown pointed out that it was the occupiers who were shining lights at his house, interfering with his right to what is called in law the peaceful of enjoyment of his home—not the other way around.

In fact, the government never disputed that much of the lawless conduct that was alleged had actually happened. But as Julian Fantino insisted, in the face of overwhelming evidence to the contrary, that Caledonia would be peaceful but for McHale, so was the government in court suggesting that Brown and Chatwell had somehow brought all this misery upon themselves. If only they had just behaved better. Throughout the piece, that is a constant theme: The victims were blamed for having provoked the occupiers to lawless behaviour.

Still, this was just one aspect of the government's defence. The first prong was that native land claims require delicate handling, and if the assertion of a land claim turns violent, traditional policing (contemporaneous arrests and enforcement) can't be used; the second was that, if natives terrorized Brown and Chatwell, the government wasn't responsible; and third, the couple was, in the vernacular, asking for it anyway.

The final plank in the government strategy was to attack Brown and Chatwell by suggesting that, as they and their family unit deteriorated—under the pressure of constant threats and intimidation, of course, with both of them drinking far too much, Brown using drugs, and the couple snapping like cornered rats at one another and anyone who came near them—they were unreliable witnesses.

This was revealed in Feliciant's minute examination of their MasterCard records, where he indicated a special interest in their liquor purchases. The tactic reached its nadir when, on the last day of the trial, he asked Chatwell about an instance of infidelity on her part.

Did the government settle to bring an end to the publicity, limited as it was, that was largely sympathetic to Brown and Chatwell?

That may have been one of the issues in play, but more significant was the fact that the settlement came less than a week before the case was scheduled to resume—and, among other witnesses, including eighteen-year-old Dax Chatwell, a number of OPP officers were slated to testify.

Because of the discovery process and disclosure rules, there are few surprises in Canadian courts; the government knew full well what those officers (some of whom had been interviewed several times over by government lawyers as if they couldn't quite believe their ears) were going to say, if asked, and that they would have told the truth.

In the middle of the trial, word spread through the courthouse that Judge David Marshall had died, unexpectedly, on November 20 at the age of seventy. A week later, his funeral service was held at St. Paul's Anglican Church in Dunnville; the trial didn't sit that day, and most, if not all, of the lawyers attended the funeral.

The man who had done so much for the people of Haldimand County and had acted so bravely in defence of the rule of law would never know of the small measure of justice dispensed to Dave Brown and Dana Chatwell.

———

There's one thing that makes Toby Barrett proud.

"I give Caledonia credit, especially in the first six months or so," he says. "They literally, physically, fought for their town, with their fists. The young guys, all the hockey guys and baseball teams, down at the barricades. No, Caledonia fought."

He credits native youth, too. "The Six Nations guys and the young guys in Caledonia, it was always fists. No knives, no handguns, nothing like that. We are of the same culture as far as that. No one else has anywhere [the other Haldimand towns where developments were stopped], as far as I'm aware. Caledonia did. I give them credit for that."

During the worst of it, he had a few lads on his own speed dial, for unofficial security. "You have a community here," he says, "with no government to help out, no police, no assistance. Everything has purposefully and completely been put into their own hands," he says.

"They [Caledonians] didn't take the law into their own hands. It was forced into their hands. And what do you do? How do you protect your kids when you have to go to work every morning, you've got to drive to Mississauga and your wife's home alone? Or your kids, they're at the school? You can't hang around every day."

People looked to those few fellows, Barrett says, who were "our law."

"Is it *Lord of the Flies*, or maybe *Survivor*? I don't watch that shit. But where the community is on its own, the real world kicks in, and then you turn to those people who have the skills or the muscle."

Out of necessity, he says, townspeople looked to the handful who would step into that void: the toughs at the barricades; Doug Fleming and his brother Randy (both widely believed to have been among those who shimmied up flagpoles at night to remove some of the Mohawk Warrior flags that so offended townspeople); and, in an entirely different way, to Gary McHale.

When we met on a warm day late in the spring of 2010, just down the road from DCE, Barrett had already had a couple of hundred responses to a survey he'd sent out to sixty thousand homes in the riding. There was no Caledonia question per se, he says. "It was just,

'What do you want Toby Barrett to work on?'" Yet the overwhelming response, in addition to the usual plea to get rid of taxes, was Caledonia. Often, in big letters, people wrote, "BRING IN THE ARMY!"—even now, with the occupation in its fifth year.

"It's unconscionable what has happened here," he says. "Good people around here, including me, we always thought we had government for a reason. We always thought government was there, or somebody was there, especially when the shit really hits the fan. It turns out, they're the ones that leave first—government [itself] or represented through the OPP or other stuff. They're just not there. It's like, 'Dive for the office and close the door.'

"It's a stereotype, but that is exactly what happened here," he says. "When you most needed help from societal institutions for whatever reason, they were gone—political reasons. You know, in a Cabinet minister's office, it's like the first thing is, 'Okay, we gotta do this and cover our ass and say this,' to all the way down the line."

Toby Barrett knows his riding inside out. He does a lot of knocking on doors, year in and year out, and always has. What he has noticed since DCE is an absence of noise.

"You never hear Skil saws or hammers in Haldimand County," he says mournfully. "Nobody's building anything. People would tell me—like, in Dunnville—they want to do a back porch. [Now,] they don't even do that. They're afraid someone might come and tell them you can't do that."

In the Legislature, oddly enough, it's much the same; it is the absence of sound that now greets mention of Caledonia. Barrett draws a parallel to the time when he was part of the Harris government and the Liberals would raise the subject of Ipperwash. The government would hold its breath, and "you could hear a pin drop. When I raise Caledonia, basically, you can hear a pin drop. And I don't raise it so much now, because we're now in a stalemate—the kind of burned-out stage, in a way."

"What should happen now?" I ask. "Should people just move on?"

"Appeasement? Move on? No no. That's not an option. That's

very dangerous to think that way. I refer to it as the burr under the saddle. You have to get that burr out from under the saddle, or you have other serious problems that can develop.

"No, you can't move on, [sing] kumbaya, [say,] 'Let's all be friends.'

"That's fine," he says, "that's one approach, but you can't, because of that symbolic occupation.

"The barricades are still right there, in front. The gantry, the power towers. The Hydro One power tower should not be lying right beside the main street of Caledonia. The burned-out trailer is still there. I can see the power towers from here. There's no wires on those towers."

He struggles, as do others in town, with the fact that he often seems not to be believed.

Once, for instance, he raised in the legislature an incident in May of 2007, in which a Six Nations man named Donald VanEvery had been spotted on DCE with an AK-47, which he then used in a shooting at an illegal smoke shop (nearly taking off a man's arm in the process). VanEvery was charged; the incident is documented as having happened. Yet, Barrett says, "I raise these issues in the Ontario Legislature and am mocked. There's these expressions of 'Shock!' [from the government benches] and 'Barrett's lost it—he's too involved with this.'

"No," he insists, and here he is practically yelling, "it's an AK-47!"

———

I first met the Rauschers at the Brown/Chatwell trial in the fall of 2009. They came frequently, and throughout Brownie's testimony, I often could hear Maria sobbing in the row behind me. As an easy crier myself, I dared not look at her very much. But I told them about the book, got their number and promised to call.

In the spring of 2010, I went to two rallies in Caledonia, one organized by Gary McHale, the other a Doug Fleming smoke shack protest. These surely rank among the strangest events I've ever attended.

After years of being at one another's throats, filled with mistrust, virtually everyone now videotapes everyone else.

McHale supporters record the "anti-racists" (consisting of many students from out of town—or, in Fantino-speak, interlopers) and natives who show up to shout them down. The "anti-racists" and natives videotape the McHale side. Often, the OPP is there, videotaping both sides videotaping one another.

I even found myself having what I thought were normal and private conversations a couple of times, only to realize I was also on camera. In one instance, I was chatting away with a *Spectator* reporter—I thought as colleagues—when I noticed a tape recorder in the palm of his hand.

"Are you taping me?" I asked.

He was. He hadn't asked if he might. He had just gone ahead and done it.

In any case, I saw the Rauschers at these rallies too. So, though I'd heard they'd left town and were living elsewhere, they still seemed to be very much a part of the Caledonia furniture. On some level, I now think, I had avoided talking to them because I suspected how wrenching the experience would be. Again, I got their number.

With Dieter's careful directions in hand, I drove to their apartment in Burlington, just off busy Plains Road, at about 2:30 P.M. on Friday, April 23. They were my last planned interview. I don't think I left the apartment until after six o'clock that evening.

By this point, I'd gone past their former place, the graceful and sprawling house on the Sixth Line, a number of times. I'd seen Maria's splendid gardens, noticed how the trees they'd planted decades earlier had grown up tall and straight. I was unprepared for their new quarters: a nice and perfectly serviceable two-bedroom apartment, but a far cry from the four-bedroom country house on more than two acres.

They had the house up for sale for two and a half years; it took that long even to get an offer. The deal closed on May 20, 2009. They got $215,000 for a property that, according to what real-estate brokers call a comparative market analysis, ought to have been worth $420,000 (though Dieter, frank to a fault, says he thinks $380,000 would have been fairer). Minus the usual fees, not to mention the money they'd poured into it before they left—aware that, as Maria says, "We had to make it as nice as possible"—they couldn't, as two retired folks in their sixties, afford to buy another place.

I noticed there were no plants on the balcony. Near tears, Maria nodded in confirmation. Just two days earlier, at her behest, they had driven by their old place so she could see the flowers coming up. She burst into tears as she told me that.

A lot of my tape from that day is of Maria, sobbing so hard I could barely make out what she was trying to say. When she composed herself, we looked at pictures of the house and garden, which seemed to calm her. I asked if they had one of Pete, their old dog, and they found some.

"Now when you drive by, you see all the spring flowers," she said. "You garden; you know yourself. A garden looks different every year. We must have put in thousands of bulbs on one side of the house, tulips and daffodils. They're blooming right now, and the magnolias too."

Maria tried to explain a few things to the Hamilton couple who bought the house. They're nice, she said. "He was hugging me the one time, said how beautiful it was. I said to her [the wife], 'Don't let that [the size of the garden] overpower you. You can always close things up. You don't have to do this. It's your house' . . .

"So many things come in your head," she said. "We couldn't stay there anymore.

"When we were moving, I was so distraught. I think I most likely had a little stroke at one time [the previous August]. I was writing a card, tried to write this one letter and I couldn't—I couldn't do it. Then—it took a while—all of a sudden, I could do it again.

"But I couldn't let on; I didn't even tell him [Dieter]," Maria said.

They never left one another alone. "If I went into town to meet my friends, he would go for a walk."

Even Pete wouldn't go outside by himself anymore; he knew there was something outside. The sudden boarding-up of windows; the times he was left with friends; the omnipresent tension had aged the Lab beyond his years.

"It didn't take much, and I would start bawling in Tim Hortons," Maria said.

One of her really bad days was when the people came from the Ontario housing ministry.

"We really thought we were going to get something," Dieter said, "because they were there and they seemed to be genuinely listening to you. But they just take the notes . . ."

They were asked the civilian version of what the OPP would always ask: "Did they [the occupiers] physically hurt you?"

"That was the first question," Dieter said. "'Were you physically hurt?' That was the police."

"And you would look and say, 'But that's my biggest fear!'" Maria said. "I'd rather be dead right away than be like that builder [Sam Gualtieri], be crippled. That was our biggest fear."

They told me about an experience they had, when they lived in Hamilton, with a bad neighbour. There were drugs and motorcycles, Maria said, "and I was quite feisty." She did a little research and found out that only a petition from area residents would do the trick. "So I went to the whole neighbourhood," she said, laughing. "'The bitch next door,' that was me, right? And I got rid of them.

"But that was when I was young," she said.

"That was when you lived in a place where the rule of law applied," I said. "You played by the rules, and the rules worked."

"That's why your blood pressure goes through the roof," Dieter said, "and you just hold on."

There were times, Maria said, "when I really thought I was going to do myself in, and I said so. Because, yeah, we will never really be the same people anymore. I had the papers to become a Canadian citizen; I ripped them up. I will never be a Canadian citizen. If I was younger, even fifty years old, I would leave this country."

Dieter said in his quiet way, "You heard sympathy; you heard empathy. You hoped something is going to happen. Nothing."

So they moved, because finally they got an offer and because, finally, they had to leave.

"I know it must have been sad," I said, "but was there any relief?"

"Calling this a home," Dieter replied calmly, his level gaze taking in the apartment, "is not there yet."

"We're better now," said Maria. "But in the beginning, I could never say, 'We're going home.' We'd say, 'We're going back to the place.' I would wake up and think I'm in a hotel. I didn't want to be here."

They went out almost compulsively. They put fifty thousand kilometres on the car, driving to casinos, where Maria would play the slots to keep her mind off her life, and then on road trips—to the Maritimes, to northern Ontario. They liked that.

"They stole four years of our life—all of our lives," Maria said. "Years which we cannot afford. We are actually old. I never felt old before, but now I'm old. I cannot afford a day out of my life and you stole those years from me!"

At another point, crying again, she said of the apartment, "All you see here now is—I live here. I do it for him. For me, I could live in one room. I could care less. I just do it because, well, I guess life goes on. But my heart is not in it. And I tell you, so help me God, every morning I wake up and I'm thinking, 'Am I dead? No, I'm not dead. Why don't you kill me kill me dead dead dead?' I have to live because of him—I don't want to.

"I'm a broken person, I'm just broken."

They hardly see their grown-up children anymore. This is the worst of their story. "I don't know what to say to them," Maria said, sobbing. "I'm a broken person." If it gets too bad, sometimes she talks to her friend Pauline. "But I can't say too much," she said. "You cannot burden people with all this."

Once, in front of one of her daughters, she let it all out, "because something was upsetting me, and I said I want to be dead and all there was was screaming.

"They don't even like us anymore," she said, her face red from crying, tears streaming down.

"Because we're difficult," Dieter said in his soft voice.

"We're difficult people," Maria said. "But how to get things back? How do you get your spirit back? I was always the cheerful person."

She remembered—as if talking about someone else, as if wondering when that person left the room—the farewell party when she left her job at the home for the disabled in Hamilton. The quality her colleagues mentioned most was her cheerful nature.

When the Rauschers heard, so long ago now, about the plans for Douglas Creek Estates, they were so excited. They knew, then, that they could stay for the long haul, because the isolation of the Sixth Line, which might have been more difficult for them as they grew older, would be no more.

"We wanted to live there in a comfortable home," Maria said, so they built a rear extension, with a laundry room, so she wouldn't have to hump it to the laundromat in town anymore.

The plan called for the new houses to come right up to their backyard. "And I said to him, 'We won't have to go anywhere,'" Maria said. Young families, with children, would be moving in; there would be youngsters to show through the garden. They could even pay teenagers to cut the grass. "Neighbour kids, I would say, 'You can come and look. You can help.' So I said to him, there will be lots of kids, if they want to come over and learn a bit of gardening."

"There'll be some life here," Dieter said.

"Lawnmowers going," Maria said. "We were so excited. It gave us almost a lifeline to stay. Even if something had happened to him or me, I wouldn't have been afraid to stay because there would be people. It was just so promising."

Maria remembered a day in the Zehrs supermarket in Caledonia when she saw the ex of a friend, a native man. "I said, 'Peter, we shared meals together. We were like families. Your kids were in my house, my kids were in your house. In all those times, you never came once to tell us that we didn't have to be frightened for our life, you never inquired how we were, and I just want to ask you why.'"

The man looked down, then looked back at Maria, and "all he could say was, 'I should have.' And I said, 'That's good enough for me.'"

Months later—they had the for-sale sign on the house by then—Maria ran into a relative of that man. She went over and sat down at his table.

"He goes to me, 'Your house is for sale.' I said yeah. He looks at me and goes, 'I wouldn't have to pay for your house,' meaning, because he's native, he could just take it.

"So I'm thinking, 'Did I hear this?' I said to him, 'Over my dead body.'

"You know what he responded? He said, 'This can be arranged.'"

She was still shaking when she got home.

As shattering as it was to talk to the Rauschers, as depressed as Maria was when I saw them, my hunch was they'd made the right call.

In January of 2010, on one of my trips to Caledonia, I had picked up a copy of the *Turtle Island News*, the Six Nations paper. It was the January 13 edition. Dominating the front page was a story about a group led by Dick Hill that had recently stopped the construction of a new Six Nations police station. Since Dick Hill stopping development was by then a classic of dog-bites-man, I cannot resist the impulse to ask how on earth this qualified as news.

The second piece was about a native bank taking Ottawa to court over a loan program.

Inside, on page 7 and clearly of no particular import, was a small story headlined, "Six Nations band council wants to buy land nearby." It turned out, as the lead paragraph said, that Chief Bill Montour said the idea wouldn't fly because the council didn't have any money.

What was startling was the following passage, beginning with the fourth paragraph, which I quote here without any editing:

> "Why would we buy it, why wouldn't we just take it?" asked councillor Helen Miller.

Councillor Melba Thomas added, "Shouldn't we do that too, with the house that's been vacated? At DCE?", referring to the house that was owned by Dave Brown and Dana Chatwell as part of the settlement of their lawsuit against the provincial government.

In a later interview, Montour said that council wouldn't "just take" land held by a third party. "We've always said we would never dispose third-party interest in land because it's not their fault," he said.

However, asked about Thomas' comment concerning the Brown-Chatwell house, Montour said "something" should be done.

Two days after the publication of the paper, on January 15, 2009, the government did something, all right: bulldozers moved in to raze Brownie's old house.

So it is better, probably, that Maria and Dieter Rauscher should live in a rented flat than in a part of Canada where duly elected councillors—speaking in public, on the record, before a gallery that includes reporters—feel absolutely free to muse aloud about whether council should simply take over land and property without paying for it, and where such pronouncements are deemed unnewsworthy enough not to warrant the front page.

Besides, about two months after our interview, I phoned Maria Rauscher one day to double-check on something she'd said. She was feeling much better, she told me, and her balcony was now overflowing with plants and looked like a jungle.

It takes so very little to make the garden that is the human heart flourish.

Appendix A

OPP News Realease, December 16, 2006.

Ontario Provincial Police
Police provinciale de l'Ontario

O.P.P.

Caledonia Detachment

32 Unity Side Road
Caledonia, Ontario
N3W 1Y2

news
release
communiqué

Detachment Commander Inspector Dave McLean

FROM: Sgt. Dave Rektor   RELEASE: 16 DEC 06
DE: PUBLICATION LE:

POLICE TAKE ACTION TO KEEP THE PEACE IN CALEDONIA
SEVERAL ARRESTED

(Caledonia, Ont) Members of the Ontario Provincial Police arrested two people today, Saturday, December 16th, 2006, during a demonstration at Douglas Creek Estates in Caledonia.

Protestors attended Caledonia for a flag raising rally which was to take place at the Canadian Tire store at 11:30am under the leadership of a male party from outside of Caledonia. The rally was organized under the pretext that it was in "Support of Our Troops" but was really an attempt to disrupt the peace and agitate local inhabitants in Caledonia.

The organizer of the rally had been stopped by police prior to attending the rally and questioned as to his intentions. He said to police that his intent was **"just to make you guys look like a bunch of assholes like you already do".**

Despite numerous warnings from the O.P.P. to the organizer of the event, he and another male defied police requests to stay away from the Douglas Creek site and incited a small group of peaceful protestors to become hostile toward police.

Officers from the Toronto Police Service attended the rally and assisted the O.P.P. in maintaining the peace and preventing any serious occurrences from happening. Commissioner Fantino stated" I am proud and thankful to all of the officers, they did an excellent job of keeping the peace and preventing this from escalating into something more serious. Most people used good judgment and stayed away from the rally. These demonstrations will not help to resolve the issues in Caledonia".

The Ontario Provincial Police would like to thank the Toronto Police Service and everyone for their support. Hopefully, negotiations will continue and a peaceful resolution will be reached for everyone.

-30-

Contact: Caledonia Media Office
905-765-9453

Appendix B

OPP Commisioner Julian Fantino's email to
Clyde Powless's defence lawyer, December 4, 2008

———

ⓘ You forwarded this message on 12/4/2008 6:51 PM.

From:	Fantino, Julian (JUS) [Julian.Fantino@ontario.ca] Sent: Thu 12/4/2008 5:44
To:	Joseph Di Luca
Cc:	
Subject:	Clyde Powless
Attachments:	

View As Web P

To the Honourable Court:

In my capacity as the Commissioner of the Ontario Provincial Police I have known Mr. Powless for the past two years.

As well, since taking office I have become directly involved in a number of meetings and dialogue with members of the Six Nations Confederacy in mutual effort to keep the peace in Caledonia where many flare-ups have taken place resulting from historical land claim disputes that have necessitated the deployment of an extraordinary amount of OPP resources when flare-ups and conflict has erupted.

Much of the conflict, confrontation and provocation has occurred during the times that Mr. Gary McHale and his followers have converged on Caledonia that invariably resulted in heightened tensions and conflict that has required an extraordinary deployment of police resources in our efforts to preserve the peace.

Although I am not in a position to address the specific circumstances that resulted in criminal charges being brought against Mr. Powless, I do feel that but for Mr. McHale's mischief-making forays into Caledonia, the very volatile situation that exists there would not have escalated time and again as it has virtually every time Mr. Mchale came to town.

I am not making excuses or apologies for Mr. Powless's actions about which he is accused, however, and with respect, the Honourable Court may wish to consider the volatility of the situation and provocation that simply could have been avoided but for the presence of Mr. McHale and his like minded followers.

As well, I wish to advise the Honourable Court that on a number of occasions Mr. Powless has been instrumental in diffusing serious conflict and confrontation during which times he has actually been the peace-maker.

Respectfully submitted.

J. Fantino, Commissioner
Ontario Provincial Police

Sent using BlackBerry

Acknowledgements

———

THE PEOPLE OF CALEDONIA already have my affection and regard; they also deserve my thanks.

After years of seeing their story diminished in the press, being told they were wrong or mistaken or worse by their government and after going to more meetings with more bureaucrats than any single group of human beings should have to endure, they were receptive and cooperative when I came calling.

Almost everyone allowed me to use their names, an act which in this country should never require plaudits, but in these circumstances does. There's a handful of others who can't be identified, and I thank them too. They know how much I owe them.

Special thanks to Don and John Henning, from whom I learned a little about hunting seasons and much more, and Gary and Christine McHale.

John Evans and Michael Bordin, the Hamilton lawyers who represented Dave Brown and Dana Chatwell, inspired me. On your worst days, your lawyer may be your only friend in the world; Dave and Dana were lucky to have these two in their corner.

There are several people whose particular stories didn't make it into *Helpless*, but who helped inform me nonetheless. Their omission here is no reflection upon the wisdom of what they had to tell me.

My editor at Doubleday Canada, Tim "Bond" Rostron, largely incomprehensible because of accent and bizarre Britspeak, was an absolute doll. So was my editor at *The Globe and Mail*, David Walmsley. I remain grateful to work for a newspaper which encourages its writers to write.

Friends and family were—as ever—full of humour and patience for my spectacular crabbiness. As Moose Anweiler said when he phoned the day after I'd finished and I didn't bite off his head for the first time in months, "You must be done. Your voice is different." I love you all.

Finally, to the one person I never met, the late Ontario Superior Court Judge David Marshall: He was a lonely advocate for the rule of law in Caledonia and never did he lose his courage.

A grateful nod to the great Canadian rocker Neil Young, to whom I listen compulsively. It was his fine song "Helpless" that gave me the title to the book.

Index

—

Anderson, Bill, 172, 173
  automobiles
    theft of, 4–5, 15–17, 112–13
    thrown over side of bridge, 63
    vandalism of, 25, 69–70, 121

Babbit, Acting Supt. Doug, 164
Barnsley, Paul, 144
Barrett, Cari (wife of Toby), 112
Barrett, Theobald Butler (Toby), 23–24,
    37–38, 130, 237–39
  criticism of land offer, 113–14
  disappointment with job done by
    OPP, 109–11
  loss of car, 111–12
  questions in Legislature about
    Caledonia, 145
  visits to Caledonia, 47–50, 148–49
Beatty, Steve, 92
Beechey, Chief Supt. Larry, 141–42
Bentham, Brent, 231
Best, Karen, 151, 154
Bielby, Mr. Justice Thomas, 229–30,
    233–34
Bird, Const. Jeff, 58, 80, 172, 173,
    175–76, 227, 228
Boniface, Commissioner Gwen, 30, 31,
    32, 138–41, 142, 157–58

Boniface, Gary (husband of Gwen),
    140–41
"bootstrapping," 193–94
Boxer, Cathy, 9
Brown, Barb, 228
Brown, Dave, 58
  accused of vandalizing own home,
    173–74
  arrest after Blue Jays game, 80–84
  bugging of house by OPP, 172–76, 203
  home demolished, 246
  lawsuit against Ontario government,
    12, 33, 55, 174, 175, 201, 203,
    228–30, 233–36
Brown, Dennis, 105–6, 107, 234
Bruder, Michael, 38, 40, 41, 46, 59, 87,
    106, 115, 116
Bryant, Michael, 166–67
Burke, John, 87, 115
Burns, Mary Ann, 35–38
Burtch Correctional Centre, 105–6,
    113–14
Butler, Col. John, 23–24

Cain, Supt. John, 55, 83, 173–74, 177, 210
Caledonia, Ontario. *See also* Haldimand
    County, Ontario
  advertising campaign, 2, 134–35

demonstration at Thistlemoor
  subdivision, 18–20
distrust of media, 101, 105
divide within community over blame,
  133–34
hostility towards OPP, 35–38, 79–80,
  83, 127, 154, 190
lack of confidence in OPP, 12–13, 73,
  184, 198, 216–17
non-native blockade of Argyle Street,
  88–89, 111–12
opponents of occupation labelled as
  racist, 193–94
paranoia resulting from DCE
  occupation, 12, 59, 239–40
use of "you know what," 22
Caledonia Citizens Alliance, 78, 105,
  115–16, 132–38, 152–53, 195
"Caledonia hardtack," 18
Caledonia Regional Chamber of
  Commerce, 132–33
CaledoniaWakeUpCall.com, 101–3,
  150–51, 180, 181
CANACE, Canadian Advocates for
  Charter Equality, 162, 230
Canadian Press, 228
Carr, Doug, 84
Carson, John, 34
Carter, Staff Sgt. Phil, 91, 216–17, 218
Cayuga, Ontario, 113
CBC Newsworld, 90
Chadwick, Rob, 84, 86, 87, 115
Chambers, Stephanie, 96, 145, 157, 194
Chatwell, Dana, 80–81, 82, 91, 155, 173,
  187, 205
  home demolished, 246
  lawsuit against Ontario government,
    12, 55, 174, 175, 201, 203, 228–30,
    233–36
Chatwell, Dax, 80, 173, 236
Chausse, Bo, 155
CHCH-TV, 5–11, 17, 46, 112, 199, 228
CHML radio, 87–88
Clairmont, Susan, 79–80, 200–203
clan mothers, 34, 49, 91
Clark, Jason, 78, 105, 115–16, 136–38, 155
Cohen, Stanley, 93–94, 95
Cousens, Doug, 160
Cowan, Det. Sgt. Bernie, 160–61

Coyle, Michael, 53
curfews, 71, 81–82

Dancey, Jack, 123–24
Dean, Tony, 182, 233
Deane, Ken (Tex), 57
Dennis, Chief Supt. Bill, 164–65
Deseronto, Ontario, Mohawk protests,
  216
Diana, Chris, 106–7, 117
Dickey, Steven, 14–17
Doering, Ron, 104
dog-whistle questions, 145–46
Doiron, Monique, 137
Douglas, Albert Kirk, 15–17, 225–28
Douglas, Russell, 58
Douglas Creek Estates (DCE)
  erection of blockade by natives, 29
  injunction granted against occupiers,
    38–42
  native "information session," 28
  offer to purchase from smoke shop
    operators, 43–45
  OPP raid, 52–58
  OPP told to avoid, 35–36, 219–21
  origin of name, 58
  pace of site cleanup, 138
  scope of development, 26
Doxtdator, Darrell, 106
Dudych, Chris, 129–31
Dunnville, Ontario, 109, 113
Dwyer, Denise, 107

Ebert, Const. Graham, 226
Evans, John, 174, 201, 233–34

Fantino, Commissioner Julian, 165, 199
  angry email to Mayor Trainer, 183–84
  anti-McHale press release, 163
  appointment as OPP commissioner,
    156–59
  character reference for Powless,
    210–11, 248
  charge of influencing municipal
    official, 183–85, 230
  Hamilton Spectator interview,
    200–203
  reaction to Dave Hartless article,
    178–79

speculation about successor, 224–25
targeting of Gary McHale, 181–83,
    200–201, 204–5, 207–9, 211, 247,
    248
testimony at Brown/Chatwell
    lawsuit, 201
testimony at Gary McHale trial,
    231–33
threat not to renew Haldimand
    County police contract, 182–83,
    201, 232–33
visit to DCE, 220–21
Fantino, Gregory (son of Julian), 159
federal government
    claims no jurisdiction in Caledonia,
        53
    denies validity of Plank Road Tract
        land claim, 27, 137
    lawyer's statement on progress at
        Caledonia, 106
    presence at negotiating table, 136
Feliciant, David, 175–76, 234–38
Findlay, John, 178–79
fires, 60, 63–65, 75, 76, 89
Fleming, Doug, 24, 186, 229, 237
    illegal sale of cigarettes, 189–91
    smoke shack protest, 203–11
Fleming, Randy (brother of Doug), 237
Flood, Greg, 209
Forbes, Don, 26
"Friday Night Fights," 78–79

G20 summit (Toronto), 224, 227
Garbutt, Nick, 5–12, 17, 199
Garda Siochana (Irish national police),
    140
Gates, Daryl, 208
General, David, 39, 103, 188, 199
Gentle, Supt. Ron, 12, 53, 57, 196, 204–5
George, Dudley, 31, 34, 57, 139
George, Luke (brother of Ron), 31
George, Reg (brother of Dudley), 34
George, Reg (father of Dudley), 31
George, Robert (father of Ron), 31
George, Insp. Ron (Spike), 30–34, 53, 55,
    139, 173, 192
    direction of Aboriginal Relations
        Team, 30
    impaired-driving charge, 194–95

prevents exchange of intelligence,
    145
relationship with Dick Hill, 144,
    195–96
testimony at Ipperwash Inquiry,
    32–34
George, Sam (brother of Dudley), 139, 191
George, Vince (brother of Ron), 31, 195
Getty, Insp. Mel, 39, 42, 78
Geysons, Det. Sgt. Roger, 219, 222
Golke, Guenter, 3–5, 6
Golke, Kathe, 3–5, 6
Goodall, Bob, 207
Goodman, Andrew, 162–63
Grand River Conservation Authority, 138
Grice, Craig, 180–83
Gualtieri, Joe (brother of Sam), 198
Gualtieri, Michelle (daughter of Sam),
    197
Gualtieri, Sam, 196–99
Gualtieri, Sandra (wife of Sam), 198

Hagan, Brian (father of Kyle), 209
Hagan, Gail (mother of Kyle), 205
Hagan, Kyle, 205
Hagersville, Ontario, 109
Haggith, Insp. Brian, 11–13, 18, 34, 39,
    56, 143, 145
Haldimand County, Ontario, 21–23
    advertising campaign, 2, 134–35
    condemnation of Gary McHale, 180
    denied seat at main negotiating
        table, 135
    Fantino email to Mayor Trainer,
        183–84
    Fantino threat not to renew police
        contract, 182–83, 201
    natives' interference with municipal
        services, 65, 70
    notification of Six Nations about
        DCE plans, 27–28, 29
    opposition to Hennings' injunction,
        40, 43
    relations with natives, 24–25, 46
    state of emergency declared, 90
Haldimand Law Association, 106–8
Hald-Nor Credit Union, 42
Halton Regional Police, 180
Hamilton Police Service, 179–80

The Hamilton Spectator, 17, 180
Harper, Stephen, 150
Harris, Mike, 191
Hartless, Dave, 118, 136
 arrest of wife Linda, 125–27
 articles posted on
  CaledoniaWakeUpCall, 121,
  164–65, 177–79
 designation as zero-tolerance
  enforcement target, 176–77
 gag order imposed by Hamilton
  Police, 179–80
 Night of the Rocks, 123–25
 testimony at Gary McHale trial,
  153–54
 Thistlemoor "resident response
  plan," 121–23
 vehicles vandalized by native
  occupiers, 68–70, 121
 witnessing of theft of U.S. government vehicle, 13–16, 18
Hartless, Linda, 69–70, 125–27
Haudenosaunee Confederacy Council,
 25, 39, 53, 103–4, 210
Hellingman, Tricia, 45
Henco Industries. *See* Henning, Don;
 Henning, John
Henning, Don, 25–28, 45–47
 injunction granted against occupiers,
  38–42
 job-site office broken into, 59
 media appearances, 45, 85, 87–88
 negotiations to sell DCE, 84–85,
  86–87, 104–6, 114–17
 precarious financial situation, 42–43
 reaction to OPP raid, 56
 sends children out of town, 61
Henning, Jack (father of Don and John),
 26
Henning, John, 25–28, 45–47, 89–90
 injunction granted against occupiers,
  38–42
 media appearances, 45, 85, 87–88
 negotiations to sell DCE, 84–85,
  86–87, 105–6, 114–17
 precarious financial situation, 42–43
 reaction to OPP raid, 56
 regrets seeking injunction, 58–59
 sends children out of town, 60–61

Henning, Julie (wife of Don), 117
Hewitt, Ken, 78, 132
Hill, Dick, 144, 195–96, 216, 220, 245
Hill, Gilbert (Gibber), 119
Hill, Hazel (wife of Dick), 118, 144
Hillman, Det. Sgt. Dave, 143, 172–76
Hoffman, Mitch, 226–27, 228
Hope, Jay, 153
Howe, Det. Insp. Angie, 208, 209
Humphreys, Adrian, 228
Hutchison, Ann, 140

Ipperwash Inquiry, 138–40, 171, 191–94,
 223

Jamieson, Janie, 29, 30, 38, 48, 49, 50,
 56, 112, 196
Jamieson, Chief Roberta, 27–28
Jean, Michaëlle, 49
Johnson, Brenda, 91
Johnson, Junior, 145
Jones, Robin, 52

King, Martin Luther, 151–52
Kinrade, Merlyn, 132, 183–85, 186–88, 209
Kinrade, Olivia, 188
Knapp, Philip, 15
Kohoko, Const. Monty, 145
Kwinter, Monte, 140, 157, 183–85

LaPratte, Mary-Lou, 154, 230
Lariviere, Will, 83
Laughing, Michael, 47, 93–95, 202
Leendertse, Deputy Chief Ken, 165,
 179–80
Lewis, Deputy Commissioner Chris, 63,
 204–5, 208, 219–22, 225
Linden, Mr. Justice Sidney, 171, 191–94
Lions Clubs, 152, 187–88
Lorch, Const. Steve, 228
Luimes, Ralph, 42, 78, 115–16, 136, 138,
 144

MacKay, Ken, 5–11, 17, 199
MacNaughton, Allen, 44, 103, 199
Maracle, Steve, 55
"March for Freedom," 151–55
Marin, André, 185
Marshall, Albert (friend of Hennings), 26

Marshall, Albert (son of David), 168–69

Marshall, Mr. Justice David, 21, 22, 227, 236
    concern about rule of law, 85-86, 105–8
    impatience with ongoing occupation, 115–16
    rules native occupiers in contempt of injunction, 40–42
    rulings overturned, 166–69

Masecar, Bob, 64

Matheson, Mr. Justice Barry, 38

McCarthy, Ed, 106–8

McDougall, Barbara, 104

McGuinty, Dalton
    apology for death of Dudley George, 191
    denies Cabinet directing OPP, 146
    described as spineless, 125
    failure to visit Caledonia, 150, 177
    Fantino emails to top staff, 181–82, 232–33
    premature confirmation of purchase of DCE land, 114

McHale, Brian (brother of Gary), 211–12

McHale, Christine (wife of Gary), 96–97, 98, 100, 152, 211, 212–13, 215–16

McHale, Donna (wife of Greg), 212

McHale, Gary, 150–56, 165
    arrest at flag rally, 161–63
    assaulted by Powless, 206, 210–11
    banned from Caledonia, 210
    charge of "counselling mischief not committed," 153–54, 209–10, 231–33
    charges filed by, 230–31
    childhood, 211–12
    complaint filed against Fantino, 183–85
    coverage of Brown/Chatwell trial, 229–30
    dissatisfaction with coverage of Caledonia, 95–97
    failed attempts to rent Lions halls, 152, 187–88
    Fantino email attacks against, 181–83
    flag rally, 155–56, 159–63
    launch of CaledoniaWakeUpCall website, 101–3
    "March for Freedom," 151–55
    moves to Binbrook, 211
    needling of MP Bryon Wilfert, 97–100
    religious beliefs, 213–15
    targeted by OPP, 204–5

McHale, Greg (brother of Gary), 212, 213

McHale, Leo (father of Gary), 212

McHale, Lucy (mother of Gary), 211

McLean, Insp. Dave, 127, 144, 164, 177–78, 204

McLeod, Rod, 183–85

McMaster, Jamie, 132

media
    Caledonians' distrust of, 101, 105
    coverage of Brown/Chatwell trial, 228–29
    criticism by Fantino, 200–201
    Hamilton, 5–11, 17, 46, 87–88, 112
    local, 78
    national, 90, 228
    native, 55, 144, 245–46
    Toronto, 49–50, 95–96, 102, 157

Meyer, Jim, 93

Miller, Derry, 139

Miller, Helen, 245

Miller, Scott, 91

Miller, Susie, 91

Miller, Trevor Dean, 15, 17, 226–27

Mohawk Warriors
    comparison to Hells Angels, 55
    flying of flag at DCE, 73, 88, 95, 111, 129, 155, 164, 237
    identification of native occupiers with, 50, 77
    involvement with occupation of DCE, 53–55, 102, 120, 144
    Ron George's description, 33

Montour, Chief Bill, 29, 44–45, 103–4, 245–46

Montour, Floyd, 149

Montour, Ruby, 149–50

Morley, Chris, 182, 233

Mullan, Chief Brian, 164–65

Nadel, Mr. Justice Joe, 228

native occupiers
    assault on CHCH news crew, 5–12
    blockade of Argyle Street, 2, 28, 60, 94–95

blockade of Argyle Street dismantled,
    92–93, 111–12
blockade of rail line, 60, 106, 118–20
checkpoints established by, 65
disrespect for courtroom decorum,
    225–28
fires set by, 60, 63–65, 75, 76, 89
found in contempt of injunction,
    40–42
immunity against being arrested,
    35–38, 122–25
imposition of curfews on non-
    natives, 71, 81–82
injunction against, 38–40
issuing of "passports," 72–73
protected from non-natives by OPP,
    78–80
rock-throwing, 123–27
rolling pickets in surrounding towns,
    109
spread of occupation beyond DCE,
    60, 196–99
surveillance of non-natives, 76–77
theft of automobiles, 4–5, 112–13
theft of U.S. government vehicle,
    15–17
throwing of car over side of bridge,
    63
vandalism of automobiles, 25, 69–70,
    121
Night of the Rocks, 123–25
Nolan, John, 164, 177
Norfolk County, 113–14

O'Brien, Thomas, 14–16
O'Grady, Commissioner Thomas, 32, 139
Ontario Civilian Commission on Police
    Services (OCCPS), 8–10
Ontario government
    apology for death of Dudley George,
        191
    blaming of victims, 234–35
    Brown/Chatwell lawsuit against, 12,
        33, 55, 174, 175, 201, 203, 228–30,
        233–36
    claims Caledonia is a federal matter,
        53
    effect of Ipperwash on aboriginal
        policy, 146–48

Fantino cleared of intimidation
    complaint, 183–85
financial assistance to Caledonia
    businesses, 135
funding of Caledonia ad campaign,
    134–35
influence over OPP at Caledonia,
    146–48
marginalization of critics of
    Caledonia policy, 164–66
negotiations to buy DCE, 84–88,
    104–6, 114–17
offer of land for removal of blockade,
    105–6, 113–14
Places to Grow (Greenbelt) strategy,
    23, 48–49
Public Works Protection Act, 227
reluctance to answer Caledonia
    questions in Legislature, 113,
    145–46, 238–39
slow pace of DCE cleanup, 138
unwillingness to seek military
    intervention, 92
use of outside legal counsel, 183–85
Ontario Provincial Police (OPP). See also
    Boniface, Commissioner Gwen;
    Fantino, Commissioner Julian
abandonment of officer at Sixth
    Line, 36
Aboriginal Relations Team (ART), 4,
    30, 31, 144–45, 195–96, 216, 220
apology for killing of Dudley George,
    139–40
arrest of Dave Brown, 83
attempt to enforce injunction, 52–61
blaming of victims, 124, 173–74, 210–11
bugging of Dave Brown's house,
    172–76, 203
Caledonians' hostility towards, 35–38,
    79–80, 154, 190
Caledonians' lack of confidence in,
    12–13, 73, 184, 198
confirmation that DCE is off-limits,
    219–21
"disguised discipline," 143
double standard of law enforcement
    at Caledonia, 34–38, 118, 125–27,
    141–42, 146–48, 152, 155–56,
    160–61, 190–91, 200, 222

effect of Ipperwash on policy at
    Caledonia, 147–49, 191–93, 223
failure to arrest natives, 3–5, 11
failure to assist victims, 6–8, 12
fixation on Gary McHale, 152–54
Framework for Police Preparedness
    for Aboriginal Critical Incidents,
    139–40, 192–93
Haldimand Reclamation Operations
    Plan, 52
insensitivity towards Caledonians,
    65, 72, 127, 242
insistence that law is being enforced,
    106–8
lack of familiarity with Caledonia,
    67, 117–18
lack of preparation for smoke shack
    protest, 203–4, 205
marginalization of critics, 164–66,
    178–80, 193–94
officers' confusion about orders,
    141–43, 219–22
press release on McHale rally, 247
pressure placed on Crown attorneys
    by, 162–63
protection of natives from non-
    natives, 78–80
punishment of officers criticizing
    Caledonia policy, 36–37, 143
refusal to arrest natives, 122–24
role in death of Dudley George, 191
self-investigation of complaints
    against, 8–10
Sixth Line declared off-limits,
    62–65, 70, 74, 77–78, 128–31,
    216–18, 220
spin on events at Caledonia, 125, 153,
    199, 207, 217
surveillance of select Caledonia
    residents, 176–77
targeting of Dave Hartless, 164–65
targeting of Gary McHale, 159–61,
    204–5
Ontario Provincial Police Association
    (OPPA), 35, 37, 47, 79–80,
    141–44, ,180, 219–25
Ormerod, Det. Const. Norm, 13, 14–16
Ottawa Police Service, 9–10

Parkinson, Jeff, 230
"passports," 72–73
Patterson, Tom, 90
Pearce, Bill, 40
Peel, Ken, 106
Peterson, David, 86–87, 104, 105–6, 113,
    135
Pickup, Chris, 78
Pilon, Maurice, 55
Places to Grow (Greenbelt) strategy, 23,
    48–49
Plank Road Tract, 27
Porter, Brian Jesse, 196, 209, 210
Powell, Mike, 14–16
Powless, Camille, 206
Powless, Clyde (Bullet), 16, 89, 120, 196,
    206, 209, 210–11, 231–32, 248
Public Works Protection Act, 227

RaiLink Canada, 106, 118–20
Ramsay, David, 47, 146, 191
Rauscher, Dieter, 61–65, 74–77, 239–44,
    246
Rauscher, Maria, 51, 61–65, 75–77,
    239–45, 246
Regional News This Week, 78
Renton, Det. Insp. Bill, 204
Robitaille, Ray, 28–30
Ross, Anthony, 33
Ross, Insp. Dave, 158–59, 195
Royal Canadian Mounted Police, 61
    investigation of Gary McHale, 97–98

Sandler, Mark, 193
Scott, Dave, 143
Six Nations. See also Haudenosaunee
    Confederacy Council
    belief it could "just take" property,
        245–46
    concern over overdevelopment,
        48–49
    DCE land claim, 27–28
    demand development fees on DCE,
        39
    governance problems, 103–4, 138
    infiltration by organized crime, 44–45
    land offered to remove blockade,
        105–6, 113–14, 115–16
    rejection of Canadian law, 149–50

relations with non-native neighbours, 24–25
Six Nations Police, 34–35, 44–45, 63, 117–18, 245
refusal to patrol Sixth Line, 130
Six Nations Solidarity Network, 151
Sixth Line
abandonment by OPP, 62–65, 70, 74, 77–78, 128–31, 216–18, 220
native raid, 66–67
sense of isolation, 244
Skye, Brian, 82–83, 125–26
Sloat, Buck, 230
Smith, Dawn, 29, 30, 34, 38, 40, 41, 48, 49, 56
Smith, Jason, 180–81
Smith, Neil, 87, 115
Smith, Rocky, 91
Smoke, Sgt. Dave, 130
smoke shacks, 189–91
smoke shop operators, 43–45
Sprucedale Correctional Centre, 113
Stephens, Insp. John, 204
Stewart, Jane, 104, 155, 209
Stirling Woods subdivision, 196–99
Stoneman, Frank, 132–36
Sullivan, Ken, 7
Sweeney, Al, 46, 228

Thistlemoor subdivision
demonstration by Caledonia residents, 18–20
OPP checkpoints, 13–14
"resident response plan," 121–22
Thomas, Melba, 246
Thompson, Carl, 66–67, 218
Thompson, Debbie, 66–67, 70–74, 127–29, 216–18
"Three Musky Steers," 186–91
tobacco, illegal sale of, 43–45, 137, 189–91, 239
The Toronto Sun, 95–96
Torsney, Brian, 135
Torsney, Paddy, 135
Tory, John, 111, 112, 114–15, 145–50

Tractor Supply Co. (TSC), 23, 109
Trainer, Mayor Marie, 2, 24, 39, 46, 130–31, 175
email from Fantino, 183–85
sent for sensitivity training, 90–92
Trickey, Paul, 118–21, 155
Trustees of the Mohawk Nation Grand River, 40–41
Turtle Island News, 55, 245–46
Tyendinaga Mohawk Territory, 216

U.S. Border Patrol, 14–17
U.S. Bureau of Alcohol, Tobacco, Firearms and Explosives (ATF), 14, 15
U.S. Department of Homeland Security, 14–17

Vandermaas, Mark, 162, 183–85, 186–87
Vanderwyk, Rick, 155, 156
Vanderwyk, Valerie (wife of Rick), 155, 156
VanEvery, Donald, 239
VanSickle, AnneMarie, 125, 150, 154, 155
vigilantism, 134

Walsh, Karl, 38, 47, 79–80, 141–44, 157–58, 221–25
Walton, Det. Sgt. Greg, 160, 163
Warmington, Joe, 157
Wawryk, Wayne, 193–94
West, Jamie, 87–88
Wilfert, Bryon, 97–100
Wilkinson, Peter, 182, 233
Williams, Kim, 47
Williams, Skyler, 198–99
Windspeaker, 144
Woods, Dianne, 92, 135
Woolley, Pat, 1, 19–20, 165–66
World Trade Center (New York), 93–94

York, Const. Kevin, 227
York Regional Police, 98–99

Zabel, Mr. Justice Bernd, 231, 232